Vascular Aphasia

Vascular Aphasia

Joseph M. Tonkonogy

A Bradford Book
The MIT Press
Cambridge, Massachusetts
London, England

This book was set in Palatino by the MIT Press Computergraphics Department and printed and bound by Halliday Lithograph in the United States of America.

Library of Congress Cataloging in Publication Data

Tonkonogiĭ, I. M. (Iosif Moiseevich)
   Vascular aphasia.

   "A Bradford book."
   Bibliography: p.
   Includes index.
   1. Aphasia. 2. Cerebrovascular disease—Complications and sequelae. I. Title.
[DNLM: 1. Aphasia. WI 340.5 T665v]
RC425.T66   1986   616.85′52   85-10958
ISBN 0-262-20054-6

Dedicated to the memory of Alexander Luria, Henri Hécaen, and Norman Geschwind

Contents

Foreword

It is a special pleasure to welcome Dr. Tonkonogy's book, the first by a Soviet-trained behavioral neurologist, now practicing in the United States. This book is largely a product of Dr. Tonkonogy's experience of over thirty years in the Department of Behavioral Neurology and Stroke in the Bekhterev Psychoneurological Institute in Leningrad. Dr. Tonkonogy served as Professor and Chairman of that department for fourteen years, up to the time of his departure from the USSR. In this volume, he shares with us the richness of his scholarship in the study of the anatomical basis of the aphasias. As a contemporary and a colleague of A. R. Luria, he is well versed in the sophisticated approach to the analysis of aphasic syndromes that marks current Soviet neuropsychology, in which cognitive and psycholinguistic factors are seen to interact with impairments of input and output modalities and experimental techniques are applied to probe the nature of the deficits underlying the patients presenting symptoms. Dr. Tonkonogy himself has conducted a series of experimental studies of auditory perception in temporal lobe aphasia.

This book appears at a time of a new burst of interest in aphasia, accompanied by the flourishing of the new discipline of neuropsychology. At the same time, advances in brain imaging techniques have led to more detailed and sophisticated correlations between behavioral deficits and structures destroyed by lesions. The crop of books and chapters that has emerged presents a distillation of these advances in concepts of aphasia as seen by many authors—among them, Benson, Poeck, Goodglass and Kaplan, LeCours and Lhermitte, and Brown.

In spite of this flourishing literature, there is a gap which Dr. Tonkonogy's volume addresses well. Namely, how aphasia following stroke is present clinically from the outset and how it evolves into a pattern in which the features associated with one or another syndrome become apparent. For the clinical neurologist who is faced with a patient whose picture after a stroke does not immediately fall into an ideal instance of a classical syndrome, this approach is an invaluable supplement.

The availability of detailed postmortem brain studies in a series of patients whose language was studied in detail during life is a rare extra feature, even though a number of these patients expired in the early post-onset period before the extent of their last aphasia had become apparent. This book is the product of many year's accumulation of cases by Dr. Tonkonogy at the Bekhterev Institute. Access to such material is rarely available to American neurologists.

In the chapters introducing the case material, Dr. Tonkonogy begins with an integrative historical overview of the competing views on the mechanisms of aphasia and their classification. The result is a highly balanced presentation in which considerations of neuropsychology and information processing are taken into account along with those based on neuroanatomical structure and vascular pathology. Dr. Tonkonogy's schooling in basic clinical neurology, his long study of vascular aphasia, and his first-hand knowledge of the current Soviet school of aphasiology are all apparent in this successful opening section. His own interpretive commentary unobtrusively provides a unifying view in which there is much wisdom.

It has been pointed out that vascular lesions offer the best means of studying structure-function relationships in the brain. Unlike penetrating missile wounds or closed head trauma, they do not injure sites remote from the primary lesion site. Unlike space-occupying lesions, they do not create lasting pressure effects that complicate the symptom picture. Unlike slow growing tumors, they do not appear in a brain that has already undergone some degree of functional reorganization before the appearance of symptoms.

As Dr. Tonkonogy points out in the final section on localization, the vascular system of the brain was not designed to coincide precisely with the functional subdivisions of the language. He reviews the vascular supply of the brain and the areas that are commonly implicated in a lesion, as well as the variation in size and extent of infarcts. The corresponding variants and overlaps in aphasic syndromes becomes understandable in this framework.

Harold Goodglass
Boston, Massachusetts
April 1985

Preface

Many decades distance us from Broca, Wernicke, Lichtheim, and their accomplishments, in initiating the study of aphasia in the second half of the nineteenth century, but in our diagnoses and localization of aphasia we still rely on Broca's postulates and the Wernicke-Lichtheim classification in spite of the numerous attempts to challenge this classification with its division of the main syndromes of aphasia corresponding to the cortical, transcortical, conduction, or subcortical site of the lesion. Some of these attempts, especially those based on "antilocalization" principles, attracted much attention of aphasiologists, and the ideas of Jackson, Marie, Head, and Goldstein belong to the brightest spots in the history of thought about aphasia.

This controversy between "localizationist" and "antilocalizationist" ideas, however, seems to be somewhat obsolete in our time of computers and robots, with their special systems of reliability which protects normal "intellectual" functioning of those devices from failure of single components or blocks. Our brain has to have similar systems of reliability; discussion of clinical diagnosis and localization of aphasia should be based on the assumption that such a system is implemented in the functional structure of the brain. Therefore it may be expected that a relatively small lesion of brain tissue would result in transient aphasia or that language disorder would not be manifested at all. Therefore the size of the lesion plays a substantial role in the development of aphasia.

That is why the main attention of this book is directed away from the differentiation of aphasia syndromes caused by restricted lesions of the cortical gray matter versus lesions of the white matter pathways to the discussion of aphasia resulting from relatively large lesions involving gray and white matter of particular areas in the language zone of the dominant hemisphere. Instead of a description of a so-called pure form of aphasia characterized by one or the other leading symptoms, special emphasis is given to the peculiar combinations of aphasic symptoms in the various syndromes of aphasia as well as on the mixed syndromes reflecting manifestations of the two to three single aphasia syndromes. The static descriptions of aphasia syndromes in the chronic stage of stroke that are prevalent in the literature have been replaced in this book by a dynamic approach concerned with the role of the type and course of cerebral vascular disease in the development and evolution of aphasia. Aphasia in the acute stage of stroke is followed to the chronic stage of stroke, and the diagnosis of symptoms and syndromes of aphasia and their localizing value is discussed.

Vascular Aphasia reflects more than thirty years of experience of aphasia study in relation to the diagnosis and treatment of stroke. In these years I collected 30 clinical-anatomical cases of aphasia. I followed most of those cases from the first hours of CVA until death, sometimes many years after the development of aphasia. Fifty-six clinical-anatomical cases of stroke with nonaphasic speech disorder, as well as without speech and language disturbances, are also included in our consideration. Clinical descriptions of aphasia syndromes in this book are partly based on the analysis of 154 nonanatomical cases of stroke with aphasia.

This book is concerned with the symptomatology, syndromes, and diagnosis of vascular aphasia, and many of the special problems, including neuropsychological assessment, aphasia in polyglots and deaf-mutes, and dementia as well as aphasia rehabilitation, are beyond the scope of the book. All interested are referred to the detailed review of these problems by Goodglass and Kaplan (1983), Benson (1979), Albert *et al.* (1981).

I often discussed the problem of aphasia with the late professor A. R. Luria from the very beginning of my work in aphasiology in the early 1950s, and I will never forget his brightness, ingenuity, and inexhaustible scientific curiosity until the last days of his brilliant life. I gratefully acknowledge the colleagues from the Bekhterev Psychoneurological Research Institute in Leningrad for the assistance during many years of our work on the problems of aphasia. Very special acknowledgment must be accorded the late profesor Norman Geschwind, who offered help and advice. My special indebtedness is given to Dr. Harold Goodglass and Dr. Robert Feldman and their colleagues, particularly Dr. Edith Kaplan and Dr. Martin Albert, the Aphasia Research Center of the Boston University School of Medicine, and Boston VA Medical Center for providing the possibility to study and to discuss the approach to the aphasia examination and research in this country.

I wish to thank Dr. Edgar Zurif, Dr. David Caplan, and Dr. Davis Howes, who all continually encouraged me to write this book. I am indebted to Dr. Charles Poser for his constructive comments and suggestions.

Acknowledgments

My very sincere thanks to Joan Crawford Poser for editorial assistance.

Vascular Aphasia

I
Classification and Symptoms of Aphasia

1

Classification of Aphasia

Anatomical Approach

One of the major goals in the neurological diagnosis of aphasia is the localization of the lesions, and therefore anatomical classifications of aphasia are widely used in everyday neurological and neuropsychological practice as well as for research purposes. Maybe that is why the oldest anatomical classification (Wernicke-Lichtheim), which was introduced by Wernicke (1874) and Lichtheim (1884), has survived to this day and is still the one most frequently used in neurological textbooks and research publications. According to this classification, the diagnosis of aphasia has to be based on a disturbance of expressive speech, comprehension, repetition, and reading and writing. A disorder of expressive speech or comprehension with disturbances of repetition, reading, and writing occurs in cortical motor aphasia or cortical sensory aphasia due to a lesion of the cortical motor speech center or the cortical sensory speech center, respectively. According to this scheme interrupting the connection between the hypothetical "center of concepts" and "motor speech center" or "sensory speech center" leads to transcortical motor aphasia, with a disorder of expressive speech, reading, and writing, or produces transcortical sensory aphasia with comprehension, reading, and writing disturbances if the "center of concepts" is disconnected from the "sensory speech center." Repetition is not impaired in transcortical aphasia, since the pathway between cortical motor and sensory speech centers is preserved. The connections from the cortical motor or sensory speech centers to the deep brain structures are interrupted in subcortical motor aphasia with a relatively isolated disorder of expressive speech or in subcortical sensory aphasia with a comprehension disturbance. Repetition, reading, and writing are preserved in subcortical aphasia. Conduction aphasia results from the disruption of connection between motor and sensory speech centers with a corresponding disorder of repetition and relatively spared expressive speech, comprehension, reading, and writing.

Unfortunately, this simple and attractive scheme has never been supported by reliable clinical-anatomical data, and the clinical signs, the localization, and even the existence of aphasia types described in the Wernicke-Lichtheim classification remain in question. The conception of cortical motor aphasia was challenged by Marie (1906a, b, c) relatively soon after the famous publications of Broca (1861a, b), Wernicke (1874), and Lichtheim (1884). Marie (1906b) showed that a disorder of comprehension may be noted in many cases of motor aphasia. He introduced a "three-paper" test to study comprehension ability; patients were asked to put one piece of paper on the table, another piece into a pocket, and the third piece on a chair. This test revealed marked disorder of comprehension in patients with either sensory aphasia or motor aphasia. Marie (1906a, b, c) and his colleague Moutier (1908) presented an analysis of 304 clinical-anatomical cases of aphasia described in the literature from 1861 through 1906 and added autopsied cases of aphasia of their own. They described three nonaphasic cases with isolated lesions of the posterior part of the left frontal gyrus in right-handed persons and cases with what they called motor aphasia due to the destruction of Wernicke's area combined with a lesion in the lenticular zone. The posterior frontal gyri were preserved in their cases of motor aphasia in which subcortical cerebral hemorrhages had occurred. Marie considered aphasia as a partial intellectual impairment manifested as a comprehension disorder. That is why, to him, Wernicke's sensory aphasia was the only true aphasia. Motor aphasia, according to Marie, results from the combination of sensory aphasia due to a lesion in Wernicke's area and "anarthria" due to a lenticular zone lesion. No serious investigator since has accepted Marie's theory, but almost every author has discussed it, because of his contribution to the study of comprehension deficit in motor aphasia, and the role played by lesions of the subcortical structures in the development of aphasia.

After Marie's famous papers, a new test series was introduced in order to study comprehension in patients with aphasia (Head 1926; Luria 1947; Goodglass and Kaplan 1983; Zurif and Caramazza 1976). It is now clear that disorders of comprehension occur in almost all types of aphasia. That is why Weisenburg and McBride (1935) proposed the terms "predominantly motor aphasia" and "predominantly sensory aphasia" instead of the motor or sensory aphasia of the Wernicke-Lichtheim classification. However, comprehension impairment in "predominantly motor aphasia" and the disturbance of expressive speech in "predominantly sensory aphasia" may be noticeable, and many modern authors (Brain 1965; Brown 1972; Hécaen 1972; Hécaen and Albert 1978; Albert et al. 1981) have used the term "Broca's aphasia" rather than "cortical motor aphasia" and "Wernicke's aphasia" instead of "cortical sensory aphasia" as less troublesome.

The terms "transcortical aphasia" and "conduction aphasia" are still widely accepted. Nonetheless a relative preservation of repetition in transcortical motor and transcortical sensory aphasia cannot be considered pathognomic, since repetition is only mildly disturbed in such types of aphasia as mild Broca's and Wernicke's aphasia, dynamic and anomic-sensory aphasia, and nonglobal mixed aphasia. On the other hand, what Goldstein (1948) called "transcortical" localization or "isolation of the speech area" is still unproven, because in many cases of aphasia with preserved repetition the lesion has been noted outside of Broca's and Wernicke's areas, but isolation of these areas from what Wernicke considered the "ideational field" has been described in only a few cases, usually accompanied by an additional diffuse degenerative or hypoxic lesion of the brain.

The term "conduction aphasia" has produced much confusion, since a disorder of repetition with relatively preserved expressive speech and comprehension may be seen in cases of moderate Wernicke's aphasia. That is why certain authors considered "conduction aphasia" as a stage of recovery in Wernicke's aphasia (Kleist 1934; Hopf 1957), whereas others completely excluded it from their classifications (Head 1926; Luria 1947, 1966). Aphasia with a primary disorder of repetition does seem to exist as a clinical entity (Ajuriaguerra and Hécaen 1949; Geschwind 1965; Brown 1972; Hécaen and Albert 1978; Goodglass and Kaplan 1983; Albert et al. 1981), but the existence of "conduction" disturbance as a main feature of this syndrome is still uncertain. The possibility of a special transcoding system for repetition cannot be excluded. A repetition disorder, therefore, may result from damage to that transcoding system rather than from a simple pathway interruption between the sensory and motor speech centers.

The term "subcortical sensory aphasia" was replaced by the term "pure word deafness" early in the history of aphasia study. A bilateral cortical lesion of the medial part of the first temporal gyri with partial involvement of the Heschl's gyri has been shown in most of these cases (Brain 1965; Hécaen and Albert 1978). Bastian (1897) adopted Broca's term "aphemia" for "subcortical motor aphasia"; it has often been used to describe an aphasic disorder of articulation without impairment of comprehension or of reading and writing (Brain 1965; Albert et al. 1981). The term "phonetic disintegration syndrome" was used in similar cases by Alajouanine, Ombredane and Durand (1939) and LeCours and Lhermitte (1976). The term "subcortical aphasia" has also been applied to a language disorder resulting from a lesion of the subcortical structures, predominantly striatal and thalamic hemorrhages (Mohr et al. 1975; Benson 1979; Reynolds et al. 1979; Alexander and LoVerme 1980).

Another example of the strictly anatomical approach is presented in the linguistic classification of aphasia of Kleist (1934). Kleist considered various types of aphasia as a language disorder both of expressive speech and comprehension of speech sounds, words, and phrases, including the names of objects. According to Kleist, expressive types of aphasia include "mutism of speech sounds" (*Lautstummheit*), "mutism of words" (*Vortstummheit*), "mutism of phrases" (*Satztummheit*), and "mutism of naming" (*Namenstummheit*). He believed syndromes of sensory aphasia consist of "deafness to speechsounds" (*Lauttaubheit*), "deafness to words" (*Vorttaubheit*), "deafness to phrases" (*Satztaubheit*), and "naming deafness" (*Namentaubheit*). Every type of aphasia in Kleist's classification is caused by a lesion in a specific area. In this way "mutism of speech sounds" is attributed to a lesion of the lower part of the left motor strip and "mutism of words" to a lesion of the posterior part of the third frontal gyrus and the adjacent area in the motor strip of the left hemisphere. To explain cases with "mutism of naming," Kleist postulated a lesion involving both the ascending part and the base of the pars opercularis in the left third frontal gyrus. He attributed "deafness to speech sounds" to a bilateral symmetrical lesion of the Heschl's gyri, "deafness to words" to a lesion of the posterior part of the left first temporal gyrus, "deafness to the names of objects" to the destruction of the posterior parts of the left second and third temporal gyri, and so on. Nonetheless, in spite of its linguistic simplicity and anatomical attractiveness, Kleist's classification did not attain the popularity of the Wernicke-Lichtheim classification, perhaps because it is poorly correlated to the clinical reality of aphasia syndromes.

In spite of his harsh criticism of the anatomical theory, Luria (1947, 1966) introduced his own classification based on the localization of what he termed the prerequisites of language function in specific cortical areas. In cases of what he called efferent kinetic motor aphasia the destroyed prerequisite is a "kinetic organization of motor action, particularly speech motor action," and the lesion is placed in the pars opercularis of the left third frontal gyrus. In afferent kinesthetic motor aphasia the lesion is localized in the lower part of the sensory strip and the adjacent part of the supramarginal gyrus in the left hemisphere. The leading disorder in Luria's dynamic aphasia is a deficit of speech initiation, an inability to begin speaking. Luria attributed this to a lesion in the posterior part of the left third frontal gyrus, but anterior to Broca's area. Luria listed in his classification two types of temporal aphasia: "acoustical-gnostical sensory aphasia," and "acoustical-mnestical sensory aphasia." The localization of the lesion is in the posterior part of the left first temporal gyrus in "acoustical-gnostical sensory aphasia" and in the middle part of the lateral surface of the left temporal lobe in "acoustical-mnestical aphasia." Luria also described "semantic aphasia" in cases with a lesion of the left inferior parietal lobule. Luria's classification of aphasia has earned substantial attention from aphasiologists and linguists. Jakobson (1964) adjusted his own concept of the code and context disorder in aphasia in accordance with Luria's classification. This classification, however, has not been widely recognized as a tool for regular aphasia diagnosis, and the Wernicke-Lichtheim classification still remains the principal classification of aphasia even in Luria's homeland.

Holistic Theory of Aphasia Classification

Jackson (1878, 1884) was perhaps the first to criticize the anatomical theory in the study of aphasia. Many of the subsequent holistic studies of aphasia were based on his work, although Jackson's views were disregarded at the end of the nineteenth century, when localization was most in vogue. A reawakening of interest in his work has to be attributed to Head's effort. Head published the selected papers of Jackson in 1915 and reviewed in detail Jackson's accomplishments and ideas. Jackson (1884) was mainly interested in the dynamic aspects of language. He first pointed out that symptom localization should not be confused with localization of the language function. Jackson stressed the significance not only of the disturbed language function but also of the preserved aspects of normal language in aphasia. A patient with aphasia may lose the ability to produce volitional, prepositional speech but retain emotional speech. For example, a word can be uttered by a patient under the effect of a strong emotion or in the course of an automatized sequence of words, but it cannot be volitionally produced. Jackson believed that the production of prepositional language had to be attributed to the left hemisphere and emotional language to the right hemisphere.

According to Head (1926), the basic disturbance in aphasia is one of symbol formulation and expression. This is a part of general intellectual ability and cannot be strictly localized in any definite area of the brain. Head described the types of aphasia as "morphological," "verbal," "nominative," and "semantic" aspects of the basic disturbance. Referring to Jackson's ideas on the negative and positive aspects of aphasia, Head stressed that not every response of a patient with a language disorder represents simply the loss of a certain function but rather may be considered as a reaction of the organism which is attempting to adjust itself to the new condition resulting from the deficit of the function. Recently, a similar point was made by Caplan (1981) in his detailed discussion of the cerebral localization of linguistic functions. He stressed that deficit analysis of pathological performance for functional analysis and localization can be used to represent the aphasic performance as the mis- or nonfunctioning of a component of a normal system. At the same time Caplan recognized that aphasic performances often do not represent the deficits, since lesions may modify existing mechanisms to produce new behavior. Bradley *et al.* (1980) stressed another possibility in which a lesion "releases" a normally less efficient mechanism. Head's preeminent position and brilliant presentation of his idea in *Aphasia and Kindred Disorders of Speech* (1926) struck a positive chord with the neuroscientists of his time, but neurologists, preoccupied with the problem of lesion localization in their patients with aphasia, continued to use the Wernicke-Lichtheim classification.

Goldstein (1927, 1934, 1948) tried to eliminate the difficulties of lesion localization pointed out by his opponents. He distinguished between the "peripheral" and "central" cortex. Lesions in the periphery result in more elemental neurological manifestations, according to anatomical principles of cortical structure. Goldstein believed that destruction of the cortical periphery led to the disorder of the "instrumentalities" of speech. Therefore he described peripheral types of motor and sensory aphasia as a disorder of the instrumentalities of speech resulting from a lesion located in the pars opercularis of the left third frontal gyrus and the inferior part of the motor strip in "peripheral motor aphasia" or in the posterior part of the left middle and inferior temporal gyri in "peripheral sensory aphasia." According to Goldstein, the central part of the cortex is equipotential. A lesion of any part of this central cortex leads to a disorder of ability for form abstractions and the severity of this disorder depends only on the size of the damaged cerebral tissue. Goldstein considered amnestic aphasia as a typical example of aphasia produced by the disorder of content or "abstract language." Goldstein's idea is closely linked to Lashley's (1929, 1933) conception of brain tissue equipotentiality.

Reliability of Brain Functioning and Classification of Aphasia

In spite of its obvious lack of clinical applications, the holistic approach cannot be rejected in the discussion of aphasia classifications, since this approach has been based on substantial theoretical and experimental work. Anatomical and holistic ideas of course must be discussed in the light of modern concepts of brain function instead of the postulates and dogmas of the nineteenth century.

An old discussion between proponents of the anatomical theory and those supporting a holistic approach has to be centered on the problem of the reliability of brain function derived from modern ideas of the functional structure of the brain in normal and pathological conditions. It seems reasonable to suggest that reliability of brain function is provided by a special system, so that destruction of part of the brain results in only minimal abnormality or continued normal function. From this point of view holistic and anatomical approaches represent conjectural extremes. The system is disregarded in the strictly outlined anatomical view but is very important in the holistic scheme of brain organization. The anatomical scheme of brain organization is based on the view that language function is provided by independent centers or areas for both expressive speech and comprehension. Destruction of one of the particular centers located in a small area of cortex, e.g., Broca's or Wernicke's area, results in a particular type of aphasia, such as the motor or cortical sensory aphasia of the Wernicke-Lichtheim classification. A specific operation of language function can also be attributed to each precisely localized center or area, such as word production for Broca's area and word comprehension for Wernicke's area, in Kleist's linguistic classification. According to such a classification, a patient with a lesion of Broca's area will have difficulty in word production, whereas a lesion of Wernicke's area results in a disturbance of word comprehension.

The opposite, holistic scheme, based on the principle of equipotentiality, looks like a scheme with the highest functional preservation. Unfortunately, this scheme is not applicable to such a complex device as the human brain characterized by various highly differentiated functional structures. One might expect that some sort of multipotentiality could exist in the structure of the neuronal networks of the small cytoarchitectonic areas. That network is characterized by redundance provided by the presence of parallel structures. The parallel neural channels increase many times the activity of a single channel in the network, so that partial destruction does not lead to the total functional failure of the entire network (Kandel 1982). Another type of redundancy may be provided by the interneuron connections so that damage of the high-frequency connection is compensated by the activation of low-frequency channels. A single network could not possibly exist as a functional structure of the entire language area with its highly differentiated sets of operations. Another example of an even more complex equipotentiality is the matter of information storage in the brain. Access to this storage has to be selective, and that is why the highly differentiated mechanisms for information processing may be associated with a holographic type of information storage (Pribram 1971; Gleser et al. 1975).

Reliability of brain function may also be provided for by the performance of similar operations by channels tuned to different primary alphabets of language. Recognition of language may be performed by different channels that recognize single phonemes, syllables, words, or phrases. Phoneme or syllable channels are probably useful for the study of a new language or for the recognition of little used or unknown words. At the same time, the channel working on the alphabet of words and phrases would be useful for the recognition of a relatively limited number of words and phrases. Perhaps the function of this latter channel has a specially developed system of protection since it is vital for everyday communication. The alphabet to some of these channels may also be restricted to substantive meaningful words or to grammatical functional words. It is reasonable to place the area of object naming in the vicinity of the channel responsible for visual gnosis of objects, while the channel concerned with small functional words would be conveniently located adjacent to the area controlling action. The functions of both channels might partially overlap so that the loss of the damaged channel would be somewhat compensated for by another preserved channel. The scheme would certainly account for the telegraphic style in Broca's aphasia and word salad in Wernicke's aphasia.

The statistical predictability of information processing seems to play an important role, maybe the most important role, in a system that provides for the reliability of brain function. Studies of statistical predictability are based on the assumption that normal human behavior results from statistical probability. This structure is dependent on an adequate reflection of the statistical characteristics of the environment in past experience in formulating behavioral strategies (Feigenberg 1963). The human brain is constantly confronted with an enormous number of situations, conditions, objects, actions, phrases, words, and combinations of speech sounds. Its capacity to deal with this information would be quickly overloaded in the absence of the processes that select and compact information and reduce it to a level accessible to the information-processing system of the brain (Tonkonogy and Tsukkerman 1966). The brain can store an enormous amount of information in its billions of nerve cells, but processing such large quantities of data poses an almost insoluble problem. Probability assessment, therefore, helps select the most important and relevant information for further processing by the brain (Bazhin et al. 1973). The role of such assessment in information processing has been widely recognized since Shannon's time, and probability assessment may eventually replace Head's "symbol formulation and expression" or Goldstein's "abstract language" as the basic concept of the main function of the brain. It should also be stressed that information processing, characterized by high statistical predictability, is preserved as much as possible by the brain. The mechanisms of this preservation remain unknown, but examples of it may be readily observed in the various manifestations of aphasia.

One example of this is illustrated in the relationship of the semantic field to language processing in patients with aphasia. Despite their expressive speech and comprehension disturbances, such patients may be quite successful in communicating if their language processing is restricted to a single semantic field, such as objects in the room. Probability assessment helps them reduce the number of choices so that the alphabet of the processing message consists of 10–15 items (in this case, objects in the room) instead of the thousands of objects that would require information processing without mechanisms for selection and reduction by probability assessment. In fact, when a patient is asked to point to a window and then to a table, he makes the determination of a very high probability that the next question will be related to objects in the same room. The number of choices, therefore, is restricted to those objects, and the process of word recognition is facilitated in spite of the aphasia. The same is true for comprehension of conversational speech, dealing with the patient's health, family conditions, etc. However, if the semantic field is suddenly changed, e.g., from objects in the room to body parts, a patient with aphasia will show substantially increased difficulty with comprehension.

Substitutions in the semantic field have also been found to be a leading cause of errors in patients with aphasia (Goodglass and Baker 1976; Blumstein *et al.* 1977). These substitutions may be attributed to the high probability value of semantically similar items. On the other hand, alienation of word meaning as described by Luria (1947, 1966) and Tonkonogy (1968, 1973) in the "eye–ear–nose" test seems to contradict the concept that language behavior is facilitated when it occurs in the same semantic field. In this test the patient is asked to touch his "ear . . . nose . . . eye" and then again, "eye . . . nose . . . ear . . . eye," etc. The meaning of the words is alienated by the swiftly changing sequence, so the patient with aphasia points to his eye instead of his nose; to his nose instead of his eye, etc. The theory of probability assessment may readily explain this "semantic paradox," since the probability of repeated instruction to point to the same 2 or 3 objects in the same semantic field is perhaps even lower than the probability of switching to another semantic field.

Duplication of single blocks or of the entire language system may be considered as one of the mechanisms that provide for the preservation of brain function. Typical examples of such duplication in living organisms are the lungs, the kidneys, the testicles, etc. Damage to or complete destruction of one of these organs is not often critical since the function of the damaged organ may be taken over by the corresponding organ on the opposite side of the body. Duplication of the cerebral hemispheres also seems to suggest duplication of function;

such mechanisms have been shown to exist by numerous animal experiments. Clinical-anatomical and electrophysiological studies, however, have shown that duplication of the function of the cerebral hemisphere has only a limited value in the preservation system for human brain function. This is especially true for disorders of language function. Bilateral lesions of Broca's area (Tonkonogy and Goodglass 1981) produce only a transient aphasia, and the presence of a symmetrical lesion in the minor hemisphere does not increase the severity of the aphasia resulting from infarction in the dominant hemisphere (Levine and Mohr 1979). Nonetheless, in the early stages of ontogenesis and in the case of ambidexterity, the duplication of the language functional system in the opposite hemisphere seems to play a more significant role in language recovery and preservation.

The system for the preservation of brain function is partly based on the overlapping of function of single channels. Therefore similar symptoms may result from lesions in various parts of the language area of the dominant hemisphere. A list of such symptoms includes anomic aphasia, alienation of word meaning, literal and verbal paraphasia, disorder of phrase comprehension, and many other manifestations of the various aphasia syndromes. Recently, Blumstein (1973) showed that such properties of phonemic paraphasias as the distribution of occurring phonemes and phonological distance between substituting and substituted phonemes, etc., are similar in Broca's, Wernicke's, and conduction aphasia.

Careful analysis also shows that language function may be turned off by such functional processes as Monakow's diaschisis (Monakow 1914), but this arrest of the function may be protective in conditions when the normal action of the language functional system is disrupted by the pathological process in the brain. A sick functional system, therefore, is getting relief for rest and possible restructuring. Monakow (1914) believed that transient symptoms of aphasia in the first days and weeks after stroke or injury could not be completely explained by the anatomical changes (edema, inflammation, etc.) in the parts of the brain adjacent to the lesion. Similarly, arrest of function may occur in areas located at significant distances from the pathological focus in the CNS. Monakow attributed this arrest of function to a disruption of continuity in the neural chains resulting from transient interruption of postsynaptic conduction. That is why he called such a condition "diaschisis," meaning "split." Such diaschisis differs from apoplectic shock by the absence of extension to the entire cerebral hemisphere; diaschisis extends only to the neural fibers originating in the lesion. If the cortex is destroyed in the region of the motor strip, therefore, the wave of diaschisis extends along the pathways originating in this gyrus through the midbrain to the spinal cord. Diaschisis may also extend through the association fibers to the other cortical regions in the ipsilateral hemisphere and via the commisural fibers of the corpus callosum of the opposite hemisphere. Later, Pavlov (1949) proposed the idea of "protective inhibition" to explain the inhibition of the brain regions in the opposite hemisphere in order to protect them from the devastating effect of being suddenly called into function and thus to gain the time needed for adjustment to this new condition. The existence of diaschisis or protective inhibition has never been proven in electrophysiological experiments, but it is expected that some equivalent mechanism will eventually be discovered. The clinical course of aphasia after an acute vascular or traumatic accident gives some evidence in support of Monakow's and Pavlov's ideas. Recently, Mohr (1973) reported cases with dramatically rapid amelioration of motor aphasia in spite of relatively large areas of cerebral infarction. This transient type of severe speech and language disorder following a stroke or brain injury has also been described repeatedly in patients with small lesions in the cortical language area (Tonkonogy 1968; Stolyarova 1973; Mohr et al. 1975; Mohr et al. 1978; Levine and Mohr 1979). On the other hand, diaschisis or inhibition may sometimes be overprotective, and the pathological sequelae of this overprotection are seen for a long time after the acute stage of the cerebral vascular or traumatic accident.

Neurolinguistic Classification of Aphasia Syndromes

Preservation of brain function by the special system discussed above may be especially successful in cases with relatively small lesions of the brain when a disorder of one particular operation is easily compensated for by the many other intact operations related to other alphabets of information processing, such as restrictions of choice, local mechanisms of equipotentiality in the neuronal network, etc. The clinical-anatomical consideration described in this book supports the view that there is no one basic disorder underlying the various aphasia syndromes. Our classification of aphasia focuses on the description of aphasia syndromes as combinations of relatively independent symptoms resulting from lesions occurring in at least two or three classical language areas. In this syndromic approach to aphasia classification, special attention is paid to the mixed types of aphasia which combine two independent aphasia syndromes resulting from large lesions in the language area of the dominant hemisphere. The underlying principle of this aphasia classification shifts from the matching of various types of aphasia with exquisitely localized lesions in particular areas of the cerebral cortex to a syndromic description of the characteristic combinations of aphasia symptoms and their relationship to the site, size, and type of brain pathology. The linguistic components of this classification include considerations of aphasia as a language disorder; thus special attention is paid to the careful clinical definition of the symptoms and syndromes of the language impairment in aphasia. Our classification is derived from instances of problems characterized by an acute onset and a relatively localized extent of brain damage, as in cases of cerebral infarction as opposed to the diffuse cerebral involvement in acute brain injury or infection. The size and site of the underlying brain pathology as well as the course of the disease are somewhat different in the aphasia caused by brain injury, tumor, or infection, and that is why classification of aphasia stemming from such causes deserves special consideration.

It is very difficult to separate the aphasia syndromes caused by lesions of the language areas of the brain from those resulting from interruption of the pathway between the language areas, since disconnection may be produced by a relatively small lesion and the aphasia may be transient or not even occur at all in such cases. More extensive lesions usually involve not only pathways but also cortical language areas, however, which underlines the fact that the disconnection syndromes in aphasia should be subjected to further research.

Substantial progress in the understanding of those syndromes and the role of the anatomical and physiological connections in brain function was made by Geschwind (1965). It would seem that future classifications of aphasia may be developed to further advance the study of those very important principles of brain functioning.

In our neurolinguistic classification, all aphasia syndromes are divided into three major groups: anterior aphasia, posterior aphasia, and mixed anterior-posterior aphasia. Each of these groups is related to a lesion in the large language areas, anterior, posterior, or mixed anterior-posterior, in the dominant hemisphere; a relatively wide variety of cortical and subcortical localizations of lesions is possible within those language areas. The manifestations of anterior and posterior aphasia seem to be almost equally distributed in expressive speech and comprehension at the higher "central" language level concerned with the morphological and syntactical structure and nominative functions of language. Both types of aphasia, therefore, share such common features as disorders of phrase production, word finding and production, disturbances of comprehension of complicated phrases, alienation of word meaning, disorders of phonological analysis, and reading and writing. At the same time, significant differences characterize anterior and posterior aphasia. The syndromes of anterior aphasia can be distinguished by the telegraphic style with a predominance of substantive words, lack of grammatically functional words, impoverishment of speech, which is reduced to short phrases and high-frequency words, and a relatively low degree of comprehension and naming disorders compared with the severity of the disturbances in free conversational speech, which consists mostly of literal standard paraphasias. In the syndromes of posterior aphasia, functional words are frequent in expressive speech, and disturbances of phrase comprehension, alienation of word meaning, and disorders of naming are especially frequent. Paraphasias, verbal or literal, are variable, and patients are not aware of the errors in their expressive speech.

On the other hnd, the motor and sensory components of the speech disorders are clearly different in anterior and posterior aphasia in the "peripheral" components, such as articulation production and phoneme comprehension, speech activity, prosody, and voicing. In anterior aphasia, the motor components of the disorder at this "peripheral" level are prominent. Syndromes of posterior aphasia include "peripheral" signs of sensory aphasia. Symptoms of motor speech disorder in anterior aphasia consist of deformation of articulation, motor dysprosody, aphonia and hypophonia, and decreased speech activity. Conversely, disorders of auditory phoneme and word comprehension, sensory aprosody, and increased speech activity are seen in posterior sensory aphasia.

Particular types of anterior aphasia include Broca's aphasia, dynamic aphasia, and articulation aphasia. Severe Broca's aphasia has almost all the central and peripheral symptoms of the anterior aphasia syndrome. In moderate and mild Broca's aphasia, the peripheral symptoms, especially articulation disorder, may be less noticeable or absent. Dynamic aphasia and articulation aphasia represent primarily peripheral types of anterior aphasia. Central language disorders are mild or partly absent in articulation aphasia, which is characterized by the deformation of articulation that is often combined with motor dysprosody and disturbances of phonological analysis. In dynamic aphasia the peripheral disorder of speech initiation, speech adynamia, is often associated with central symptoms of simplification, or impoverishment of expressive speech.

Syndromes of posterior aphasia include Wernicke's aphasia, anomic-sensory aphasia, repetition aphasia, and anomic-spatial and phonemic-sensory aphasia. Like Broca's aphasia in the anterior aphasia syndromes, severe Wernicke's aphasia has almost all the symptoms of central and peripheral language disorders of the posterior aphasia syndrome. In moderate and mild Wernicke's aphasia, peripheral disorders, especially disturbance of the auditory recognition of phonemes, is mild or absent. Phonemic-sensory aphasia is related to the peripheral level of disorder and is characterized by the auditory disturbance of phoneme recognition associated with only mild manifestations or even complete absence of the posterior aphasia syndrome. All three remaining syndromes of posterior aphasia have signs of primarily central language disorder. Anomic-sensory aphasia is characterized by great difficulties in naming and alienation of word meaning combined with moderate frequency of small functional words in conversational speech, a tendency to augmentation, and variable verbal paraphasias. In repetition aphasia, a disorder of the series of syllables and word repetition is associated with variable literal paraphasia and a peculiar type of anomic aphasia characterized by difficulty in finding word endings. Anomic-spatial aphasia is a peculiar syndrome related to a disturbance of spatial-temporal processing in expressive speech and comprehension combined with anomia, especially for body parts and temporospatial relationships.

Special attention is paid in our classification to mixed anterior-posterior aphasia. Global aphasia is a well-known combination of severe Broca's and Wernicke's aphasia resulting from an extensive lesion of the language areas of the dominant hemisphere. Other types of mixed aphasia include a combination of moderate Broca's or dynamic aphasia with anomic-sensory aphasia or mixed nonglobal aphasia and a combination of articulation and repetition aphasia. We believe that still other combinations of aphasias will be described as attention is turned to the analysis of various aphasia syndromes.

2

Symptoms of Aphasia and Their Relative Diagnostic Value

Most aphasic symptoms occur concurrently in the various types of anterior and posterior aphasia and cannot be considered pathognomic of any definite type of aphasia. These symptoms, therefore, have diagnostic value mainly as part of a particular aphasic syndrome. For example, fluent versus nonfluent speech is one of the most important differential signs of anterior and posterior aphasia, especially of Broca's and Wernicke's aphasia. Nonetheless, speech may be fluent enough in dynamic aphasia, mild Broca's aphasia, or in some cases of articulation aphasia. On the other hand, logorrhea and augmentation characterize most of the posterior aphasia but may be absent in almost half of the patients with posterior aphasia, especially in the acute stage of CVA. A list of the common aphasic signs and symptoms also includes such major aphasic manifestations as anomia, comprehension disorder of logicogrammatical construction and space–body relation in language, alienation of word meaning, difficulty in differentiation of phonemes and their series, etc.

This presence of the common aphasic symptoms in cases of both anterior and posterior aphasia has led to contradictions in aphasia classification. A particular type of aphasia syndrome, for example, anomia or anomic aphasia, has sometimes been described as an independent syndrome with a wide area of possible lesion localization in the left hemisphere. At the same time, anomia has been considered one of the symptoms of Wernicke's aphasia. Disorder of repetition with relatively good comprehension has been noted in repetition or conduction aphasia and often in the recovery stage of Wernicke's aphasia; therefore the clinical borderline between these two types of aphasia becomes vague. Assessment of the relative severity of the particular symptom as a part of the aphasic syndrome is important in the differential diagnosis of aphasia. For example, alienation of word meaning and impaired ability to follow commands in Head's and Luria's tests occur in both anterior and posterior aphasia, but these symptoms are more severe in posterior than in anterior aphasia when there is equal severity of the aphasia. Disturbed ability to name objects is also more severe in posterior aphasia. On the other hand, nonfluent speech is transient and less prominent in patients with posterior aphasia in the acute stage of CVA. Disorder of phoneme series repetition and differentiation may be noted in patients with phonemic-sensory aphasia, repetition aphasia, and Wernicke's aphasia, but the disturbance is much more prominent in patients with phonemic-sensory aphasia. The common symptoms also have to be examined qualitatively in the differential diagnosis. For example, the naming disorder in patients with posterior aphasia is characterized by the production of numerous verbal and literal paraphasias, attempts to explain the object's function without using the target word. Prompting of the first phonemes in the target word stimulates production of new literal and verbal paraphasias, but patients eventually find the right word, especially after repeated prompting of the first syllables. In anterior aphasia, attempts at naming objects make speech stop completely. Repeated stimulation, such as "Try to remember" or "What do you call this object?", may elicit the right answer, but patients often remain silent anyway. The same symptoms may have a different diagnostic value in the various tests. The existence of a comprehension disorder may provide a little help in distinguishing severe Broca's from Wernicke's aphasia in the acute stage of stroke. Signs of expressive speech disorder are more helpful in differentiating the anterior and posterior aphasia at that stage, since aphonia is characteristic of patients with Broca's aphasia, and a flow of unintelligible speech sounds is characteristic of patients with Wernicke's aphasia. At the same time, the presence of comprehension disturbance is very valuable in differentiating nonaphasic aphonia or severe dysarthria from the aphasic syndromes with aphonia or dysarthria.

Additional neurological symptoms also have to be considered in the differential diagnosis of aphasic syndromes. It is well known that marked right-sided hemiparesis may be seen in most patients with Broca's aphasia in the chronic stage of stroke, and that there is no weakness in the extremities or very mild weakness predominantly in the right hand in patients with Wernicke's and other posterior aphasias. This sign is also not pathognomic, however, just as in most of the aphasic symptoms, since right-sided hemiparesis may be noticeable for several hours or even days in cases of posterior asphasia immediately after the onset of stroke. In the chronic stage of stroke, patients with non-Broca's anterior aphasia also are often free from noticeable persistent right-sided hemiparesis; paresis of the right extremities is seen in less than 50% of patients with articulation aphasia.

The differential diagnosis of aphasic syndromes, therefore, must include qualitative and quantitative analysis of the symptoms and their relative severity, assess the values of the same symptoms in the various diagnostic tasks, and evaluate the main diagnostic criteria for aphasic syndromes in the acute stage compared to the chronic stage of CVA.

Symptoms of Aphasia and Their Assessment

Disorder of Expressive Speech

Information about expressive speech is mainly obtained in free conversation with the patients. This is crucial for all aphasia diagnosis, including anterior, posterior, and mixed aphasia, since free conversation with a patient gives vital information about his or her speech output. Such conversation is also very useful for the evaluation of the patient's comprehension and his mental status in general. The topics of conversation may deal with the patient's recall of the development of his illness, a description of his work, and details about his family situation. Patients may be asked, "How are you feeling today?" "How did the stroke develop?" "Where did it happen?" "Do you have children?" "What are they doing?" "Where did you work?" "Describe your profession," etc. During such a conversation patients with anterior aphasia often have to be encouraged to continue to speak with the words "Yes," "Sure," "Tell me more about this," "Don't worry, your speech will be better, it takes time." On the other hand, it is often wise to inhibit the speech of posterior aphasics with augmentation or logorrhea by saying "Sorry," or "Would you please repeat that?" since analysis of the "word salad" may be difficult in cases of nonstop speech activity. Free conversation for 10–15 minutes usually provides the examiner with the essential information for aphasia assessment. Additional information about expressive speech may be obtained by showing the patients pictures and asking them to describe the pictures or to retell a short story recounted by the examiner. More data may be derived by having the patient recite automatized sequences, such as the numbers 1, 2, 3, 4, etc., the days of the week, or the months, and sing "Happy Birthday to You" and similar well-known songs. Free conversational speech remains the most reliable source for expressive speech evaluation, so that most of the aphasic symptoms described below may be obtained in the course of a free conversation with aphasia patients.

Impoverishment of Speech The most severe manifestation of speech impoverishment is the restriction of speech output to three or four "verbal stereotypes." This is called "embolophasia" or "embolic occlusion" of expressive speech. In it a patient answers various questions with three or four stereotyped words or syllables, such as "pa-pa-pa," "ma-ma-ma," "yes," or "no." He is often trying to communicate by changing the intonation of the same embolophasic word or by a corresponding facial expression and gesture. In the less pronounced cases speech production is characterized by short, simplified phrases, so that not more than three or four words are included in the phrase. The words used in such speech are also restricted to the limited vocabulary of high-frequency words.

Speech impoverishment occurs in patients with anterior aphasia and mixed anterior–posterior aphasia and is less prominent or absent in patients with posterior aphasia. In posterior anomic-sensory aphasia, however, the degree of speech impoverishment can sometimes be matched with a corresponding level of disturbance in anterior dynamic aphasia, especially in the acute stage of stroke.

Changes in the Ratio of Nouns to Functional Words   There is an approximately constant ratio among the number of nouns, verbs, and grammatical functional words in normal speech. Fluctuation of that ratio is relatively small and depends on the circumstances. The number of nouns is higher when the matter discussed is well known to the people involved in the conversation, so that some of the verbs and small functional words may be omitted as redundant. A good example of such language is a telegram written on the assumption that the receiver of the telegram is well informed about the general condition and only needs some key words, mainly nouns, and some verbs in uninflected and declarative form, to understand the message. For example, "Flight 927 Saturday" means, "I will arrive in your city this Saturday on Flight 927. Time of arrival may be checked at the airport's inquiry office." An example of its opposite is a lecture given by an inexperienced lecturer who tries to make his subject matter more understandable by the use of numerous additional functional words.

A pathologic manifestation of changes in this ratio occurs in two major types of aphasia patients: preponderance of nouns, or telegraphic style, and preponderance of grammatical functional words, or "word salad," in more severe cases.

Preponderance of Nouns (Telegraphic Speech)   In this type, speech consists almost completely of uninflected nouns and verbs. Phrases are composed of only one or two words, and small functional words such as articles, connective words, and auxiliaries tend to be omitted (Zurif 1980). Verbs are also often dropped from these sentences and when they are retained their inflectional forms tend to be omitted. This type of speech disorder has been called telegraphic style because of the preponderance of the declarative grammatical forms and omission of the small, often redundant, functional words. At the less severe level, the number of verbs and small functional words used in expressive speech is higher, but because uninflected nounds predominate, the style still may be called telegraphic. Telegraphic style is typical for patients with anterior and mixed aphasia.

Preponderance of Grammatical Functional Words   In this, speech is characterized by the omission of nouns and some verbs and the predominance of small grammatical functional words. In severe cases such speech may be called "word salad" because of the absence of key words, content nouns and verbs, and numerous paraphasic errors, producing a mixture of senseless words. However, careful analysis may show that the patient is trying to compensate for the loss of the key words by circumlocution and may eventually be understood by the listener. In less severe cases, "word salad" is nonexistent or not noticeable, but a reduced number of content nouns and preponderance of small functional words may be noted. "Word salad" is almost pathognomonic for severe Wernicke's aphasia. A lesser predominance of small functional words may be seen in patients with anomic-sensory, anomic-spatial, and moderate to mild Wernicke's aphasia.

Disorder of Word Production and Word Finding   Literal paraphasia is one of the main manifestations of word-production disturbance. The patient cannot produce the right sequence of phonemes in the word and replaces the phoneme with other phonemes. These replacing phonemes, literal paraphasias, often have acoustical or articulatory similarity with the replaced phonemes ("p" instead of "b," "c" instead of "z," "d" instead of "t," "m" instead of "n," etc.). Sometimes literal paraphasia includes the reverse placement of correct phonemes in the word ("taleb" instead of "table"). Disorder of word production may be increased by the omission of phonemes and syllables from the word, so that "window" may sound like "wind" because the "ow" is omitted, or by the addition of a sound, such as "f" instead of "w", which will produce "find." Verbal paraphasia, replacement of the word, usually reflects a word-finding difficulty. The patient replaces the word with a word from the same semantic or phonological field. For example, "light" may be used instead of "lamp," "wash" for "sink," "table" for "desk," or "bible" for "table." Sometimes the similarity between the original and the replacing word is difficult to establish, and the replacing word seems to be accidentally chosen, but usually a connection can be found.

Word-production disorder with literal paraphasia usually occurs in patients with anterior aphasia and is less often encountered in posterior aphasia. Verbal paraphasia is much more frequent in patients with posterior aphasia, especially Wernicke's aphasia. However, numerous literal paraphasic errors are typical for patients with another type of posterior aphasia, repetition aphasia. Both literal and verbal paraphasic errors are quite predictable in anterior aphasia, so that "p" is usually replaced by "b," "t" by "d," "table" by "taleb," etc. In patients with posterior aphasia, including repetition aphasia, variable literal and verbal paraphasias are noted, and "p" may be replaced by "b," then by "t," and then by "l."

Naming Disorder Both the terms "anomic aphasia" and "amnestic aphasia" have been applied to the disorder of naming in patients with aphasia, although "anomic aphasia" more accurately reflects the main feature of this disturbance. In it a patient cannot usually remember the name of the object or the part of it pointed out for naming. Prompting of the first phonemes of the right word usually helps the patient to find it. The examination consists of having the examiner point to objects around the patient ("pillow," "floor," "ceiling," "window," "button," "sleeve") and to the body parts ("elbow," "eyelash," "eyebrow," "knee," "wrist"). The patient is asked to name each of the presented items. If he fails, a clue of two to four phonemes is given by the examiner starting with two phonemes, such as "wi," "win," "wind," for "window." The number of objects and body parts that the patient is unable to name shows roughly the degree of the naming disorder. Special sets of pictures have been developed for naming examination in the various aphasia testing batteries. Such sets include 80–100 items and are very useful for research and rehabilitation purposes, but for clinical diagnostic examination, the presentation of 8–10 objects and 5 or 6 body parts usually provides the examiner with the essential diagnostic information. An additional examination may include action naming ("walking," "standing," "eating," etc.) as well as what is called responsive naming ("What do you call the source of illumination in this room?" for "lamp").

Anomic aphasia may be seen in patients with various types of anterior and posterior aphasias. In patients with approximately equal levels of spontaneous speech disorder, however, naming disorder is more prominent in those who have posterior aphasia, including anomic-sensory aphasia, with naming disturbance as one of the main symptoms of the aphasic syndrome. On the other hand, prompting is often less helpful for naming in anterior aphasia than in posterior aphasia. Patients with anterior aphasia usually need a clue consisting of two or three syllables out of three- or four-syllable words. In posterior aphasia a prompting of one or two phonemes may lead to correct naming.

Naming disorder is usually distributed equally for objects and body parts, but in patients with anomic-spatial aphasia, the disturbance is often more noticeable with regard to naming body parts. In most patients with repetition aphasia, anomia is characterized by difficulty in finding the word ending, so that patients have easy access to the beginning of the appropriate word but use literal paraphasias when trying to finish naming the object. The usual type of anomic aphasia may also be noted in patients with repetition aphasia.

Disorder of Automatized Speech   Patients with aphasia usually have little difficulty in producing sequences of the weekdays (Monday, Tuesday, . . .), months (January, February, . . .), and especially single digits (one, two, . . .). Even in cases of severe aphasia with embolophasia or "word salad," some preservation of automatized speech may be revealed. That is why extreme disorder of automatized speech is noted only in patients with very severe aphasia.

Anosognosia of Speech Disorder   In this disorder the patient is not aware of the errors and changes in his speech output. In spite of his pronounced "word salad," a patient with severe Wernicke's aphasia speaks as if his speech were completely normal and everybody should understand what he is talking about. A patient often becomes angry when the examiner asks him to explain what he means. Anosognosia, or lack of awareness of speech disorders, is usually moderate or mild in patients with moderate Wernicke's aphasia or other types of posterior aphasia. In anterior aphasia, anosognosia of speech disorder is absent, and efforts, tension, and slowness of the nonfluent speech stress the active attempts of the patient to overcome the speech disorder.

Speech Hyper- and Hypoactivity   Hyperactive, "nonstop" speech is called "logorrhea." The patient speaks without any external stimulation. Sometimes the seemingly endless flow of speech contains many paraphasic errors and many small functional words, so that the term "logorrheic word salad" properly describes this fluent stream of senseless words. In the most severe cases that stream consists of indistinguishable sounds and may be called "mumbling." In less severe cases only a tendency to logorrhea may be noted. The patient answers a question with circumlocution and useless redundance. Augmentation may also be seen in such cases. Asked to repeat two syllables (pa-ba) or words ("table–house"), the patient adds two or three extra syllables or words to the end of the series. Therefore "pa-ba" will be repeated as "pa-ba-da-ta" or "table–house" will become "table–house–chair–dog," etc. Attempts to overcome the naming difficulty lead to the augmentation of the word ending with numerous literal paraphasias. Hyperactive speech should not be confused with festinating speech in the Parkinsonian syndrome, when speed of the speech is markedly increased, but no tendency to logorrhea, augmentation, or high speech activity may be noted.

Hypoactive speech, or dynamic speech disorder, is characterized by decreased speech initiation. The patient starts to speak only after external stimulations, and repeated encouragement is needed to keep him speaking. Articulation ability and normal speech volume is usually preserved, whereas in patients with the Parkinsonian syndrome the bradykinesia of speech is accompanied by slurring dysarthria and hypophonia.

Logorrhea and augmentation occur in posterior aphasia, especially in patients with Wernicke's aphasia, but also may be noted in repetition and anomic-sensory aphasia. Dynamic speech disorder is seen in patients with anterior aphasia and is a main symptom of dynamic anterior aphasia. Hypoactive speech may also be noted in patients with posterior anomic-sensory aphasia in the acute stage of stroke. The presence of augmentation is helpful in differentiating anomic-sensory aphasia from anterior aphasia in such cases.

Aphonia and Hypophonia   Complete loss of voice (aphonia) was not included in the aphasia syndromes in the early aphasia studies. Recently, an active approach to the diagnosis and treatment of acute CVA led to a more careful description of the neurological symptoms and syndromes in the first stage of stroke. It is now known that global and anterior aphasia may be manifested as a complete aphonia in the first hours and days of CVA (Tonkonogy 1964; Tonkonogy 1968; Mohr *et al.* 1978; Albert *et al.* 1981). The patient does not produce any sound; he is completely mute. He makes an effort to answer a question by moving his lips and tongue, but has no voice. He may moan when asleep. The patient's tongue movement is slow and he cannot protrude his tongue from his mouth. Aphonia differs from the severe dysarthia called "anarthria" in patients with bulbar and pseudobulbar disorder by the fact that swallowing is preserved. Patients with anarthria also have a severe dysphonia and a hoarse voice when speech starts to recover, while phonation after a period of aphonia in aphasic patients is produced in a clear, nondysphonic voice. Normal phonation replaces aphonia after a period of hypophonia, or low volume of speech. In some cases of aphasia, hypophonia becomes a persistent symptom during all stages of the acute and chronic periods of stroke.

Aphonia occurs in patients with mixed, mainly global aphasia, and anterior (usually Broca's) aphasia in the acute stage of CVA. Posterior aphasia does not manifest itself as an aphonia, and a "mumbling" stream of indistinguishable sounds may be perceived in some patients with severe Wernicke's aphasia right after the onset of the stroke.

Motor Dysprosody   Patients with motor dysprosody have a distorted rhythmical-melodic structure of speech. A free flow of speech, or melodic line, is interrupted; speech is characterized by effort, tension, arrest between words and while pronouncing a word. Speech output is nonfluent and laborious, and intonation changes sharply from low to high pitch and back to low pitch, so that the normal fluctuation of low and high pitches is disrupted. Dysprosody is increased by the frequent arrest of speech after pronunciation of one to two words and disturbed breathing control during speech.

Motor dysprosody is one of the most valuable signs of anterior aphasia in spite of being part of the nonlanguage disorder of speech. However, it has to be kept in mind that speech prosody is closely connected with language function, since intonation and a rhythmical-melodic line play a significant role in the process of language communication. Motor dysprosody may also be considered a symptom secondary to difficulty in word-finding and phrase production. However, patients with posterior aphasia have disorder of word-finding and production but retain the rhythmical-melodic structure of their speech output. Motor dysprosody is also seen as an independent type of anterior aphasia without a marked language disturbance, so that it can occur as a primary disorder of speech-language output. Motor dysprosody is usually prominent in patients with severe Broca's aphasia. Patients with dynamic aphasia and motor agrammatism and some patients with articulation aphasia show mild motor dysprosody or disorder of the rhythmical-melodic line of speech, but these may be absent. In patients with posterior aphasia the prosodic line of speech is preserved, but in some cases with anomic-sensory aphasia, especially in the acute stage of CVA, arrests for word-finding sometimes resemble motor dysprosody in dynamic aphasia.

Perseveration and Palilalia   Perseveration may be defined as repetition of the same word or phrase in answer to a question or command. The patient says "table" when the table has been pointed out by the examiner. He then continues to say "table" when a chair or a window is pointed out. After two or three minutes of rest, the patient begins correctly with the word "window" but continues to call the next presented objects "window." Perseveration also exists in following commands; for example, after a correct response to the command, "Close your eyes," the patient continues to close his eyes in answer to the subsequent commands, "Raise your hand," "Show your nose," "Touch the pillow." Palilalia is the repetition of the same word or phrase many times in answer to one question, as, "good—good—good . . .," or "I am doing well, I am doing well, I am doing well" in answer to the question, "How are you feeling?" Perseveration is often seen in patients with aphasia, especially anterior aphasia. Palilalia is typical for sub-cortical structure lesion and has been described in patients with pu-taminal lesion. Palilalia frequently occurs in patients with Parkinsonian dysarthria.

Articulation Disorder   Two main types of articulation disorder may be seen in patients with aphasia. One is slurring dysarthria, an articulation disorder developing secondary to paresis of the muscles used in speech production. In the other, movement of speech muscles is preserved, and the articulation disturbance occurs at the language phonemic level.

Slurring dysarthria is characterized by slurred, effaced nasal speech, so that the patient speaks as if he has "a hot match in the mouth." Slurring dysarthria usually occurs in patients with pseudobulbar disorder due to paresis of the speech muscles. The same muscles are used in swallowing, and disorder of swallowing often accompanies slurring dysarthria as well as nasal accented speech caused by paresis of the soft palate and uvula. In patients with aphasia, slurred pronunciation may be noticeable. This slurring dysarthria is seen in patients with anterior aphasia, especially Broca's aphasia. Its relation to pseudobulbar disorder remains unclear, however, since the lesion is usually unilateral in cases with aphasia, and no other pseudobulbar signs may be noted. Therefore swallowing is preserved and nasal accent is absent in such cases with aphasia and slurring dysarthria. Difficulty of muscle move-ment in speech production can be explained as a sequela of unilateral central paresis of the facial and hypoglossal nerves with a corresponding disorder of mouth and tongue motion in patients with aphasia.

Articulation production disorder seems to be a more essential aphasic symptom than slurring dysarthria. In cases of severe aphasic disorder, especially in the acute period of CVA, articulation production may be almost completely lost, and the patient cannot produce volitionally any articulation requested for repetition or needed for conversation. He opens his mouth, moves his lips and tongue, and produces a standard embolophasic word or syllable, "pa-pa," "ma-ma," "ta-ta-ta," "yes" in answer to every question. When articulation production begins to improve, repetition of some speech sounds, especially vowels, becomes possible, and the patient also produces some consonants in his reduced speech output. The vowels and consonants are often distorted and some of their differential features are missed. One of the most frequently omitted features is voicing, so that the patient utters instead of "b" a distorted sound resembling "p"; "z" is replaced by "s"; "ch" by "sh," etc. Sometimes articulation resembles a child's pronunciation with "l" instead of "r," "s" instead of "t," and so on. This omission of the differential features has to be distinguished from literal paraphasia, since a patient with the deformation of articulations produces a distorted, deformed speech sound. For example, "k" sounds somewhat like "h," but it is neither a "k" or "h"; it is a distorted, deformed speech sound resembling "k" more than "h." The term "literal paraphasia," therefore, cannot be applied in such a case. Distorted articulations often give the impression of a foreign accent, e.g., native English–American or Russian speakers sound as if they have a Scandinavian accent characterized by the soft pronunciation of "ch," "z," "k," and similar sounds.

Articulation production disorder is present in almost every patient with severe Broca's aphasia and is frequently seen in the milder cases In some patients articulation production disorder is a main manifestation of aphasia, and therefore the term "articulation aphasia" is useful.

Comprehension Disorder
Comprehension of ordinary conversational speech is usually preserved in most cases with moderate and mild anterior aphasia and disturbed in many patients with more severe Wernicke's aphasia, even in the chronic stage of stroke. In the past this led to the description of Broca's and Wernicke's aphasia as motor and sensory aphasia, respectively. Special testing of comprehension ability was first introduced by Marie (1906c) and revealed a comprehension disorder in patients with motor aphasia. To do this, Marie proposed the test of "the three pieces of paper." The patient was told, "Here on this table are three pieces of paper of different size; give me the largest one, crumple the middle-sized paper and throw it on the floor, and put the smallest one in your pocket." Based on the difficulty aphasics experienced in performing this test, Marie came to the conclusion that every aphasia is Wernicke's aphasia with or without expressive speech disorder, which depended on the presence of an additional lesion in the anterior "lenticular" speech zone. Marie's theory has not been well supported by later aphasia studies, but the testing of comprehension that he started has been carried further by many authors and plays a valuable role in aphasia diagnosis. For example, the disorder of expressive speech is best evaluated by assessing the free conversational speech of the patient. On the other hand, special testing is essential to evaluate properly the disorder of comprehension. Evaluating comprehension of conversational speech is included in this examination, but its role is less important than evaluation of conversational speech in an expressive speech dis-

order. An enormous number of tests to study comprehension may be devised, since almost any grammatical rule can be used to construct a new test. That is, the diagnostic value of the comprehension subtest must be proven before introducing it into the aphasia test battery. A detailed review of the methods of assessment comprehension deficit in aphasia was recently done by Boller *et al.* (1977).

Comprehension Disorder of Conversational Speech   This disorder may be manifested at the language and nonlanguage level, but most often it is related to language disturbance. Examination of expressive speech presents a good opportunity to assess the comprehension of conversational speech, since the patient has to understand questions about his illness, work, and family condition. If the patient does not understand the question, asks the examiner to repeat it, or answers a given question incorrectly, it is evident that he has a disorder of comprehension. Such a disorder occurs in patients with severe Wernicke's aphasia or in cases with phonemic-sensory aphasia ("phoneme or word deafness"). Comprehension of conversational speech is usually preserved in most patients with anomic-sensory aphasia, repetition aphasia, and mild to moderate Wernicke's aphasia, as well as in patients with anterior aphasia. Difficulties in comprehension may be revealed, however, when the patient tries to understand a conversation between other persons which is not directly related to his problem. Listening to a radio broadcast also presents difficulties for such a patient. Certainly, a precise evaluation of the disturbance in conversation comprehension is not easy, since the degree of disorder revealed often cannot be accurately assessed and the origin of the comprehension disturbance (phonemic, word, or phrase level) remains unclear.

Disorder of Word Comprehension   A primary disorder of word comprehension may occur on either the auditory or the semantic level. A disturbance at the auditory (verbal) level consists of difficulty in making the appropriate phonological identification of the word based on its auditory characteristics. At the next step of word recognition, this phonological identification has to be associated with a corresponding object, notion, or action; this process too may be disturbed, causing what is called alienation of word meaning. The secondary disorder of word comprehension may be related to a disturbance of the phonemic level (phonemic-sensory aphasia) or to a more basic hearing loss.

   The disorder of word comprehension is tested in the following way: The patient is asked to follow simple commands such as to point to an object or part of the body; for example, "Show the table," "window," "floor," "ceiling," "door," "lamp," "carpet," or "elbow," "knee," "eye," "ear," "nose." Some simple, two- or three-word phrases may also be used for testing word comprehension, such as, "Close your eyes," "Open your eyes," "Open your mouth," "Close your mouth." In comprehension testing, the examiner has to be careful not to give a clue to the patient by unconsciously looking at the corresponding object or body part, such as looking at the eyes when he asks the patient to close his eyes, or at the mouth when the task is to open or close the mouth.

Alienation of Word Meaning   Complete inability to follow any command is seldom seen, except in the acute stage of stroke. In a patient with severe comprehension disorder, the first simple command is usually comprehended and he opens his mouth or closes his eyes correctly according to the order. The next command, however, cannot be carried out, and the patient continues to close or open his eyes regardless of the subsequent commands. After resting for a few minutes, the patient may again carry out one or two simple commands and then becomes bewildered and unable to follow the commands. Such disorder of word comprehension has been called (Luria 1966; Tonkonogy 1968) alienation of word meaning and represents one of the most important signs of comprehension disturbance.

In less severe cases, alienation of word meaning is manifested after a few correct responses to the commands to show the floor, door, window, elbow, knee, foot, etc. A special test with variations can also be used to reveal a symptom of alienation in the moderate or mild disorder of word comprehension. The basic test consists of the command to show without repetition his or her nose . . . then his or her ear . . . then his or her eye . . . ear . . . eye . . . nose . . . eye. In such a condition the patient with aphasia starts to alienate the meanings of the words and to indicate instead of his or her nose, his or her eye when asked to touch the nose, etc. This test is called "the eye–ear–nose test with one component." In the same test with two components, the patient has to show his or her "ear, nose," then "eye, ear" . . . "ear, eye" . . . "nose, ear" in the same order as commanded by the examiner. This variation is more sensitive, so it may be used to reveal even a mild disorder of word comprehension.

Alienation of word meaning in a sense presents the mirror image of verbal paraphasic errors. Patients with paraphasic errors replace the right word with a similar but wrong word; in cases of alienation, a wrong object is indicated instead of the object named in the command.

It should also be stressed that operation within the same semantic field does not reduce alienation of word meaning as it does in comprehension disorder of conversational speech. On the contrary, alienation may be elicited if the commands are repeatedly confined to the same three or four objects, such as "eye–ear–nose." At the same time, the patient cannot easily change the semantic field from body parts to pieces of furniture, etc. But even when he is being tested in one definite semantic field, repetition of a restricted number of commands also reveals the alienation disorder.

Alienation of word meaning is noted in almost every patient with aphasia, but it is more prominent in patients with posterior aphasia and in severe Broca's aphasia.

Disorder of Auditory Word Recognition   This disorder can be considered to be the mirror image of literal paraphasia and phoneme omission in expressive speech. In it the patient cannot make a correct auditory phonological analysis of the word he or she hears. Some of the phonemes may be omitted or replaced by other phonemes in his or her perception, so that "bread" sounds like "bed," "table" like "cable," "bible," or "gamble," etc. Evaluating this disorder is much more difficult than assessing the paraphasic errors in expressive speech, since the patient's word perception can be evaluated only by indirect testing. In the past this led to controversy in the discussion of phonological disorders and their role in the disturbance of word comprehension. Some authors considered such a disorder a basic disturbance in Wernicke's aphasia (Luria 1940, 1947, 1966). On the other hand, Blumstein *et al.* (1977) showed that patients with lesions located below the Sylvian fissure make approximately the same number of errors in phonemic discrimination as patients with nonfluent aphasia, and therefore the degree of comprehension impairment does not correlate with the deficit on a phonemic discrimination test. These authors came to the conclusion that the phonemic processing deficit in patients with Wernicke's dysphasia is not at the perceptual or hearing level but at the level in which linguistic significance is associated with adequately perceived phonemes.

The controversy may be partly resolved by changing the focus from the theoretical-analytical level of the basic mechanisms of aphasia to the more clinical description of the auditory phonological disorder as a symptom of the comprehension impairment in aphasia. This disorder was repeatedly revealed when words spoken by the examiner had to be matched with objects, and patients with aphasia often responded to a phonemically similar word ("cable" instead of "table") included in the same series of oral word presentation (Schuell *et al.* 1964; Gardner *et al.* 1975). The role of the phonological disorder in comprehension impairment depends on numerous factors including the degree of the associated alienation of word comprehension and the level of the deficit in understanding the more complicated grammatical structures. Use of the quantitative combined assessment of general comprehension impairment is also very important, since the understanding of conversational speech cannot be used alone as an indicator of the degree of comprehension deficit.

The presence of a phonological deficit in auditory word comprehension may be suspected when a patient with a disorder of word comprehension shows difficulty in the repetition of words. Numerous literal paraphasic errors, or omission of phonemes, are noted in repetition of one- or two-syllable words, such as "cat," "table," "chair," "house," "window." The number of errors increases when the patient is asked to repeat a long, multisyllable word such as "industrialization" or a nonsense series of two or three syllables, "be-de-te," "ta-da-za," "rel-run," "dan-seez." Repetition disturbance may also be related to the disorder of expressive speech in patients with anterior aphasia, to the reduced word span in repetition aphasia, and to the primary deficit in auditory phonemic perception in phonemic-sensory aphasia ("word deafness").

Difficulty in Differentiation of Words and Series of Syllables   This may be tested to rule out any connection of the repetition disorder with the impairment of the speech output. The patient is asked to raise his hand if the two auditory presented words are the same ("table–table") and not to raise his hand when these words are different ("table–cable," "table–gamble"). Words that sound very much alike, as well as those that sound different, are used in this test. Series of syllables are presented in the same manner and include phonemically similar as well as dissimilar syllables: "ba-da-ta" versus "pa-za-ga" or "ba-da-ta" and "pa-ta-da." A variation of this test includes matching the auditory presented word with its picture. Phonemically similar words are used to test for the disorder of phonological analysis. Therefore word-comprehension impairment associated with the disorder of repetition and differentiation of the words and nonsense series of syllables may be considered a manifestation of the auditory phonological deficit in word recognition.

Phonological Analysis   Short and long words are said aloud and the patient is asked to spell them: for example, "cat," "dog," "table," "book," "watch," "pneumonia," "description," with or without repetition. A variation of this test requires complete exclusion of expressive speech. The patient is asked to raise his hand if, for example, "b" is present in the auditory presented word and not to raise his hand when "b" is absent ("table," "bread," "dog," "chair," "trouble," "cat"). Disorder at the phonetic level may be ruled out in testing if the patient correctly repeats and differentiates single vowels and consonants. Preservation of reading and especially of writing is also considered a sign that phonological analysis has been preserved.

Phonological disorder of auditory word recognition is prominent in patients with Wernicke's aphasia. It may also be present in Broca's aphasia as a secondary manifestation of the impairment in phonological analysis. In Wernicke's aphasia, the auditory component of the phonologial analysis is probably disturbed and a corresponding phonological deficit of word recognition is manifested. In Broca's aphasia, disorder of the motor component of the phonological analysis may result in the secondary disturbance of word recognition based on the phonological analysis. This type of comprehension impairment at the syntactical level was shown in patients with Broca's aphasia by Zurif and Caramazza (1976), and the existence of similar mechanisms at the phonological level cannot be excluded.

There is usually no phonological disorder of auditory word recognition in patients with posterior anomic-sensory and spatial-sensory aphasia or in patients with anterior dynamic or articulation aphasia.

A mild degree of phonological disorder in auditory word recognition may be noted in patients with repetition aphasia. This may stem from difficulty in the short-term retention of words during the time needed to complete the phonological analysis. Further psycholinguistic study may clarify the nature and mechanism of the phonological disorder in auditory word recognition.

Disorder of Auditory Phoneme Discrimination   In this disorder the patient cannot repeat or differentiate between single vowels or consonants. He repeats "e" as "o," "b" as "k," and "t" as "j," or refuses to repeat at all. He makes many errors when asked to raise his hand if both single speech sounds are the same ("a . . . a," "o . . . o") and not to raise his hand if they are different ("a . . . o," "t . . . k"). In less severe cases, a patient may correctly repeat and differentiate individual vowels but has great difficulty in doing so with consonants. Comprehension of words is noticeably disturbed in such cases, so that the term "word deafness" has been used to indicate the fundamental nature of this disorder of word comprehension. "Word deafness," however, occurs only when repetition and differentiation of single phonemes is disturbed; therefore the term "phonemic-sensory aphasia" or "phonemic deafness" seems to be more appropriate for this disorder. Nonauditory phonological analysis is usually preserved in such cases. At the same time, in patients with a phonological disorder of auditory word recognition a disturbance of the nonauditory phonological analysis of written words is usually present.

Disturbance of auditory phonemic discrimination is an important manifestation of phonemic-sensory aphasia or phonemic or "word deafness." In some patients with severe Wernicke's aphasia or global asphasia, however, auditory phonemic discrimination is markedly disturbed, especially in the acute stage of stroke.

Disorder of Phrase Comprehension   Various syntactical rules may be used to construct the phrases for the comprehension examination. Most of these phrases remain useful for research purposes, but some of them have been included in the regular clinical examination of aphasia. In general, such phrases reflect a body–space–time relation in language. They consist of the two major types of the tests developed by Head (1926) and Luria (1940, 1947, 1966). Head's and Luria's tests may be called "hand–ear–eye"and "logicogrammatical structures," correspondingly.

The "hand–ear–eye" test was first proposed by Head (1926) for examining the semantic component in language comprehension. The test originally included a set of pictures showing the left or right hand pointing in different ways toward the left or right ear or eye. The patient had to copy this position exactly, not to reverse it in order, for example, to touch his right ear with the index finger of the left hand if the picture showed this body-part relation. According to Head, mirror reflection of the hand–ear–eye relationship does not require the direct participation of the inner language, since the patient uses only his visual perception to imitate the corresponding relation. Therefore if the sample picture shows the right hand pointing to the left ear, the mirror reflection will be the left hand to the right ear, and this reflection can be done without language participation. On the other hand, Head suggested that reverse pointing cannot be performed without a semantic operation in the inner language to define the right–left relation between the hand and the appropriate part of the face. The same task is also presented by the examiner, who shows the various hand–ear–eye positions while sitting in front of the patient and asks him to copy these positions with the same hand and point to the same ear or eye as the examiner did. A third variation of this test consisted of the oral command by the examiner to perform the same task, i.e., "touch your right ear with your left hand," "left eye with the left hand," or more complicated, "left ear with the index finger of your left hand," "right eye with the ring finger of your left hand," "left eye with the little finger of your right hand" (if the patient does not have a right-sided hemiplegia).

The last, third, variation of Head's test eventually became a very useful tool in evaluating the phrase-comprehension deficit. The degree of comprehension impairment in this test correlates well with the general level of comprehension deficit in patients with aphasia. If a patient performs this test well, it is doubtful that he has aphasia. That is why Head's test is very important in differentiating aphasia from a non-aphasic disorder, especially in the acute stage of stroke. The "hand–ear–eye" test also shows the presence and the degree of comprehension disorder in patients with anterior aphasia and in some cases with posterior aphasia when comprehension of conversational speech is mostly preserved. The basic comprehension disorder, however, shown by failure to perform this test, remains unclear. The role of the syntactical language operation needed for such phrase comprehension also cannot be ruled out, since the word order in Head's command does not express the logical sequence of the task. His phrase, "show your right ear with the index finger of your left hand," has the words in reverse sequence ("right ear–index–left hand") to evoke the action, "left hand–index finger–right ear." Certainly, further study is needed to clarify the basic mechanisms involved in the performance of Head's "hand–eye–ear" test, but the clinical importance of this test for phrase-comprehension evaluation remains quite clear.

Comprehension of the logicogrammatical structures seems to be somewhat compromised in Head's test, since the logical sequence of the presented phrase does not usually correspond to the sequential order of the words in the phrase, especially in the phrase with prepositions "after," "before," and "with," and to the inverted, passive subject-object order.

The prepositions "after" and "before" can be tested with the phrases: "I ate lunch after I called my friend: What did I do first?" "Do you put your shoes on before your socks?" "Do you have lunch after dinner?" The preposition "with" is tested in the phrase, "With the key, touch the pencil" or "Touch the pencil with the key," "Touch the key with the pencil," etc. The passive order is, "A fox was killed by a wolf: Which animal is dead?" or "A boy was eaten by the steak. Is this phrase right or wrong?" and "A steak was eaten by the boy. Right or wrong?" Therefore, in all the presented types of phases the logical sequence differs from the sequence of the words. For example, in the phrase, "A fox was killed by a wolf," the grammatical sequence is "fox–wolf" and the logical order is "wolf–fox." In the phrase "Touch the pencil with the key" the grammatical order "pencil–key" is presented versus the logical sequence "key–pencil," etc.

Comprehension of such structures is especially difficult for patients with aphasia even if their understanding of conversational speech seems to be almost completely preserved. Aphasia patients have a similar difficulty with comprehension of a phrase in which the logical structure of the object's relation or position in space is not defined by the order of the words. There are two main types of such phrases. In one type a possessive relationship is vague and reversible, e.g., "Who is my husband's sister, a man or a woman?" or "My sister's husband," "My brother's wife." The possessive relationship can also be used to reveal a striking disorder, as when a patient with aphasia is asked to show "my nose," "your ear," "my shoulder," "your elbow."

Another type of difficult logical structure is presented by phrases that describe the spatial relationship between two objects, as expressed by the terms "to the right of," "to the left of," "behind," "on," "under," "in front of," "in back of." Most of the patients with anterior and posterior aphasia show a comprehension impairment for all the types of described phrases, so that comprehension of these phrases can be used for a more precise quantitative–qualitative assessment of the phrase-comprehension disorder. The degree of this disorder usually corresponds to the level of disturbance shown by Head's "hand–ear–eye" test. In some types of aphasia, however, comprehension may be especially difficult for particular types of phrases. For example, the relative position of the two objects in the space described by the phrases "to the right of," "on," "under," "behind," etc., is especially difficult for patients with anomic-spatial aphasia to understand. At the same time, these types of phrases are less difficult to comprehend compared to other logicogrammatical structured phrases, for patients with anomic-sensory or moderate Wernicke's aphasia.

Disorder of Gesture Comprehension   In some patients with severe Wernicke's or global aphasia, comprehension of gesture is disturbed. Patients cannot understand such simple commands as "open your mouth," "close your eyes," "raise your hand," "follow me," or "leave this room." A total disorder of gesture comprehension occurred in one of our patients with "phonemic deafness" and bilateral superior-temporal infarction.

Disorder of Word Span Retention   Repetition and pointing span includes 7 ± 2 words in normal subjects. This span is restricted to one to three words in patients with aphasia. Patients are asked to repeat a series of three or four words, such as "dog–cat–pen" or "dog–cat–pen–chair." Most aphasia patients who are able to repeat one word repeat two or three words, sometimes changing the order of the presented words in the series. When repetition is disturbed, the pointing word span is evaluated. In the simpler series, patients are instructed to point to three or four objects in the room, for example, "show the window . . . door . . . carpet," then "show the ceiling . . . the washstand . . . the curtain . . . the chair." A set of ten or twelve cards with pictures of objects is often used in the pointing-span test for changes in the position of objects in new presentations, since objects in the room are permanent and their position in space may orient the patient and help him to perform the pointing-span test.

A disorder of word-span retention is evident in patients with global, Broca's, or Wernicke's aphasia. Word-span retention is often restricted to one or two or two or three words. A marked disorder of word-span retention may also appear in posterior anomic-sensory aphasia and especially in repetition aphasia, whereas in anterior, dynamic, or articulation aphasia word-span retention is less limited and includes four to five words, and in some cases six words.

Repetition Impairment
A disorder of phoneme repetition may be revealed when the patient is asked to repeat "a," "o," "u," "e," "k," "g," "j," "p," "b," etc. Most of the consonants and some of the vowels are actually said as a syllable "key," "gi," "jay," "ou," etc. An irregular order of phonemes in such syllables may also be used, i.e., "key," 'e-e-k," "gi," "ig." This repetition of the isolated phonemes is disturbed in patients with a problem in articulation production because of difficulty at the motor end of the repetition processing. Repetition disorder for a single phoneme may also be secondary to disturbance of the auditory phoneme processing. In both articulation and auditory types of repetition impairment, the patient cannot correctly reproduce the requested single speech sound. In more severe cases with deficit in articulation production, the patient will try to find the appropriate position of the muscles used in speech, but only a restricted number of "embolophasic" vowels or consonants may be produced. At the same time, auditory differentiation of the single phoneme is preserved and a patient may be seen to correctly raise his hand when two phonemes are the same and not to raise his hand if the phonemes are different. This differentiation is performed with many mistakes and often only by chance when the auditory part of repetition processing is disturbed. The patient tries to listen carefully to the speech sound. He is asked to repeat it but reproduces another speech sound sometimes quite different from the requested phoneme. In less severe cases the articulation deficit in repetition appears as a deformation, a distortion of articulation, or as a foreign accent in expressive speech. Auditory sensory impairment of phonemic repetition processing is characterized by literal paraphasic errors during attempts to reproduce a presented phoneme. The disorder of phoneme repetition is one of the major symptoms of anterior articulation aphasia and posterior phonemic-sensory aphasia. The difficulty of articulation production leads to repetition disorder in articulation aphasia and impairment of auditory phoneme recognition produces a repetition

deficit in phonemic-sensory aphasia. Similar articulation problems may be responsible for phoneme repetition disorder in severe Broca's aphasia, and a deficit in auditory phoneme recognition leads to the disorder of phoneme reproduction in severe Wernicke's aphasia. Both of these mechanisms are probably responsible for the noticeable disorder of single phoneme repetition in global aphasia. At the same time, repetition of the single phoneme is preserved in moderate and mild Broca's and Wernicke's aphasia, and in anterior and posterior aphasias, including repetition aphasia, in which repetition disturbance appears at the level of the series of phonemes and word reproduction.

Disturbance of Word Repetition   In more severe cases the patient cannot repeat without mistakes, omission of the phonemes, and literal paraphasic errors a simple well-known one- or two-syllable word ("table," "dog," "cat," "door," "book," "chair"). A milder disorder of word repetition may be revealed when the patient is asked to repeat multisyllable and low-frequency words ("electroencephalograph," "Gibraltar," "industrialization," "geographic," "statistical," "hippopotamus"). Word repetition is disturbed mainly in Broca's and Wernicke's aphasia, including moderate and sometimes mild forms of aphasia. Repetition of low-frequency and multisyllable words may actually be noted in all types of aphasia, including so-called transcortical anomic-sensory and dynamic aphasia.

Repetition Disorder of Phonemes and Syllable Series   These series include three vowels ("a-o-u," "u-o-a") or three syllables with the same consonant and various vowels ("ba-bo-bu," "bu-bo-ba"). Repeating a series of oppositional phonemes ("pa-ba," "da-ta," "va-fa," "fa-va") is also difficult for patients with aphasia. In all types of aphasia, a repetition disorder of such series is present, but this disorder is more prominent in Broca's and Wernicke's aphasia, probably secondary to the impairment of phonological analysis. A deficit in retention of the phonemes or syllables span may also play a role, especially in patients with repetition aphasia.

Disorder of Phrase Repetition   This is more noticeable for prolonged and more complicated phrases ("The car parked in the garage is an old Plymouth"). Phrases with a preponderance of small functional words ("he is the one who did it") are equally difficult for patients with aphasia. Disorder of phrase repetition is especially severe for patients with Broca's, Wernicke's, and repetition aphasia. Complicated phrases, however, may also be difficult for repetition in various types of anterior and posterior aphasia. Therefore repetition of isolated vowels, consonants, and syllables is impaired in phonemic-sensory aphasia ("phonemic deafness"). Patients with Broca's and Wernicke's aphasia have a phonological, syntactical, and semantic disorder of word and phrase comprehension and a corresponding disturbance in repetition. During repetition a motor dysprosody with laborious speech may be seen in Broca's aphasia, and augmentation, a tendency to logorrhea, and fluent paraphasic speech in Wernicke's aphasia.

On the other hand, repetition is preserved or mildly disturbed in patients with "transcortical" dynamic and anomic-sensory aphasia, probably because of preserved phonological analysis and less prominent disorder at the syntactical level and in word-span retention. That is why testing repetition is useful in the diagnostic evaluation of these types of aphasia. Mild repetition disorders, however, occur in other various types of anterior and posterior aphasia, including mild Broca's and Wernicke's aphasia, nonglobal mixed aphasia, and anomic-spatial aphasia, so that aphasia diagnosis cannot be made only on the basis of repetition study, and other tests and methods of evaluation have to be used for diagnostic purposes. Therefore the old Wernicke-Lichtheim term "transcortical aphasia" for patients with relatively preserved repetition seems to be inappropriate for the more detailed differentiation of various aphasia syndromes. The same is also true for patients with marked repetition disorder, since a deficit in single phoneme repetition may be noted in articulation aphasia and phonemic-sensory aphasia as well as in severe Broca's and Wernicke's aphasia, where the nature of repetition disturbance may be quite different.

A primary disorder of repetition cannot be completely ruled out in some cases with so-called repetition or conduction aphasia. Disorders of expressive speech and comprehension are not noticeable in such cases, and marked repetition disorder with literal paraphasia are the major clinical manifestation of repetition aphasia. These repetition disorders are mainly characterized by difficulties in reproduction of words, phrases, and series of phonemes and syllables, and preserved repetition of the single vowels, consonants, and syllables. At the same time, comprehension of words and phrases is only mildly disturbed, and disorder of expressive speech is restricted to literal paraphasic errors.

Disorder of Reading
Reading of single letters is disturbed in relatively severe cases of Broca's and Wernicke's aphasia and in cases with mixed, especially global aphasia. Unusual difficulty is encountered in reading different styles or fonts of printed letters. This literal alexia is secondary to the language disorder in patients with aphasia and usually has no relation to the primary disturbance of letter-reading in so-called agnostic alexia. Literal

alexia in patients with aphasia manifests itself in many cases as an anomia for letters, but nonrecognition of the letters may also be seen in severe global Broca's or Wernicke's aphasia. Such patients fail in letter-matching, especially when the same letter is presented in the various types of characters.

Reading words is disturbed in most of the anterior and posterior aphasias with the disorder of phonological analysis. Impairment of reading is more often seen in multisyllable and low-frequency words ("Gibraltar") than in short, well-known words ("wood," "carpet," "dog," "cow"). In severe cases (Broca's, Wernicke's, global aphasia), reading seems to be impossible, but patients may correctly match cards with the name and picture of an object if the set includes cards with names and pictures of three or four objects. This "global" reading may be used for the restoration of phonological analysis and of reading and writing ability in patients with aphasia. In severe aphasia, reading is often preserved for so-called ideographs or words well known to the patient such as "U.S.A.," "Washington," "America," his or her last name. Some patients show greater ability in silent reading than in reading aloud, since an expressive speech disorder often increases the reading difficulties.

Reading phrases reflects the difficulty in word and letter reading, but in less severe cases of aphasia, disordered reading of prolonged and complicated phrases may be more noticeable, especially if the patient shows a marked syntactical deficit in his oral language.

The reading disorder is usually secondary to or at least concurrent with aphasia, maybe due to the underlying impairment of phonological analysis. In more severe cases of Broca's, Wernicke's, or global aphasia, however, the role of the lesion extension to the primary parietal or occipital center of reading cannot be excluded, since the degree of alexia does not often correspond to the severity of Broca's or especially of Wernicke's aphasia.

Disorder of Writing
Writing may be disturbed at the same literal, word and phrase level as alexia. In some cases, however, dissociation occurs between writing on dictation and copying written material. Test examples for writing are similar to those in reading examination. The patient is asked to write on dictation and copy a single letter, one or two syllables, high-frequency words and multisyllable low-frequency words, short and prolonged phrases, and simple and complicated ones.

Impairment of writing is usually more severe than the reading difficulty in patients with aphasia. A marked agraphia may be revealed not only in Broca's, Wernicke's, or global aphasia but in cases with dynamic or even articulation aphasia, where writing is often disturbed along with the phonological analysis. Reading is usually preserved in these cases.

Calculation Disorders
The most difficult operations for patients with aphasia are:

1. Reading and writing complicated digits, such as 1004, 100014, 1515, 710017;
2. The multiplication table, especially using numbers from 5 on up (5×6, 7×9, 6×7);
3. Subtraction of numbers, such as $32 - 17$, $48 - 29$, $83 - 47$, without writing these figures during the operation of subtraction.

Calculation disorder occurs in almost every patient with anterior or posterior aphasia. Certainly the severity of this disturbance markedly differs in the various aphasias and, in general, is more prominent in Broca's, Wernicke's, and corresponding mixed, especially global, aphasia. In articulation and phonemic-sensory aphasia, acalculia is mild or absent in most of the cases. On the other hand, in some patients with Broca's, Wernicke's, or global aphasia, acalculia is so severe that patients cannot perform a simple addition with single digits ($2 + 3$, $4 + 5$). An extension of the lesion to the left inferior parietal lobe is suggested in those cases.

It should also be stressed that acalculia in patients with aphasia significantly depends on the language disorder. These patients sometimes show a completely preserved calculation ability when playing cards or using real money, since assessment of the cards and money value can be based on the recognition of the corresponding picture without phonological analysis of the corresponding spoken or written word.

Apraxia and Agnosia
Detailed reviews of the various types of apraxia and agnosia are beyond the scope of this book, and the reader is referred to the publications of Critchley (1953); Luria (1966); Brain (1965); Tonkonogy (1973); Hécaen and Albert (1978). In this book the description of apraxia and agnosia is restricted to the problems of impairments that are closely related to aphasia.

Apraxia   Buccofacial apraxia is characterized by the inability to carry out the requested facial movement on command or to imitate the examiner's movement as requested. Most of the movements a patient performs involuntarily without difficulty so that automatic movements of the facial articulatory muscles are preserved. Volitional response is impaired, however, and the patient cannot show on verbal command or by imitating how to "blow out a match," "sip through a straw," "cough," "lick the lips," "whistle," "sniff," "click the tongue," etc.

Buccofacial apraxia is present in almost every patient with anterior aphasia, being especially notable in Broca's and articulation aphasia. No direct correlation has been noted between the severity and the type of aphasia and buccofacial apraxia (DeRenzi *et al.* 1966; Tonkonogy 1968). Buccofacial apraxia may be noted in some patients with posterior aphasia when the lesion extends to the inferior parietal lobule with probable central gyri involvement. Buccofacial apraxia is more often present in patients with anterior aphasia and may be considered one of the most valuable additional signs in the differential diagnosis of anterior and posterior aphasia.

Symbolic and ideomotor apraxia is the name given to the inability to respond with appropriate movements to the commands "Salute like a soldier," "Show how you wave good-bye," "How would you beckon to come here?", "Make a fist," "How would you flip a coin?", etc. This apraxia is often seen in patients with anterior aphasia and in some cases of posterior aphasia. Dynamic apraxia has been described by Luria (1947, 1966) and is characterized by a disorder of serial movements of the hands and/or legs. The patient cannot carry out the requested series of movements, "Show your palm, rib, fist," "Rib, palm, fist," or "Show your left fist, your right palm," "Left palm, right fist," etc. Dynamic apraxia may be seen more often in patients with anterior aphasia.

Positional apraxia may be revealed when the patient is asked to imitate the hands' relative positions to themselves or to the various parts of the face. The examiner requests the patient to imitate his hands' position; for example, the patient has to imitate touching with the index finger of the left hand the left corner of the mouth or the left corner of the left eye or the left ear lobe. The same may be done for the right side of the face. Two hands may also be placed in the various positions, including touching with the tips of the fingers of one hand, the palm of the other hand, etc. Positional apraxia is a very useful clue indicating extension of the lesion to the inferior parietal lobule, especially to the supramarginal gyrus, in patients with anterior, posterior, or mixed aphasia.

Constructional apraxia has attracted much attention in recent years, and so many sophisticated tests have been devised to evaluate it that this type of apraxia has become unreliable in localizing brain pathology. Severely impaired constructional praxis for two-dimensional figures, however, can still be used as a sign that the lesion extends to the left inferior parietal lobule. That sign includes impairment in drawing on verbal command or in imitating two-dimensional geometric figures, such as a triangle, a diamond, a star, or a simple scheme of a face, a house, etc. Evidence of "close-in" symptoms may also be seen in such a drawing when, e.g., the patient's copy of the star is almost "closed in" to the star he had to copy. A somewhat different type of constructional apraxia has also been described in patients with a right parietal lobe lesion or frontal lobe pathology. Right parietal lesion produces apraxia in construction of two- or three-dimensional blocks and geometric figures based on these blocks (Hécaen and Albert 1978). Frontal lobe pathology is responsible for constructional difficulty secondary to a disorder of goal-directed behavior. Clinical evaluation of the constructional apraxia due to right parietal or frontal lesion seems to be more difficult, however, since it is less definite than a simple apraxia in construction of the two-dimensional forms and figures resulting from the lesion of the left inferior parietal lobule.

Agnosia   Auditory agnosia for the sound of objects may be revealed when the examiner stands behind the patient and asks him or her to identify the sound of jingling keys, rubbing paper, or applause produced by the examiner when the patient cannot see the objects. A tape recorder is also used to present the sounds of wind, a car engine, a train, a cow, a cat, a dog, a crying child, etc.

Auditory agnosia sometimes accompanies a phonemic-sensory aphasia and severe Wernicke's aphasia, but recognition disorder of an object's sound has been described in cases without any sign of aphasia (Hécaen and Albert 1978). Auditory agnosia for emotional and intonational characteristics of speech is discussed below in chapter 4 in the section Phonemic-Sensory Aphasia.

Recognition and reproduction of rhythmic patterns is often disturbed in patients with aphasia, especially in cases of posterior aphasia. The patient cannot differentiate such patterns as a l-l-s-l from l-s-l-l (l = long, s = short signal) and has difficulty in reproducing them. A series of both simple and complex patterns may be used to evaluate the rhythmic recognition. However, assessing the results for tests with complicated rhythmic patterns is more difficult and vague because of the additional factors involved in the performance of these tasks (general memory disturbance, amusia, frontal lobe syndrome, etc.).

The disorder of topographic orientation is often seen in patients with aphasia. Such a patient does not show any noticeable sign of impairment in real space orientation (the hospital ward, his home, streets near his home, etc.), but his mental geographic orientation is disturbed. The patient cannot show on a blank sheet of paper the direction of north, south, east, or west, or when asked to pretend that the paper is a map of the United States he cannot indicate the state of Florida with reference to Alaska, Detroit, and Miami; Los Angeles and New York; or the Atlantic and Pacific oceans. Difficulty in orientation in the patient's room on the ward may also be found. This disorder of orientation in the topographic or space scheme seems to be secondary to the impairment in the language formulation of the relationship between the objects in space ("to the right of," "behind," "on the top," etc.).

Finger agnosia, described by Gerstmann (1924, 1927) is a type of somatognosia. The patient cannot stretch out or bend on command the same finger as the examiner, such as the index or ring finger. The ability to point to the particular finger touched by the examiner is also disturbed. Finger anomia completes this picture of somatognosia, apraxia and anomia, called finger agnosia. The presence of finger agnosia usually depends on the lesion extension to the left inferior parietal lobule.

Finger agnosia is a feature of Gerstmann's syndrome, which also includes acalculia, right-left disorientation, and agraphia and occurs in patients with a lesion of the left angular gyrus.

Right-left disorientation often occurs in an aphasic syndrome due to the language disturbance. A sign of such disorientation can be seen in almost every patient with aphasia when Head's "hand–ear–eye" tests ("touch your right ear with your left hand," etc.) is given to the patient. A primary difficulty of the right-left orientation is also seen, especially in the acute stage of stroke. The patient has to touch his right or left arm or the right or left arm of the examiner when the arms are lying at the sides of the trunk, or crossed on the chest. A number of more complicated tests have been introduced to evaluate right-left disorientation. The results of such tests, however, often depend on additional factors, including the language disorder, the visual complexity of the test, or a memory problem, so that those results only partly reflect a primary impairment of the right-left orientation caused by the lesion of the left inferior-parietal lobule.

Astereognosis is characterized by a deficit in the tactile recognition of objects, such as a key, a pen, a pencil, a coin, etc., and occurs in patients with a lesion of the left supramarginal gyrus. Astereognosis accompanies aphasia with extension of the lesion to the anterior-inferior parietal region.

Evaluation of aphasia patients may be facilitated by using a rating scale for aphasia symptoms. Such a rating scale may help build a bridge from the constantly growing number of neuropsychological batteries of aphasia tests to the clinical symptomatology of aphasia. This is especially important, since the assessment of neuropsychological testing can be adjusted by such a scale to the clinical needs and bedside reality.

One of the first rating scales for aphasia evaluation has been included in the test battery developed in the 1960s and early 1970s by Goodglass and Kaplan and entitled the "Boston Aphasia Diagnostic Examination" (Goodglass and Kaplan 1983). A similar scale was developed for computer application in aphasia diagnosis by Frantsuz *et al.* (1964). A rating scale for aphasia may also be used in the future to develop a special score for differential diagnosis of aphasia syndromes based on clinical examination and neuropsychological testing.

Rating Scale for Aphasia Symptoms

A. Articulation and prosody
    1. Articulation disorder
       (a) Deformation of articulation, "foreign accent"
           (3) Most words distorted by the deformed articulations
           (2) Many words with one or two distorted articulations
           (1) Occasional distorted articulations
           (0) Normal
       (b) Slurring dysarthria
           (3) Severe slurring speech
           (2) Slurring, nasal speech
           (1) Mild slurring speech
           (0) Normal
    2. Voicing disorder
           (3) Aphonia
           (2) Hypophonia, mumbling, and whispering
           (1) Mild hypophonia
           (0) Normal
    3. Motor dysprosody
           (3) Severe tension and effort with distorted breathing control during speech; speech nonfluent, slow, interrupted by arrests and sudden changes of volume and accent
           (2) Moderate tension, slowness, and distortion of the prosodical, rhythmical-melodic structure of speech
           (1) Same changes, but fewer
           (0) Normal fluent speech
    4. Speed of speech
       (a) Increased
           (3) Very fast, slurring speech
           (2) Moderate increase of speech speed
           (1) Mild increase
           (0) Normal
       (b) Decreased

      (3) Very slow bradykinetic speech

      (2) Moderate bradykinesia

      (1) Mild bradykinesia

  5. Speech activity

    (a) Increased

      (3) Severe logorrhea, nonstop speech

      (2) Moderate logorrhea, augmentation of words

      (1) Augmentation of words in naming and repetition

      (0) Normal

    (b) Decreased

      (3) Severe adynamia, absence of attempts to speak

      (2) Decreased speech initiation; the patient starts and continues to speak after repeated verbal stimulation

      (1) Mild decrease of speech activity

B. Paraphasia and perseveration

  6. Literal paraphasia

      (3) Most words markedly distorted by literal paraphasias

      (2) One or two literal paraphasias

      (1) Occasional literal paraphasias

      (0) No literal paraphasia

  7. Verbal paraphasia

      (3) More than 50% of words replaced by verbal paraphasias

      (2) One or two verbal paraphasias in a phrase of six or seven words

      (1) Occasional verbal paraphasias

      (0) No verbal paraphasia

  8. Standard or variable paraphasias, verbal and literal

      (3) Marked variability of paraphasias, verbal or literal

      (2) Stable, similar paraphasias, verbal or literal

      (1) No clear impression

      (0) No difference

  9. Perseveration

      (3) Often, 30–50%

      (2) Moderate, 10–20%

      (1) Occasional

      (0) Normal

C. Agrammatism

  10. Impoverishment and simplification of speech

      (3) Embolophasia

      (2) Short sentences of two or three mostly high-frequency words

      (1) Sentences of four to six words, rarely auxiliary phrases, and many high-frequency words

(0) Normal
11. Telegraphic speech
   (3) Almost complete absence of small functional words; mostly one or two word phrases, usually nouns
   (2) Prevalence of nouns and verbs, marked reduction of small functional words
   (1) Mildly telegraphic
12. "Word salad" and circumlocution
   (3) Numerous verbal paraphasias, many incomprehensible small functional words, "word salad" speech
   (2) Predominance of small functional words, decreased number of nouns, verbs, and circumlocution
   (1) Mildly decreased number of nouns, tendency to circumlocution
   (0) No "word salad" or circumlocution

D. Naming
13. Anomia
   (3) Anomia for 60–80% of all objects presented for naming
   (2) Anomia for 30–50% of presented objects
   (1) Anomia for 10–20% of presented objects, especially objects with low-frequency names
   (0) Normal

E. Repetition
14. Repetition disorders
   (a) Single phonemes
      (3) Inability to repeat 50–80%
      (2) Inability to repeat 20–40%
      (1) Inability to repeat 10–15%
      (0) Normal
   (b) Series of phonemes and syllables
      (3) Inability to repeat 50–80%
      (2) Inability to repeat 20–40%
      (1) Inability to repeat 10–15%
      (0) Normal
   (c) Words
      (3) Inability to repeat one-syllable words
      (2) Inability to repeat longer and lower-frequency words
      (1) Inability to repeat only a few longer and lower-frequency words
      (0) Normal
   (d) Sentences
      (3) Inability to repeat two- or three-word sentences

(2) Disorder of repetition of longer (4–5 words) and more grammatically complicated sentences

(1) Difficulty in repeating phrases with a higher proportion of small functional words

(0) Normal

F. Pointing Span

15. Disorder of word-series retention

(3) Disorder of retention of two-word series

(2) Retention limited to two or three words

(1) Retention of four or five words

(0) Normal

G. Serial speech

16. Impairment of automatized speech

(3) Severe disorder of serial speech for such memorized sequences as counting up to 20, and reciting the days of the week and the months of the year

(2) Errors, prolonged stops, especially for reciting the months of the year

(1) Some errors, slowness of verbal performance in serial speech

(0) Normal

H. Differentiation of speech sounds

17. Disturbance in differentiation of speech sounds

(a) Single speech sounds

(3) Disorder of distinguishing 60–80% of single vowels and consonants

(2) Disorder of distinguishing 30–50% of single speech sounds

(1) Disorder of distinguishing 10–15% of single speech sounds

(0) Normal

(b) Phoneme and syllable series

(3) Errors in differentiation of 60–80% of two- or three-vowel or -syllable series

(2) Errors in differentiation of 30–50% of the same series

(1) Errors in differentiation of 10–15%

(0) Normal

I. Comprehension of speech and gestures

18. Disorder of speech and gesture comprehension

(a) Simple commands

(3) Severely disturbed comprehension of simple commands; patient cannot follow them completely or can follow only the command given at the beginning of the examination

          (2) Patient can follow most simple commands in one category of objects but not in new category

          (1) Mild impairment of comprehension when changing from one category of objects to another

          (0) Normal

    (b) Complex commands

          (3) Errors in 70–90% of Head's "hand–ear–eye" test and Luria's logicogrammatical tests

          (2) Errors in 20–60% of Head's and Luria's tests

          (1) Errors in 10–15% in the same tests

          (0) Normal

    (c) Conversational speech and gestures

          (3) Complete or almost complete impairment of comprehension of conversational speech and gestures

          (2) Difficulty in comprehension of speech over telephone or radio or conversation between two persons which is not directed to the patient

          (1) Disorder manifested only if patient has to comprehend rapid speech, especially when speech is not directed to the patient

          (0) Normal

19. Alienation of word meaning

          (3) Severe alienation of word meaning in following simple commands, especially those shifted from one object to another

          (2) Alienation of word meaning in "eye–ear–nose" test with one component

          (1) Alienation of word meaning in same test with two components

          (0) No alienation

J. Phonological analysis, reading, and writing

    20. Disorder of phonological analysis

          (3) Inability to assess number of phonemes in short, one-syllable words or differentiate between words with or without certain phonemes

          (2) Difficulty in assessment of number of phonemes in multisyllable words; errors in differentiation of words with or without certain phonemes

          (1) Mild impairment

          (0) Normal

    21. Alexia

          (3) Complete or almost complete loss of ability to read with preservation of reading for three to four ideographs

        (2) Reading is slow; literal and verbal paralexias

        (1) Some slowness of reading; occasional literal and verbal paralexias

        (0) Normal

22. Agraphia

        (3) Complete or almost complete loss of ability to copy, to write volitionally, or on dictation

        (2) Slow copying, with errors; writing on dictation and volitional writing markedly disturbed

        (1) Some slowness of writing; occasional literal and verbal paragraphias

        (0) Normal

K. Associated symptoms

23. Buccofacial apraxia

        (3) Severe disorder of volitional movement; preserved involitional motion of the tongue

        (2) Failure to perform many tests of buccofacial praxis

        (1) Occasional errors and slowness of buccofacial praxis

        (0) Normal

24. Hemiplegia: (a) right, (b) left

        (3) Complete or almost complete loss of movement

        (2) Moderate hemiparesis, more prominent in distal parts of the extremities

        (1) Mild weakness, predominantly in hand and foot

        (0) Normal

25. Hemihypesthesia: (a) right, (b) left

        (3) Hypesthesia to pinprick and touch; loss of position and vibration sense

        (2) Hypesthesia to pinprick only

        (1) Vague hypesthesia to pinprick

        (0) Normal

26. Hemianopia: (a) right, (b) left

        (3) Complete or almost complete hemianopia

        (2) Loss of vision in upper or lower quadrant

        (1) Incomplete quadrant hemianopia

        (0) Normal

II

Syndromes of Aphasia and Stroke Evolution

3
Anterior Aphasia

Anterior aphasia is characterized by a disorder of expressive speech and comprehension resulting from a lesion of the anterior part of the language zone of the dominant (in most cases) left hemisphere. The major structures of the anterior part of the language zone include the gray and white matter of the posterior portion of the third frontal gyrus, the Rolandic operculum, and the insula. Involvement of the posterior part of the first and second frontal gyri has also been recorded in patients with anterior aphasia, especially in those with a primary disorder of speech initiation, as well as extension of the lesion to the subcortical structures, including the caudate nucleus, the putamen, and the globus pallidus, which may often be seen in cases of persistent anterior aphasia.

The basic signs of the various types of anterior aphasia include anterior motor agrammatism with mainly substantive content words and a diminished number of small functional words in the expressive speech, disorder of word-finding and word production, motor dysprosody, articulation disorder, lack of speech initiative, and difficulty in comprehending complex grammatical constructions. Each of the basic signs may be more or less prominent or even completely absent in individual cases. In general, however, these signs form a common syndrome with various manifestations in the particular types of anterior aphasia, including Broca's aphasia, articulation aphasia, dynamic aphasia, and motor dysprosody.

Broca's aphasia is the most frequently observed and studied type of anterior aphasia. In severe cases of this aphasia most of the basic signs of anterior aphasia are pronounced, including anterior motor agrammatism, disorder of word-finding and production, motor dysprosody, articulation disorder, and difficulty in speech initiation.

It seems reasonable to use the term "severe Broca's aphasia" for such cases involving severe language disturbances and "moderate Broca's aphasia" for a milder form, primarily related to the disorder of word and phrase production.

It seems useful to replace the widely used terms "transcortical motor aphasia" and "aphemia" by names reflecting more clearly the main clinical features of those syndromes, with further division into syndromes that often have been grouped under the same names in spite of their clinical differences. The term "transcortical motor aphasia" is controversial from the anatomical point of view and may refer to at least two syndromes of anterior aphasia, including "dynamic aphasia," with a disorder of speech initiation and difficulty in phrase production. The term "aphemia" was first used by Broca (1861b) to describe what three years later was called "aphasia" by Trousseau (1864). Trousseau pointed out that the word "aphemia" means "infamy" in modern Greek and proposed to replace it with the Latin word "aphasia," which was widely accepted in spite of Broca's opposition. Later, Bastian (1897) used the term "aphemia" to describe an articulation disorder in patients with aphasia. Two different syndromes, however, were called "aphemia" by Brain (1965), Albert et al. (1981), and Schiff et al. (1983): the syndrome of "motor dysprosody," with a disorder of melodic line, rhythm, and accent, and the syndrome of "articulation aphasia," characterized by a primary difficulty in articulation production. A third syndrome called "aphemia" was described by Petit-Dutaillis et al. (1954) and by Penfield and Roberts (1959) in patients with disorders of speech initiation due to a lesion of the supplementary motor area at the mesial surface of the left frontal lobe. The term "dynamic aphasia" seems to describe better the clinical features of that syndrome.

Broca's Aphasia

Symptomatology Broca's aphasia is the most common type of aphasia that results from a cerebrovascular accident. Patients with Broca's aphasia may be seen in almost every neurological ward. In such cases the disorder of word production is one of the leading features of language disturbance. That disorder is usually associated with the symptoms of anterior motor agrammatism. Articulation production is relatively less disturbed, but motor dysprosody occurs in almost every case of Broca's aphasia. A dynamic disorder of speech initiation may also be seen in patients with Broca's aphasia mainly in the acute stage of stroke due to postictal somnolentia resulting from a transient edema around the brain lesion. The disorder of language production occurs in association with a comprehension deficit and a disturbance of reading, writing, and calculation. Right hemiplegia or marked right-sided hemiparesis is another prominent neurological manifestation in most of these patients.

In the acute stage of stroke, Broca's aphasia often started with aphonia, or complete loss of voice. A patient with aphonia does not produce any sound and rarely makes any attempt to vocalize. Sometimes he moves his lips or tongue or opens and closes his mouth, but the patient often cannot protrude his tongue out of his mouth, and the tongue moves slowly and feebly in the mouth. In spite of aphonia and difficulty in moving the tongue, swallowing is preserved. Usually no sign of pseudobulbar disorder can be noted, so that the entire picture of aphonia reflects more a dynamic disorder of voice initiation than primary paresis of voice-production muscles. That is why vocalization often occurs during an involuntary cough and groan or during a larynx examination, when the patient is asked to say, "ah . . . ah . . . ah" and his attention is focused on the examination rather than on the vocalization. In some cases with Broca's aphasia, embolophasia or verbal stereotype develops in the first hours and days of the stroke. Articulation and word production are reduced to two or three syllables or words: "ta . . . ta . . . ta," "ma . . . ma . . . ma," "na . . . na," "Ann," "yes," "no." The patient produces a restricted number of the same stereotypic combination of speech sounds under different circumstances, sometimes trying to use intonation for better communication. The patient's emotional state may be recognized by the modulation of his voice, which is hypophonic and dysprosodic, with a sudden change from high to low pitch and absence of the melodic flow typical of normal speech. A disorder of comprehension is striking at the onset of the stroke, especially in cases with postictal somnolentia, but comprehension of simple commands and conversational speech about his or her personal life usually returns in five or six days. The patient often answers, nodding "yes" or "no" to the simple questions about his family ("Are you married?" "Do you have children?" "How many children? One? Two? Three?" etc.), city ("Do you live in Boston? New York? Arlington?" etc.), everyday activity ("Did you have dinner? lunch?", "Did your wife visit you yesterday? today?" etc.). He or she may follow some simple commands ("Close your eyes," "Open your eyes," "Open your mouth," "Raise your hand," etc.), but alienation of word meaning (disconnection of words from their meanings) usually develops after one or two correct performances, and the patient begins to perseverate in the performance of the first task; e.g., to open and close his eyes on all following commands. This disturbance seems especially prominent if the request has shifted from one category to another, e.g., from body part to furniture, or when the same body part has been presented repeatedly in commands: "Show your nose," "eye," "ear," "eye," "ear," "nose," etc. The patient, however, usually follows the same command easily when presented by gesture. Reading, writing, and calculation are practically impossible in the first days after the onset of the stroke.

Right hemiplegia or marked hemiparesis develops after a stroke in patients with Broca's aphasia. Right hemihypesthesia alone may be revealed in approximately one-third of the cases. The visual fields are usually preserved.

Speech begins to improve in the first days after stroke. Aphonia persists in some cases for 14 to 15 days; the first sounds appear in most patients three or four days after the onset of the stroke and in some cases in one or two hours after onset. Recovery is also usually made from the embolophasia (verbal stereotype) sometimes accompanied by hypophonia and whisper. This combination of embolophasia, hypophonia, and whisper may be called mumbling and usually lasts from minutes and hours to a few days. Mumbling persists and becomes a steady symptom in only a few patients with Broca's aphasia. On the other hand, embolophasia persists more often for months and even years. Some recovery of expressive speech may be noted in the late stages of stroke, including the ability to say several nonstereotypic words and to repeat some phonemes, syllables, and simple words. Comprehension usually improves faster, especially for conversational speech and simple command. In more than half of the cases severe Broca's aphasia in acute CVA is lessened to moderate within two or three weeks after onset. Recovery of reading, writing, and calculation is also characterized by the improvement from severe disorder to moderate difficulty, especially in reading and calculation.

Tongue movement usually is recovered completely in 7 to 14 days after the onset of the stroke, but buccofacial and limb ideomotor apraxia persists in the chronic stage of CVA. In one to three weeks motor function begins to improve slightly, and severe spastic hemiparesis with a predominant disturbance of motor function in the distal part of the right arm and leg is noted for a long time after the stroke.

In the chronic stage of stroke a patient with severe Broca's aphasia has almost complete loss of articulation and word production. He or she answers any question or repeats phonemes, syllables, or words with the same stereotypic series of syllables or words; e.g., "du-du," "a-tu-tu," "yes, yes," "ma-ma-ma," "va-va," "na-na-na," etc. He or she can say "Yes" with a negative, positive, or interrogative intonation supported by approximate gestures and facial expression. Reciting well-known verses or automatized sequences usually is impossible, but often the patient can sing the melody of a popular song with some of the words.

Sometimes a patient with severe Broca's aphasia in the chronic stage of stroke answers questions with nonstereotypic words, but the words are still restricted to the echolalic repetition of one of the words from the question, usually the last one, e.g., "Do you have pain?"

"pain . . . pain," "What is your main problem?" "problem . . . problem." Some patients can repeat correctly or with literal paraphasia vowels and syllables such as "ma," "pa," or "ca," but seldom short words like "cat," "ear," or "table." Naming of presented objects takes place rarely, usually after a clue (the first phonemes of the word) is given.

In patients with moderate Broca's aphasia, conversational speech is impoverished and simplified. Phrases include not more than two or three words and often only one word. The patient has difficulty in word production and tries to find the right sequence of the phonemes in the word, but often he fails and skips over the phonemes or replaces them with the wrong phonemes, producing so-called literal paraphasia. Verbal paraphasia, the replacement of words, occurs less frequently than literal paraphasia in these patients. Literal and verbal paraphasia, characterized by a relative stability of replaced phonemes or words, the so-called standard paraphasia, may be noted in cases with anterior aphasia, including Broca's aphasia, as distinguished from the variable paraphasia of posterior aphasia. A patient with standard paraphasia quite regularly changes "v" to "f," "z" to "j," "table" to "cable," "house" to "home," etc. The replacement in variable paraphasia is unstable, and the patient may change "v" to "f," then "v" to "s," "v" to "b," and so on.

Another feature of moderate Broca's aphasia is perseveration of a phoneme, syllable, or word. The patient continues to pronounce "be-be-be," "a-a-a," or paired words in an effort to produce various words and phrases during conversational speech. This perseveration is different from that in subcortical palilalia. A patient with perseveration shows some difficulty and effort in producing the perseverating sounds. Palilalia, on the other hand, is characterized by the fast and somewhat dysarthric repetition of the same word, e.g., "ear-ear-ear-ear" or "table-table-table-table."

Motor dysprosody is one of the most persistent features of moderate Broca's aphasia. The melodic line, rhythm, and intonation of conversational speech is distorted by effort, tension, frequent and prolonged pauses between single words or two- or three-word phrases. Sometimes moderate Broca's aphasia is accompanied by hypophonia and slurring dysarthria, which may mask these dysprosodic features, but careful analysis of the pauses and the intonation in the patient's speech usually shows motor dysprosody. Articulation aphasia may also occur in combination with Broca's aphasia in some patients. A disorder of word production is often associated with the symptoms of anterior motor agrammatism in patients with Broca's aphasia. This agrammatism is called "telegraphic style," since the usual phrase consists of one or two words and includes a noun and a verb or a single noun, and small functional words are almost completely omitted.

The disorder of naming is not as noticeable as word-production difficulty in conversational speech. Most patients cannot remember the name of an object recalled with relatively low frequency, so that naming "plague," "eyelash," or "hangnail" are much more difficult for them than "table," "glasses," or "cat." A marked improvement of naming upon prompting with the first few phonemes of the object's name is typical for a patient with posterior anomic aphasia. A patient with Broca's aphasia, however, usually improves on naming only if prompting includes most of the syllable of the word or the complete word.

Repetition is particularly difficult for multisyllabic, low-frequency words, such as "industrialization" and "electroencephalography," and more prolonged and complicated phrases like "The car is parked in the garage behind the house," as well as phrases with many small functional words: "He is the one who did it."

Automatized sequences are usually preserved, but difficulty often occurs in naming the months of the year. Singing and recitation are not markedly disturbed.

Comprehension of conversational speech about familiar subjects is usually adequate in patients with severe or moderate Broca's aphasia. The patient follows simple commands but shows mild alienation of word meaning if the command shifts from one word category to another or when the same body parts are presented repeatedly in a series of two word commands: "Show your nose . . . ear," "eye . . . ear," "ear . . . nose," "nose . . . eye," etc. Comprehension of the same commands for a body part in a sequence is preserved: "Show your nose," "ear," "nose," "eye," "ear," "eye," "nose," etc. Comprehension of complex grammatical constructions is very much disturbed: "Point with the pencil to the key"; "to the key with the pencil"; "with the index finger of your right hand to your right ear," etc. Differentiation of the vowels and their series is preserved. After one to five learning trials the patient can distinguish "a" by raising his hand from "o" by keeping the hand still or "i" from "u," "a-o-y" from "o-y-a," etc. The patient's auditory language gnosis remains intact, but the retention of a word span of two, three, or four words is possible only for two words, such as "Show the table and the door," "window and ceiling," "sink and floor."

Phonologic analysis (spelling) is usually destroyed in patients with severe or moderate Broca's aphasia. The patient cannot estimate the number of phonemes and syllables in a given word, especially if the word consists of three, four, or more syllables. Estimating the number of phonemes in the word is difficult, and the patient makes many mistakes when asked if a certain phoneme is present or absent in a word or to list words that contain a "t" or an "r." The patient's difficulties in performing this test may be avoided if the patient is asked to raise the left hand when the requested phoneme is present in the word pronounced by the examiner; e.g., "t," and not to raise the hand if another phoneme is in the word, such as "r." This helps to avoid difficulties in communication related to expressive speech disorder. The number of mistakes diminishes if the examiner stresses the phoneme while pronouncing the word: "t-t-t-able," "c-ross," or the patient says the presented word aloud.

Reading and writing are strikingly disturbed in patients with severe Broca's aphasia. A patient can only read silently and write very familiar words, such as his or her last name, sometimes the first name, or copy letters, syllables, and short words, but often omits letters and produces many literal paralexias. In some cases, copying is actually "slavish imitation" performed very slowly but correctly. Calculation only is preserved up to 10 (3 + 2, 7 − 3, 2 × 4, etc.).

A patient with moderate Broca's aphasia has a moderate degree of difficulty in reading aloud and even less in silent reading. The patient reads easily a series of two or three words. He can read more words and longer phrases but with literal paralexias and omission of the phonemes. A disorder of writing on dictation and volitional writing is much more striking than is a reading disturbance. Most patients can only write on dictation some phonemes, syllables, and ideographs. Certain patients can write many words on dictation, but only those of two or three syllables. Copying is preserved, although some patients only draw a slavish copy of the presented word sample.

Oral arithmetic performance is very difficult for patients with severe and moderate Broca's aphasia, although written arithmetic, including subtraction with a transfer over 10, e.g., "15 − 7, 22 − 8, 27 − 13," can be performed without mistakes but takes more time than usual. Some forgetting of the multiplication tables can be noted, especially for multiplication of numbers from 5 on up, e.g., "6 × 9, 9 × 8, 7 × 9." All our 26 patients with severe and moderate Broca's aphasia showed buccofacial apraxia and to a lesser extent, ideomotor apraxia. A patient cannot follow such suggestions as, "How would you blow out a match?", "Try to whistle," "Try to cough," "How would you suck through a straw?", or "Make a fist," "Salute like a soldier," "Wave good-bye," but performs this command much better or does it correctly if he or she copies the examiner or uses a real object in a real situation.

Associated neurologic symptoms in most patients include severe, right-sided spastic hemiparesis with almost complete absence of movement in the right arm, hand, and foot and incomplete loss of motion in the right leg. The patient walks slowly with circumduction and other typical difficulties of spastic hemiparetic movement. Preservation of movement is noted only in a few patients with moderate Broca's aphasia in the chronic stage of CVA. In such cases, a transient right-sided hemiparesis occurs in acute stroke. Most of the patients show right-sided hemihypesthesia for pinprick and some for vibration and position senses. Visual field defects have not been noted in our cases with severe and moderate Broca's aphasia. Patients with moderate Broca's aphasia in the acute stage of CVA often have a striking recovery of speech and language. In such cases, aphasia is transient or lessened from moderate to mild in the chronic stage of CVA. Severe Broca's aphasia in acute CVA usually becomes moderate in the chronic stage or remains severe in cases with more extensive cerebral damage.

Localization of Lesions An isolated lesion of Broca's area in the posterior part of the third frontal gyrus does not produce stable aphasia syndrome. Only transient or no aphasia have been described in most such cases, including our own clinical-anatomical case with transient Broca's aphasia and bilateral lesions confined to the posterior part of F_3 in both hemispheres. That case was recently described in detail by Tonkonogy and Goodglass (1981); therefore only the main data are presented below:

Case 1, RA: A 57-year-old, right-handed woman suffered sudden mild weakness in her right extremities, predominantly the hand, and moderate aphasia. Her medical history was remarkable for 18 years of hypertension and atrial fibrillation of several months' duration. In the first days after the stroke she had difficulty in spontaneous speech and in word-finding, had reduced and hesitant speech output, shortening and simplification of sentences, some comprehension difficulties, and reading and writing disturbances, but her articulation was preserved. Her speech and movement began to improve gradually by the fourth day and recovered completely after a month. No obvious signs of aphasia, dysarthria, or paresis were observed at this time.

Ten months later, she suddenly developed left hemiplegia and slurring of speech. On admission to the hospital the next day, a neurological examination revealed moderate left central facial paresis, slight deviation of the tongue to the left, difficulties in swallowing, complete left hemiplegia, and left hemihypesthesia without visual field defects. Motor and sensory functions in the right extremities were completely preserved. Moderate pseudobulbar dysarthria with slurring pronunciation was noted, but there were no signs of aphasia.

During the next few days, neurological and neuropsychological examination showed no change, and no signs of aphasia developed; dysarthria, left hemiparesis, and left hemihypesthesia persisted. On the eleventh day after admission, the patient died of pneumonia.

Anatomical diagnosis: Left ventricular hypertrophy and atherosclerotic nephrosclerosis, as well as atherosclerosis of the aorta and cerebral arteries, were present, as was atherosclerosis causing stenosis of the intracranial portion of the internal carotid artery. The area of infarction of the gray matter in the territory of the cortical branches of the left middle cerebral artery involved in part the pars triangularis, the pars opercularis, and the pars orbitalis of the third frontal gyrus. The infarction in the territory of the cortical branches and lenticulostriate divisions of the right middle cerebral artery involved the white matter of the posterior part of the third frontal gyrus, the insula, the white matter of the anterior part of the temporal lobe, and the dorsal part of the anterior limb of the internal capsule; this lesion was connected to an additional hemorrhagic infarct in the striatum (Fig. 3.1).

The histopathological examination showed only slight diffuse changes in the lower parts of the motor and sensory strips (areas 6 and 43), including the Rolandic operculum and posterior part of T_1 in the left hemisphere, and microscopic foci of softening in the cortex of the pars triangularis and especially the pars opercularis of the third frontal gyrus of the left and right hemisphere.

In this case a small infarction confined to Broca's area in the left hemisphere produced only transient Broca's aphasia that did not recur after a second stroke with a lesion of the symmetrical zone in the right hemisphere. Similar anatomical cases with left hemisphere or bilateral lesions of the posterior part of the third frontal gyrus have been collected from the literature or originally described by Marie (1906b), Moutier (1908), Niessl von Mayendorf (1911, 1926), and Victoria (1937) in support of Marie's postulate that the third frontal gyrus does not play any role in the language function. Recently, Mohr (1976), Mohr et al. (1978), and Levine and Mohr (1979), on the basis of the review of the literature and personal cases, stressed that in the focal lesions, including those confined to Broca's area, only a faint degree of language deficit was evident.

Mohr et al. (1978) observed that infarcts limited to the posterior part of the left frontal gyrus resulted in a transient mutism with recovery in a few days or weeks to almost normal speech with some mild articulation disturbances. According to Levine and Mohr (1979), a symmetrical destruction of Broca's area in the opposite hemisphere does not produce a global or severe Broca's aphasia, and notable pseudobulbar dysarthria develops only in a few cases. Mohr (1973, 1976), Mohr et al. (1978), and Levine and Mohr (1979) demonstrated that in Broca's aphasia the severity and persistence of the deficit, as stated by Mohr et al. (1978), is proportionate to the size and distribution of the infarction over the opercular, insular, and adjacent cerebral region. Levine and

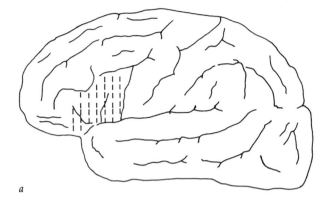

a

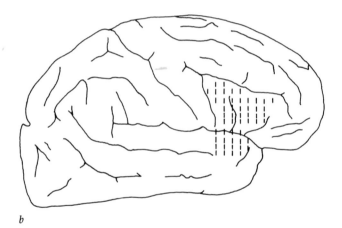

b

Figure 3.1
Case 1, RA, Transient Broca's aphasia. *a*, Infarction in the cortex of the left hemisphere (anatomical and histopathological data). *b*, Infarction in the cortex of the right hemisphere (anatomical and histopathological data). *c*, Coronal section through symmetrical infarcts in pars opercularis of the third frontal gyri. *d*, Pars opercularis of the third frontal gyrus in the left hemisphere. Microscopic focus of the cortical infarction in the phase of cicatrization (hematoxylin-eosin stain, × 140). *e*, Microscopic area of cortical infarction in the pars opercularis of F_3 of the right hemisphere (hematoxylin-eosin stain, × 140), early stage of cicatrization.

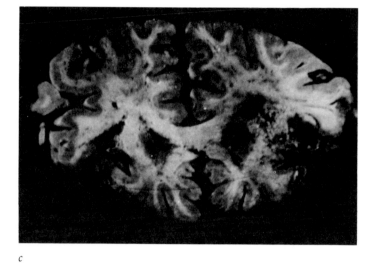

c

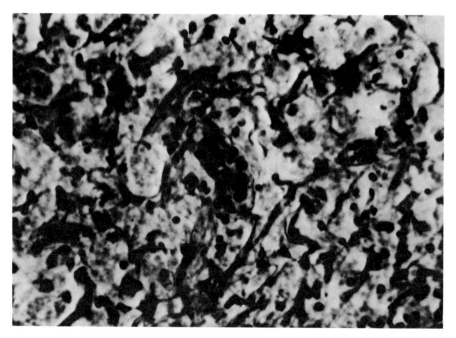

d

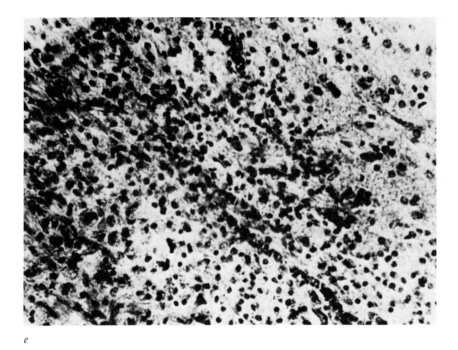

e

Mohr (1979) indicated that recovery in cases with a limited lesion of the dominant third frontal gyrus is mediated by the adjacent areas of the dominant hemisphere.

Our own data are almost completely consistent with the Mohr *et al.* (1978) and Levine and Mohr (1979) conclusions. In our personal cases aphasia was transient if the lesion was restricted to the posterior part of the left third frontal gyrus (Case 1, RA); patients with extensive lesions had a more persistent aphasia. In our cases with moderate and severe Broca's aphasia, therefore, the lesions involved not only the posterior part of the third frontal gyrus, but also the Rolandic operculum and the insula, with extension, especially in cases of severe Broca's aphasia, to the adjacent cortical and subcortical areas of the frontal lobe and the central gyri as well as in many cases, in depth to the putamen, the caudate nucleus, and the globus pallidus. In the acute stage of stroke, the area of brain tissue softening may be more restricted, and the severity of Broca's aphasia depends on the edema and other reversible pathological processes which develop around and in the vicinity of the primary infarction foci. These are still relatively large and are usually located in the cortico–subcortical zone consisting of Broca's area, the Rolandic operculum, and the insula. Extension of the infarction to the striatal structures and the internal capsule often occurs.

Table 3.1 Localization of the Left Hemisphere Infarction in Cases with Severe Broca's Aphasia

Case Number and Initials	Posterior Part of F₃		Rolandic Operculum		Insula		Anterior T₁		Posterior T₁		Supra-marginal and Angular Gyri		Posterior F₁ and Cingulate Gyrus		Corona Radiata, Subcortical Structures, and Capsula Interna		Lumen of Left Carotid Artery		Lumen of Left Middle Cerebral Artery	
	A	H	A	H	A	H	A	H	A	H	A	H	A	H	A	H	A	H	A	H
Case 2, FN	–	3	3	3	2	2	–	–	–	2	–	–	–	2	–	2	–	2	–	–
Case 3, GA	3	3	3	3	3	3	–	–	–	1	–	–	–	–	2	2	3	–	–	–
Case 4, SA	3	3	–	–	3	3	–	–	–	–	–	–	–	–	3	3	–	–	–	–
Case 5, CA	3	3	–	1	3	3	3	3	–	–	–	–	3	–	2	–	2	2	2	2

All four patients died within one month after the onset of the stroke.
Anatomical (A) and histopathological (H) data: 3, complete destruction; 2, moderate pathological changes; 1, mild pathological change; 0, intact.
Lumen of the vessel: 3, complete obliteration; 2, severe stenosis; 1, mild stenosis; 0, normal.

Clinical and anatomohistopathological examination has been done in four of our personal cases with severe Broca's aphasia. All four patients died in the acute stage of stroke 10 to 20 days after the onset. The area of infarction (Table 3.1) involved the cortical branches of the left middle cerebral artery, including the orbitofrontal branch and the arteris of the precentral and cental sulci. The infarction destroyed the gray and white matter of the posterior part, the pars opercularis and triangularis of the third frontal gyrus, the adjacent areas of the second frontal and orbitofrontal gyri, and the inferior part of the central gyri, including the Rolandic operculum and the insula.

In two out of four cases the additional areas of infarction were revealed in the territory of the anterior cerebral artery, at the mesial surface of the left hemisphere, in the posterior part of the first frontal gyrus, and in the anterior-medial part of the cingulate gyrus and the corpus callosum. In one case the area of infarction involved in part the temporal lobe and the gray and white matter of the anterior part of the first temporal gyrus. The histopathological examination of the posterior part of the first temporal gyrus (Wernicke's area) showed mild changes in one case and moderate changes in another case which did not exceed the level of changes relating to the processes of aging. The gray and white matter of the left supramarginal and angular gyri were anatomically preserved in all four cases. In all cases the area of infarction extended to the territory of the lenticulostriate branches of the middle cerebral artery and involved the internal capsule and striatum in three cases and the corona radiata of the frontal lobe in all four cases.

Thus, in cases with Broca's aphasia, the large area of infarction was revealed in the territory of the cortical and lenticulostriate branches of the left middle cerebral artery. In the gray and white matter of the anterior-inferior part of the left hemisphere, including the inferior-posterior portion of the frontal lobe, the Rolandic operculum, and the insula, the lesion extended to the corona radiata, the internal capsule, and the striatum. A large anterior infarction is responsible for the severity of Broca's aphasia in the chronic stage of stroke. In such cases aphasia is accompanied by a severe right-sided hemiplegia and hemihypesthesia, which can be related to an extension of the lesion to the internal capsule and the surrounding subcortical structures. On the other hand, most of the patients with acute CVA have a more restricted, partial lesion of the anterior zone, and severe Broca's aphasia subsequently improves to a moderate aphasia in the chronic stage.

Such types of more restricted lesions occurred in one out of our four anatomical cases with severe Broca's aphasia. The patient had severe Broca's aphasia and died eleven days after onset, but recovery to a moderate aphasia could have been expected in that case, since a hemorrhagic infarct occupied the gray and white matter of Broca's area, the Rolandic operculum, and the insula with extension to the corona radiata with sparing of the subcortical structures and the internal capsule.

Case 3, GA: A 56-year-old right-handed woman suffered sudden weakness in her right extremities and loss of speech. She could not say any words or make any sound except a moan. In answer to a question she produced a short, slurring sound, somewhat like "a." She understood conversational speech speech fairly well. The patient also followed commands to show many objects and some of the body parts but with alienation of word meaning for some commands, such as to touch her ear, right or left. Her ability to read, write, and calculate was impaired. Her tongue was protruded slowly with deviation to the right. A moderate right hemiparesis was primarily confined to the hand; right hemihypesthesia to pinprick occurred with preservation of deep sensation. No visual field defects were noted. On the eleventh day after the onset of the stroke, the patient died of pneumonia.

Anatomical Diagnosis Insufficiency of the mitral valve was evident, with left ventricular hypertrophy. Complete thrombosis of the intracranial portion of the left internal carotid artery was revealed. Hemorrhagic infarction in the corical division of the left middle cerebral artery (Fig. 3.2) involved the lower part of the pars triangularis (F_3) extending to the cortical and subcortical areas of the lower pars opercularis (F3), the adjacent part of the pars orbitalis and in depth through the corona radiata to the anterior horn of the lateral ventricle. The area of infarction continued to the insula and the Rolandic operculum and could not be seen behind those structures.

The histopathological examination showed multiple microscopic foci of infarction in the anatomically preserved area of the left pars opercularis (area 44).

In cases with Broca's aphasia due to a cerebral hemorrhage, the localization of the lesion is much less predictable than in aphasia due to a cerebral infarction. Anterior cerebral hemorrhage usually occurs from the lenticulostriate branches of the middle cerebral artery occupying the internal capsule and adjacent subcortical structures, including the caudate nucleus, the putamen, and the globus pallidus without a direct involvement of the crucial cortical areas in the anterior speech zone. The Broca's area, the Rolandic operculum, the insula, and the adjacent gray and white matter are free from hemorrhage, but edema extends from the site of hemorrhage to those and other cortical areas producing severe Broca's aphasia, or more often, global aphasia, since edema and other reversible pathologic processes reach not only the anterior but also the posterior language zone. Aphasia in such cases is usually transient and nonstable, and the patient regains almost com-

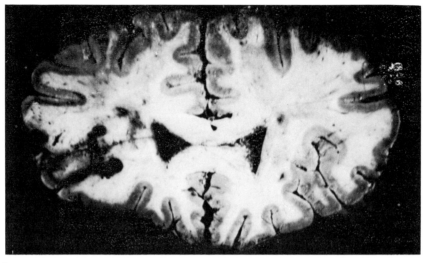

a

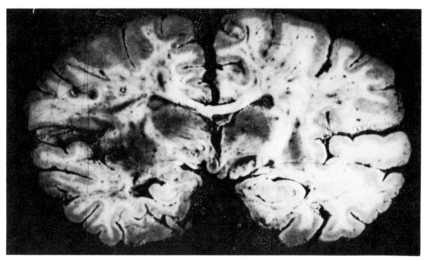

b

Figure 3.2
Case 3, GA, Severe Broca's aphasia. *a*, Coronal section through the pars opercularis of the third frontal gyrus. Hemorrhagic infarction in the pars opercularis of F_3 and corona radiata of the frontal lobe of the left hemisphere. *b*, Coronal section at the level of the chiasm. Infarction in the hemisphere spreading to the insula and lower part of motor strip.

pletely his or her language ability if he or she survives the acute stage of stroke without neurosurgical intervention, which inevitably leads to the operative damage of language-related cerebral tissue in most such cases.

A small hemorrhage in the Broca's area and the adjacent white and gray matter can also produce a moderate and transient Broca's aphasia, but cerebral hemorrhage usually takes place in the lenticulostriate branches of the middle cerebral artery and hemorrhage from the cortical branches seldom occurs. Perhaps it is for this reason that we did not observe such cases in our patients with CVA.

Articulation Aphasia and Motor Dysprosody

Both articulation aphasia and motor dysprosody usually are differentiated from the common types of aphasia by the complete or almost complete preservation of comprehension, reading, calculation, and writing. The disorder of expressive speech, the main manifestation of aphasia in such cases, is also distinguished from the usual aphasia by only mild disturbance or by almost complete sparing of word and phrase production. Their similarity to ordinary aphasia is related only to the disorder of speech prosody and articulation as well as to the frequent presence of mild difficulties in writing and calculation in patients with articulation aphasia or motor dysprosody. Lichtheim (1885) called these disorders "subcortical motor aphasia," since in such cases he supposed an interruption of the white-matter pathway from the preserved Broca's area to the corresponding motor centers. The difference between these and common types of aphasia was stressed by the names given to them by later writers: "aphemia" by Bastian (1897) and Albert et al. (1981); "anarthria" by Marie (1906c); "pure motor aphasia" by Déjerine (1914); "mutism of speech sounds" by Kleist (1934); "phonetic disintegration syndrome" by Alajouanine et al. (1939) and LeCours and Lhermitte (1976); "afferent motor aphasia" by Luria (1947, 1966).

In 1947, Monrad-Krohn added a new term, "dysprosody," stressing the disorder of melodic line, rhythm, and accent in speech. His patient, a native Norwegian speaker, had never left Norway in her life, but after a stroke she developed a "German" accent. Later, the development of a "German" accent was described in native English speakers by Critchley (1952) and Whitty (1964).

Motor Dysprosody

Symptomatology This disorder is characterized by the distortion of the normal smooth flow of speech, which becomes slow and effortful, with long pauses between single syllables or words and poor breathing control. Motor dysprosody occurs in almost every patient with Broca's aphasia and sometimes as a single syndrome with mild word-finding difficulty or anterior motor agrammatism in conversational speech. Comprehension, reading, writing, and calculation are almost intact. The phonological, morphological, and syntactical structure of the speech seems to be almost completely preserved, and mild anterior aphasia can only be revealed after a detailed examination. Motor dysprosody differs clearly from dysphonia in patients with bulbar or severe pseudo-bulbar dysarthria. Dysphonia is characterized by a relatively stable, high- or low-pitched voice with reduced regular melodic changes in the pitch and some hoarseness of the voice.

Motor dysprosody changes the entire melodic line and intonation of speech flow by the rapid rising or decreasing of the voice pitch with the interval between high and low pitch filled with indications of effort and tension. The phonological and morphological structures of words are preserved, however. Cases with pure motor dysprosody differ from Broca's aphasia by the spared ability to find the right sequence of the phonemes and syllables in words, and words in phrases, in spite of the slowness, effort, and other indications of dysprosodic speech output.

Transient aphonia and moderate right-sided hemiparesis with hypesthesia often occur in cases with a single syndrome of motor dysprosody immediately after stroke, but voice and movement in the right extremities recover within hours or in a day or two, so that motor dysprosody is accompanied by a mild paresis in the right hand with complete or almost complete recovery of movement in the right leg. Right hemihypesthesia to pinprick remains stable in approximately half of the cases. The visual fields are usually intact in patients with pure motor dysprosody.

Immediately after the onset of the stroke, tongue movement is slow and restricted, but swallowing is preserved. Within two or three days, tongue movement recovers completely, but buccofacial and limb apraxia for intended motion remains prominent in the acute stage and later in the chronic stage of stroke. Motor dysprosody also occurs as one of the symptoms in patients with Broca's aphasia. The clinical picture of this more complex aphasia syndrome, however, also includes disturbances in word-finding and production, comprehension, and other language disorders, as well as motor dysprosody. That is why some authors consider that the word-finding and articulation disorder in Broca's aphasia is caused by dysprosody. Others explain dysprosody as a result of word-finding and production difficulty. But cases with a relatively isolated syndrome of motor dysprosody defy both theories and show that dysprosody can be considered only as a symptom that attenuates or increases some of the articulation or word-production difficulty, but which has its own origin and corresponding site of localization.

Cases with isolated motor dysprosody studied histopathologically have been described by LeCours and Lhermitte (1976) under the name "phonetic distintegration syndrome" which was applied to a carefully investigated case by Alajouanine *et al.* (1949). An autopsy revealed an infarct in the gray and white matter of the inferior part of the motor strip and the dorsal part of the insula. Motor dysprosody occurred together with Broca's aphasia, and the authors stressed the role of a lesion in Broca's area. The lesion in cases with stable Broca's aphasia, however, usually extends from Broca's area to the Rolandic operculum, the lower motor strip, and the insula. It seems, therefore, that the lesion in these areas is primarily responsible for pure motor dysprosody. In our case of motor dysprosody combined with transient articulation aphasia, a postmortem examination revealed an area of infarction in the inferior one-third of the motor strip and the anterior part of the Rolandic operculum with extension to the extreme capsule. An additional small area of infarction in subcortical structures had also occurred (see Case 6).

Articulation Aphasia

Symptomatology Speech is characterized by the deformation or distortion of phonemes as well as by missing some of their differential features, giving rise to what is considered a "foreign" or "childish" accent. The patient most often seems to develop a Scandinavian accent if his or her native language is Russian and a German accent if his or her native language is English. The Scandinavian accent in patients with articulation aphasia is characterized by the omission of voicing in the phonemes. The patient softens "f" to "v," "k" to "h," "ch" to "sh," etc. At the same time, his pronunciation of "c," "h," or "sh" is abnormal; a deformation of articulation occurs and the phoneme sounds somewhat like a "v" or "h," but has also some resemblance to "f" or "k." This is not a literal paraphasia, therefore, with simple replacement of one phoneme by another, since the new phoneme is distorted and does not completely replace the old one. Literal paraphasia with normal pronunciation of a new phoneme seldom occurs in patients with typical articulation aphasia. Literal paraphasia seems to reflect a disorder of word production rather than a disorder of articulation production.

A patient with a "childish" accent replaces "r" with "l," "ch" with "c," and "sh" with "c," as well as softening and slurring other vowels and consonants. This phenomenon often accompanies such Broca's aphasia symptoms as difficulty in word or phrase production and comprehension. Patients with a "foreign" accent do not usually show any pronounced sign of word-finding or production difficulty. Articulation aphasia with a "foreign" accent often appears alone. However, mild anterior motor agrammatism and motor dysprosody with slow, effortful speech occurs in some cases with articulation aphasia.

Repetition of the single distorted phoneme or syllable improves articulation, and most of the deformation disappears, but the distortion can be revealed again when the patient is asked to repeat the same consonant in the vowel–consonant and consonant–vowel syllable, e.g., "ar" and "ra," "el" and "le," "em" and "me," "ec" and "ce," or to switch to the opposite phoneme, e.g., "k" to "h," "b" to "p," "ec" to "ce," etc. Repetition of a word or phrase is slightly difficult in some cases for a long, multisyllabic word ("pneumoencephalography," "Popocatepetl") or complicated phrases.

Recitation and automatized speech show the same pattern of "foreign" or "childish" accent but not so noticeably as in conversational speech. Naming is completely preserved, even for a low-frequency word, but the distorted accent remains unchanged when the patient pronounces the name of the presented object or action. Comprehension of conversational speech, single words, phrases, and following of commands is preserved. Mild difficulty sometimes occurs in following the more complicated of Head's commands, "With the middle finger of your left hand, show your right eye," or Luria's logicogrammatical constructions, "Using a pen, point to a pencil; using a pencil, point to a pen," etc. Alienation of word meaning occasionally occurs in the "eye–nose–ear" test, especially when the command contains two nouns: "Show your ear–nose," "eye–ear," "nose–eye." Many patients with articulation aphasia rarely manifest any difficulty in comprehending; the slight difficulty can only be revealed when they are tired, usually at the end of the day. Patients usually have good retention of phonemes, syllables, and word span in a series of three or four items and sometimes five or six items.

Phonological analysis and silent reading are preserved or only slightly disturbed. However, reading aloud reveals all the distortion and deformation of phonemes of their conversational speech, with a striking increase of the number of literal paralexias in comparison to the few true literal paraphasias in speech. Writing is often very much disturbed, much more so than would be expected in cases with only slight disorder of reading, phonological analysis, word production, and comprehension ability. The nature of this discrepancy has to be yet explained, but there is no doubt that patients with articulation aphasia often cannot write on dictation single phonemes, syllables, words, or even well-known ideographs. Copying remains preserved or slightly disturbed by literal paragraphia and omission of phonemes, especially in longer, grammatically complicated words and phrases. Some patients write without any difficulty, including writing on dictation. They do not use writing instead of oral speech for communication even, however, with severe articulation disorder combined with motor dysprosody. In contrast to this, a patient with severe dysarthria due to a brain-stem bulbar or pseudobulbar lesion prefers to write or to use alphabet cards for communication and tries to avoid talking.

Calculation is only slightly disturbed. The patient has difficulty in performing without writing a complex operation, such as subtracting numbers consisting of two or three digits or multiplying numbers from 5 on up ($5 \times 7, 8 \times 7, 9 \times 6$).

Buccofacial and ideomotor apraxia does not differ in severity from that in patients with Broca's aphasia. There is no direct correlation between the severity of articulation aphasia and apraxia.

Moderate or severe, right-sided hemiparesis occurs in less than one-half of the patients with articulation aphasia. In most cases, only a mild spastic hemiparesis, predominantly in the right hand, can be revealed, or movement is completely preserved. That is why articulation aphasia may be called "anterior aphasia without hemiparesis or with mild hemiparesis" since Broca's aphasia is "anterior aphasia with severe hemiparesis." Right-sided hemihypesthesia with disorder of sensation to pinprick is revealed in approximately every second patient with articulation aphasia. Some of them also show a right-sided disturbance of the position and vibration senses. A patient with articulation aphasia usually develops severe anterior aphasia with aphonia and right-sided hemiplegia in the acute stage of stroke. A fast recovery to the stage of a moderate articulation aphasia and often complete recovery of movement or mild right hemiparesis is usually seen in hours or one to two days after the onset of the stroke.

Localization of the Lesion It is quite difficult to locate the lesion site in articulation aphasia apart from the lesion in motor dysprosody, since both syndromes frequently overlap. Indeed, in the following case (for detailed description, see Tonkonogy and Goodglass, 1981) articulation aphasia occurred together with motor dysprosody. A lesion of the lower motor strip and the anterior Rolandic operculum was noted.

Case 6, DC: A 63-year-old, right-handed man developed slight right hemiparesis, predominantly in the right arm, and slowness of speech with dysprosodic alteration of speech melody, involving both stuttering and poor control of pitch. His articulations were deformed but not slurred; they sounded like altered speech sounds, omitting characteristic differentiating articulatory features, primarily voicing. Moderate word-finding difficulties were also present. Comprehension, reading, and writing were practically intact. After three weeks, speech and motor function had recovered remarkably, but some mild dysprosody that resembled stuttering and weakness in the right hand lasted until the next episode, two months later. At this time, sudden aphonia and right hemiplegia developed, which lasted until his death of pulmonary edema ten days later. During this time, the patient understood most questions related to his illness and family, as well as simple commands ("Close your eyes," "Open your mouth," etc.), but moderate impairment of word comprehension was observed in more complex commands, or when the commands to show the object had been shifted back and forth between room objects and body parts. The patient had difficulty in comprehending longer words and sentences. He could write with his left hand but with many omissions of letters.

The patient had a moderate right central facial paresis. The patient's tongue movement was remarkably disturbed; he could not protrude his tongue, and the tongue movements within the mouth were slow and weak, with deviation to the right. In spite of the severe right hemiplegia he had no sensory deficit or visual field abnormality.

Anatomical Diagnosis The left cardiac ventricle was hypertrophied with atherosclerosis of the aorta, coronary, and cerebral arteries. No visible changes were seen in the right hemisphere. Several foci of infarction were noted in the left hemisphere. The first and most prominent infarction was in the corona radiata of the frontal lobe. This infarction extended to the anterior part of the corpus callosum and more posteriorly to the cortex of the central gyri, appearing at the surface of the motor strip and destroying it between its midpoint and the lower third. The size of this superficial infarction was 1.0×1.5 cm, and it was linked to an infarct in the anterior limb of the internal capsule. Two other small zones of infarction were situated in the extreme capsule. There was no visible pathology in the cortex or white matter of the first, second, or third frontal gyri or in the temporal lobe.

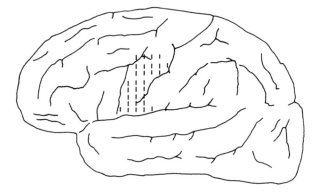

Figure 3.3
Case 6, DC, Articulation aphasia. Infarction in the left hemisphere (anatomical and histopathological data).

A histopathological examination showed infarction in the lower part of the motor strip, including the anterior part of the Rolandic operculum (area 6 and area 43). Slight histopathological changes were noted in the posterior parts of the third frontal gyrus (area 44) and in the caudal end of the first temporal gyrus (area 22).

It can be concluded that the dysarthria, dysprosody, and slight paresis of the right hand after the first stroke were related to the infarction in the lower motor strip, including the Rolandic operculum (Fig. 3.3), since mild paresis, restricted predominantly to the hand, is typically caused by an infarction of the cerebral cortex. The extension of the infarction to the corona radiata of the frontal lobe and anterior part of the corpus callosum after the second stroke presumably brought about the right hemiplegia and aphonia.

The fact that the articulation disorder cleared up quickly but the mild motor dysprosody remained may be used as a basis for speculation about possible differences in lesion sites in articulation aphasia and motor dysprosody. Motor dysprosody may be primarily related to the more anterior lesion of the Rolandic operculum and the adjacent part of the motor strip, and articulation aphasia may develop because of a more posterior lesion in the Rolandic operculum and adjacent areas of the sensory strip and the supramarginal gyrus. Certainly an essential lesion site in articulation aphasia and motor dysprosody still has to be elucidated, including the possible role of the insula and the pathology of the subcortical structures.

Dynamic Aphasia

Symptomatology Dynamic aphasia often starts with aphonia at the onset of the stroke and is similar to the other anterior aphasia syndromes in the acute stage of CVA, but shortly afterward, usually after two or three hours or a day or two of aphonia, a dynamic disorder of speech initiation is manifested as a major symptom. The patient lacks the starting impulse to initiate speech; he cannot engage in free conversational speech. An energetic stimulation or incentive to speak produces an appropriate but short, simple answer with mild signs of motor dysprosody and articulation disorder. The patient speaks with arrests resembling stuttering or mild deformation or slurring of speech sounds as well as with occasional paraphasias, mainly literal, and perseverations. It is difficult to get an answer from a patient with dynamic aphasia, but when it is elicited there is usually complete preservation of phonological, morphological, and syntactical structure. At the same time the patient tries to replace an active full-scale answer with a short, abbreviated answer or with the echolalic passive repetition of the last word of the question. Moderate or mild motor agrammatism is manifested in such cases as a partial loss of small functional words and a tendency to use substantive uninflected words. A sharp difference also has to be noted between the almost complete absence of conversational speech and only slightly disturbed repetition, naming, and reading with, however, increased hesitation, especially for naming and reading. When naming is more disturbed, e.g., during the first days after the onset of stroke, the low-frequency names of objects, such as "eyelash" and "hangnail," are sometimes used by the patient more easily than high-frequency words, such as "watch" and "elbow." A contrasting relationship can usually be seen in patients with Broca's aphasia who manifest their major difficulties in language performance with the low-frequency words.

The dynamic disorder of speech initiation often occurs as a symptom in various aphasia syndromes, including Broca's and articulation aphasia, especially in the acute stage of stroke. This symptom becomes prominent but transient in some cases with mild Broca's or articulation aphasia in the first days and weeks after stroke onset because underlying pathological conditions (edema of the surrounding cerebral tissue, inhibition of the language functional system of the brain, poststroke somnolentia, etc.) are reversible. Such cases have often been described as "transcortical motor aphasia," since repetition is much better preserved than spontaneous speech in both syndromes. The localization of the lesion, however, is quite different in dynamic aphasia, mild Broca's, or articulation aphasia, and careful clinical analysis, especially a repeated examination on subsequent days after the onset of the stroke, can be very helpful in distinguishing those syndromes, since patients with dynamic aphasia show a completely preserved or only slightly disturbed phonological, morphological, and syntactical structure of language when the blocking of speech initiation can be overcome by corresponding stimulation.

During the first days after the stroke, comprehension is badly disturbed in patients with dynamic aphasia and may be secondary to the speech and motor akinesia. Most patients do not even try to follow simple commands, such as "Close your eyes" or "Raise your hands," and start to move one of their hands which has been placed by the examiner on their face only after repeated commands, "Show your nose," "Show your ear," etc. Later in the course of stroke, comprehension improves notably, much faster than conversational speech, to the point of almost complete restoration.

Difficulty in reading, writing, and calculation in patients with dynamic aphasia may also be related to the general lack of initiation. Movement of the tongue is usually preserved in such cases, even immediately after stroke onset. Mild buccofacial apraxia occurs, however, especially in the acute stage of CVA. Right-sided hemiplegia after stroke is followed by right-sided hemiparesis, more prominent in the right leg in many cases. Hypesthesia and visual-field defects have not been noted in most dynamic aphasia cases. Dynamic aphasia usually develops with a background of general lack of initiation and motor activity, but dynamic disorder of speech initiation seems to be especially noticeable in cases with dynamic aphasia.

In the chronic stage of stroke, dynamic aphasia more often is manifested as a relatively moderate disorder. The patient speaks fluently, but his or her language is somewhat agrammatic and improverished; his or her phrases are short and simple, characterized by arrests. These arrests are partly related to the lack of speech initiative, but there is often some manifestation of motor dysprosody. The patient cannot recount in detail the content of a story or his or her own biographical data and has to be repeatedly stimulated for more detailed description of a picture in the series of pictures. He or she prefers to use only one or two words or an idiomatic expression, e.g., "Train not crashed . . . that's it, what I can say," when asked to describe a series of pictures showing children's attempts to prevent a train crash. He or she continues to describe details of the story only when stimulated by additional questions, such as, "Who stopped the train from crashing?", "Why were the children near the railroad?", etc., showing that a mild

motor agrammatism with predominance of substantive words in simplified phrases is typical of these cases.

Repetition ability is almost completely preserved or only slightly
distorted. Difficulty occurs only in repeating long phrases or phrases
mainly consisting of small functional words. Repetition of the oppositional phonemes, "p-b," "v-f," "t-d," etc., is also difficult in some
cases. Naming is mildly disturbed, sometimes for high-frequency words,
but more often for low-frequency words. Automatized speech is usually
preserved.

Comprehension is not disturbed for conversational speech, isolated
words, or differentiation of a series of phonemes, such as "a–o–u,"
"a–u–o," "o–u–a," etc. The infrequent errors occur only in following
one of the complex commands of Head or a logicogrammatical construction of Luria. In some cases alienation of word meaning appears
in the "eye–ear–nose" test with two components: "Show your
eye . . . ear," "nose . . . ear," "eye . . . nose," etc. Most patients have a
preserved retention for a word series of four or five words or even six
words.

Phonological analysis is completely preserved or only slightly difficult
in assessing the presence or absence of certain phonemes in a word,
especially if the presented words have to be divided into two groups,
e.g., one group including the words with the phoneme "z," another
with the phoneme "t." Reading aloud is done somewhat slowly with
infrequent literal paralexias and omission of letters. Silent reading is
usually preserved. Writing on dictation and volitional writing is characterized by literal paragraphia and letter omission, but copying is
performed without difficulty.

A mild disorder of calculation usually manifests itself as partial for-
getfulness of the multiplication table, especially from the numbers 5
on up, and errors in more complex mental subtraction, such as 32 − 16,
47 − 23, etc.

Buccofacial apraxis is not observed in most cases, especially when
the patient is asked to repeat the examiner's movement. But the patient
often shows mild or moderate difficulty when asked to carry out a
movement in response to commands such as "blow," "whistle,"
"cough," etc.

Associated neurologic disorders include a mild right-sided hemiparesis. Right-sided hemihypesthesia for sensation to pinprick is infrequently noted, but the position and vibration senses are usually
completely preserved.

Localization of the lesion in dynamic aphasia has been placed in the
dominant frontal lobe, and most authors agree that the lesion spares
Broca's area. Luria (1947, 1966) located this lesion anterior and superior

to Broca's area. Kleist (1934) believed that his "Adynamia der sprach" developed after a lesion in the posterior second frontal gyrus just above Broca's area. Earlier, Lichtheim (1884) suggested that a lesion of the white-matter pathways under the motor speech area produced a transcortical motor aphasia with primary disorder of spontaneous speech and good repetition, resembling a dynamic disorder of speech. Goldstein (1927, 1934, 1948) distinguished two types of transcortical motor aphasia. The first type was attributed to a mild partial lesion of Broca's area, the other to the interruption of the pathway from the frontal lobe to the motor speech area. In recent years the role of the posterior mesial surface of the first frontal gyrus has been pointed out in the discussion of transcortical motor and dynamic aphasia, especially after Penfield and Rasmussen (1950) had described a supplementary motor area at the mesial surface of the hemisphere anterior to the motor representation of the leg in the area 6 α, β of the Vogts. Electrical stimulation of that area in the right or left hemisphere caused, in addition to peculiar movement of the extremities, a persistent phonation or perseveration of the same word. Stimulation of that area in the dominant hemisphere also produced an aphasic response. These data have increased the interest of clinicians in the speech disorder related to a superior-posterior lesion of the frontal lobe. The old literature has been reviewed again, and new cases have been described by Petit-Dutaillis *et al.* (1954), Guidetti (1957), Botez (1962), Rubens (1975), Alexander and Schmitt (1980).

The first anatomohistopathologically studied case of dynamic aphasia with a proven lesion of the supplementary motor area seems to have been published by Tonkonogy and Ageeva (1961). In this case, an infarction in the left anterior cerebral artery in the mesial surface of the left hemisphere extended into the posterior part of the first frontal gyrus and the adjacent area of the cingulate gyrus.

Case 7, MC: A 67-year-old, right-handed man suddenly developed right-sided weakness with complete paralysis of the right leg and mild weakness in the right arm with slow but preserved movement. He had had hypertension and TIA for many years and had suffered a transient left-sided hemiparesis nine years before the CVA. On the third day after the recent onset of stroke, he developed severe paresis of the right arm in addition to the existing plegia of the right leg, and his speech became impaired. Normal speech activity decreased; the patient answered questions only after repeated stimulation. His phrases were short and simplified, but the phonological and morphological structure of the language was preserved. No slurring of speech as in dysarthria or motor dysprosody was noted. The patient's motor activity also decreased. He lacked initiative and spontaneity and did not move without much urging so that his speech disorder appeared to be part of the more general disturbance of initiation and drive.

The patient's comprehension was relatively better than his spontaneous speech, and after active stimulation he could follow the repeated commands to show his "ear, nose, eye, nose . . . " and even similar commands with two components: "Show your ear–nose," "eye–ear," "nose–ear," etc. The patient correctly read the word "hand" and smiled on seeing his last name shown to him by the physician. Other written words did not elicit any reaction from the patient, although they were repeatedly shown him. He had no sign of apraxia in his left arm.

By the fifth day, the general aspontaneity and slowness in following commands had increased. The patient still followed the physician's movements with his eyes but followed only a few commands upon being urged to cooperate. He did not speak or make any sound. He developed bilateral pneumonia and died of acute cardiac failure on the sixth day after the onset of the stroke.

Anatomical Diagnosis Left ventricular hypertrophy and atherosclerosis of the aorta and cerebral arteries were noted at autopsy. The area of recent infarction involved the territory of the left anterior cerebral artery, the white matter of the cingulate gyrus and part of the first frontal gyrus on the mesial surface of the hemisphere. In the orocaudal direction the infarction began from the level of the genu of the corpus callosum and completely disappeared at the posterior part of the paracentral lobule (Fig. 3.4). The areas of infarction in the right hemisphere were older and adjacent to the external wall of the lateral ventricle, the caudate nucleus, and the anterior limb of the internal capsule. The more recent infarction was also seen in the symmetrical area of the left hemisphere. A myelin stain showed that the infarction in the left hemisphere involved primarily the corona radiata of the left frontal lobe extending to the white and gray matter at the borderline of the cingulate gyrus and the first frontal gyrus in the area anterior to the paracentral lobule. A more posterior area of infarction involved the cortex of the medial surface of F_1, corresponding (area 6) to the supplementary motor area of Penfield, and the anterior part of the paracentral lobule (area 4). A histopathological examination did not reveal any area of infarction in the pars opercularis and pars triangularis of the left F_3. Two similar cases were reported by Rubens (1975) and Alexander and Schmitt (1980). Localization of the infarction in the territory of the anterior cerebral artery was confirmed by radioisotope brain scans in Rubens's report and with CT imaging in cases presented by Alexander and Schmitt (1980).

In spite of these papers, a number of question remained unsettled. Dynamic disorders of speech and difficulty in speech initiation were

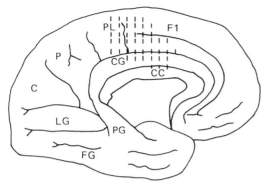

a

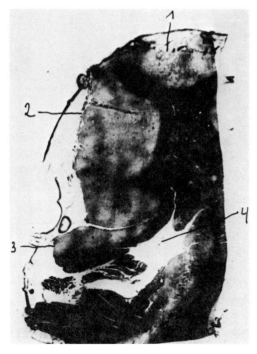

b

Figures 3.4
Case 7, MC, Dynamic aphasia. *a*, Infarction in the cortex of the medial surface of the left hemisphere (anatomical and histopathological data). F1, first frontal gyrus; PL, para-central gyrus; CG, cingulate gyrus; CC, corpus callosum; LG, lingual gyrus; C, cuneus; P, precuneus. *b*, Myelin stain of the infarction at the border of the first frontal and cingulate gyri with extension to the corpus callosum. 1, posterior F_1 convexital surface; 2, medial surface of posterior F_3; 3, cingulate gyrus; 4, focus of the infarction. *c*, Mesial surface of the posterior F_1 in the cortical area of the microscopic infarction with prominent cell loss and in the early stage of cicatrization (hematoxylin and eosin, × 140).

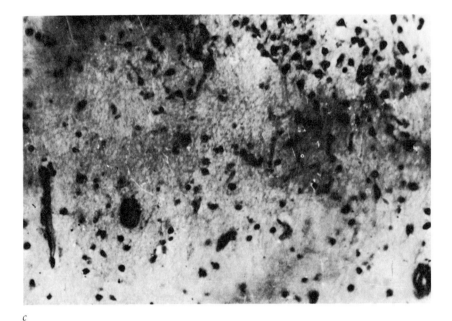

c

also described in cases with lesions of the posterior part of the second frontal gyrus. Cairns *et al.* (1941) and Daly and Love (1958) described "akinetic mutism" somewhat similar to severe dynamic aphasia in their cases with lesions of the periaqueductal gray matter. The role played by a lesion of the ventral lateral nucleus of the thalamus in the later development of "akinetic mutism" was also stressed.

Dynamic aphasia is manifested as a primary disorder of speech initiation, since general motor activity is not reduced in most of the patients, especially in the chronic stage of stroke. On the other hand, in cases with akinetic mutism, general activity, including motor activity, is markedly diminished, and lack of speech initiative may represent a secondary manifestation of the general aspontaneity. Dynamic aphasia as a primary disorder of speech initiation may therefore be attributed to a lesion of a specific region in the superior-posterior part of the frontal lobe. In cases with a lesion of the posterior part of the second frontal gyrus, dynamic aphasia may be explained as resulting from edema and other pathological processes developing around the primary focus of cerebral infarction in adjacent areas of the first frontal gyrus. The manifestation of motor agrammatism and other mild signs of Broca's aphasia may be attributed in such cases to the cortical involvement by the pathological processes of the adjacent Broca's area. This type of marked dynamic aphasia associated with simplification and impoverishment of speech occurred in our Case 8.

Case 8, MA: A 64-year-old, right-handed male with a long history of hypertension and atherosclerosis had two myocardial infarctions fourteen years and eight years, respectively, before his first CVA. Later, he developed a thrombotic occlusion in his right femoral artery and had his right leg amputated at the middle portion of the thigh. Five months after surgery, the patient lost consciousness for one hour and developed a mild weakness and hypesthesia in the right hand.

Two months later, the patient had transient difficulty in word-finding and production which lasted several hours. No sign of agraphia and alexia was noted at that time. A mild paresis of the right hand did not change noticeably in the course of this TIA.

On the seventeenth day after the TIA, the patient developed CVA with a pronounced speech disorder, severe paresis of the right arm, and plegia of the stump of the right thigh. Three days later the patient had difficulty in making general conversation, although the phonological, morphological, and syntactical structure of expressive speech was preserved. He repeated the last one or two words of any question asked and had a tendency to perseveration of these words. His speech was fluent, free of tension and effort. After repeated encouragement the patient correctly answered questions, but his answers were short and simplified, with long pauses between the questions and his responses. His ability to repeat syllables, words, and phrases was mainly preserved. The patient repeated phrases consisting of seven or eight words using oppositional phonemes, but sometimes he failed to repeat phrases with many small functional words and a series of three syllables. Naming was characterized by strikingly increased latency and occasional verbal paraphasias: he called "coat," "shirt," and "eyebrow," "wig." Prompting of the first phonemes of the word helped to improve naming. Comprehension of conversational speech and simple commands was moderately disturbed. Alienation of word meaning was noted in the "eye–ear–nose" test with one component. The ability to read was preserved, but he could not write with his left hand. The patient wrote one or two letters and then refused to continue writing. He had no sign of finger agnosia or of general akinesia, and he participated properly in the examination of motion and sensory function. Tongue movement and buccofacial praxis were spared, and swallowing was preserved. Severe paresis of the right arm and plegia of the right leg stump were present. Right-sided unsteady hemihypesthesia was noted for pinprick, but position and vibration senses were intact in the right hand. The visual fields were normal.

On the twenty-third day the patient developed pneumonia and died on the thirty-eighth day.

Anatomical Diagnosis Hypertonia was present with hypertrophy of the left cardiac ventricle and moderate arteriolonephrosclerosis. Atherosclerosis of the aorta, the cardiac, and the cerebral arteries was noted. Multiple myocardial scars after repeated infarctions were seen.

A large recent cerebral infarction was observed in the territory of the left anterior cerebral artery. The infarction was 0.6 × 0.7 cm anterior to the paracentral lobule in the posterior part of the first frontal gyrus corresponding to the supplementary motor area. This infarction extended posteriorly to the lateral surface of the gray and white matter of the motor strip measuring 4.0 × 2.5 cm in the largest part of the lesion (Fig. 3.5). The focus of the infarction disappeared 0.5 cm posterior to the sensory strip. The length of the infarction from the anterior tip to the posterior end was 5.5 cm. No visible changes were seen in the cingulate gyrus and in the corpus callosum.

Two additional old small foci of cerebral infarction were noted in the left hemisphere. One of them was seen in the territory of the left middle cerebral artery which had destroyed the gray and white matter of the posterior part of the second frontal gyrus. Another small focus of infarction, measuring 1.2 × 1.2 × 0.7 cm lateral was observed in the territory of the left posterior cerebral artery on the lateral surface of the occipital lobe at the borderline with the inferior parietal lobule.

The histopathological examination of the posterior part of the third frontal gyrus (area 44) in the left hemisphere showed that the structure of the cortical layers was preserved in this area. Mild edema was noted only in a few cells in the immediate vicinity of the cerebral infarction in the posterior F_2. A small microscopic focus of the cerebral infarction with glial proliferation was seen in the second and third cortical layers of area 44. In general, the histopathological changes in the posterior part of the third frontal gyrus were moderate. The histopathological examination showed only minor changes in the pars triangularis (area 45) of the third frontal gyrus, as well as in the cingulate gyrus anterior to the paracentral lobule of the left hemisphere.

Therefore the development of dynamic aphasia in Case 8 may be attributed to the large infarction in the posterior part of the first frontal gyrus in the left hemisphere. This infarction extended from the level of the supplementary motor area to the paracentral lobule and the upper part of the motor and sensory strip. The notable movement disorder in the leg reflected this lesion after CVA accompanied by the development of persistent dynamic aphasia. A transient speech disorder

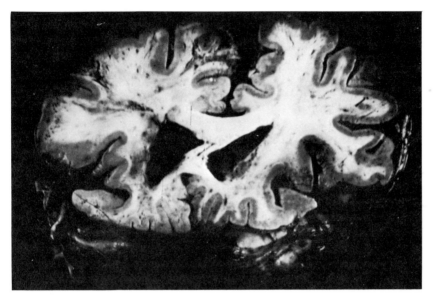

a

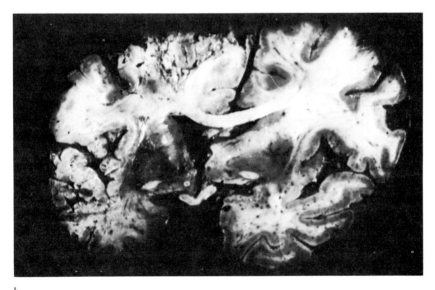

b

Figure 3.5
Case 8, MA, Dynamic aphasia. *a*, Coronal section at the level of the temporal poles. Infarction in the posterior part of the first frontal gyrus on the medial surface of the left hemisphere. A second small infarction is seen in the posterior part of the second frontal gyrus in the homonymous hemisphere. *b*, Coronal section at the level of the chiasm. Infarction on the medial surface of the left hemisphere spreading to the convexital part of the upper portion of the motor strip and the adjacent white matter. No visible changes in the middle and lower portions of the motor strip.

and mild paresis of the right hand in the initial vascular accidents recorded in this case may be attributed to the old small infarction of the posterior part of the second frontal gyrus in the left hemisphere. This additional infarction in the posterior F_2, as well as microscopic changes in the adjacent area (44), may have caused the slight motor agrammatism, naming disorder, and alienation of word meaning. Surprisingly, there was no sign of agraphia at the time the small infarction developed in the posterior F_2 corresponding to Exner's center of writing.

General akinesia and signs of motor aspontaneity were absent in Case 8. Nonetheless, these disturbances were prominent in Case 7. It seems, therefore, that dynamic aphasia clearly represents a primary disorder of speech initiation in Case 8, but primary adynamia of speech in Case 7 is probably combined with the secondary disorder of speech initiation due to the general akinesia. This distinction may also be explained by the differences in lesion localization in both cases. In Case 8, a large infarction in the left hemisphere occupied the posterior part of the first frontal gyrus corresponding to the supplementary motor area, but the cingulate gyrus was spared. On the other hand, in Case 7, MC, the infarction of the cingulate gyrus in the left hemisphere partly extended into the adjacent area of the posterior F_1 on the mesial surface of the hemisphere. The lesion of the supplementary motor area and the adjacent posterior part of the left hemisphere is probably responsible for the development of the dynamic aphasia, a primary disorder of speech initiation. At the same time, a lesion of the cingulate gyrus leads to general motor akinesia with a secondary disorder of speech initiation.

4

Posterior Aphasia

Syndromes of posterior aphasia develop in cases with a lesion of the posterior part of the language zone in the dominant hemisphere, usually the left hemisphere. The posterior language zone includes the gray and white matter of the middle and posterior part of the first, second, and third temporal gyri, Heschl's gyri on the internal surface of the temporal lobe, and the supramarginal and angular gyri of the parietal lobe. This zone is connected through the temporal isthmus with the thalamic nuclei, but the role of the lesion in these areas in language disorder still has to be clarified.

Posterior aphasia was originally described by Wernicke (1874) as a sensory aphasia in contrast to Broca's motor aphasia. Later, Marie (1906c), using a complicated test for comprehension ability, showed a comprehension deficit in patients with Broca's aphasia but attributed that deficit to the additional lesion in Wernicke's area. Marie's theory notwithstanding, the presence of a comprehension disorder in patients with Broca's aphasia has been repeatedly confirmed, and special tests for comprehension ability in Broca's aphasia have been developed. Therefore patients with motor aphasia show disorder of comprehension, and patients with sensory aphasia have a disturbance of expressive speech as a constant feature of language disorder. The terms "motor" and "sensory" aphasia have been abandoned by many authors. From our point of view, the terms "anterior" and "posterior" aphasia are most appropriate for the groups of aphasia syndromes developing after lesions of the anterior or posterior portions of the language zone in the dominant hemisphere.

Posterior aphasia is characterized by a disorder of expressive speech and comprehension. This disorder includes posterior motor agrammatism with lack of the substantive content words and prevalence of the small functional words, anomia, increased speech activity, and alienation of word meaning, difficulty in comprehension of conversational speech and of gestures in more severe cases, and disorder of auditory word and phoneme recognition. Various combinations of these symptoms in the different types of the posterior aphasia syndrome include Wernicke's aphasia, anomic-sensory aphasia, phonemic-sensory aphasia or "phoneme deafness," repetition aphasia, and anomic-spatial aphasia. The names of these various types of posterior aphasia indicate mostly clinical features related primarily to language disorder. The site of the lesions in various types of anterior and posterior aphasia cannot be defined precisely at present, and it is reasonable to reflect in the name of those types the clinical features of a particular aphasia syndrome.

For various posterior aphasia the old term "Wernicke's aphasia" may be conserved, since this term reflects a relatively well-defined entity and has been widely accepted in the literature. The other terms, such as "transcortical" or "subcortical sensory aphasia," or "conduction aphasia," are dubious from the point of view of localization, since the disruption of transcortical and conduction pathways occurs almost in every case of aphasia, and a pure cortical lesion without involvement of adjacent white matter has not been described in cases with persistent aphasia or in the opposite condition with a lesion of the white matter but no extension to the cortical pure language areas. The terms "transcortical" and "conduction" also reflect the presumable brain mechanisms of language and its disorder, but those mechanisms are still to be clarified in spite of more than one hundred years' study of aphasia. Terms reflecting the clinical features of aphasia syndromes are preferable at present, and localization of lesions has to be described in more general terms related to the destroyed lobe of the hemisphere without pinpointing the transcortical or conduction pathways. Such a description is especially difficult in cases with persistent aphasia, which usually results from a large cortico–subcortical lesion.

The term "transcortical sensory aphasia" has been applied to two forms of posterior aphasia: (1) anomic-sensory aphasia, with disorder of naming and alienation of word meaning as a major feature, and (2) mild Wernicke's aphasia. Some cases with semantic or anomic-spatial aphasia have also been described as transcortical sensory aphasia. "Conduction aphasia" includes "repetition aphasia" with disorder of word-span retention and literal paraphasia as main symptoms, some cases with moderate Wernicke's aphasia, and cases with a combination of repetition aphasia and articulation aphasia. The term "word deafness" also should be abandoned, since in these cases a phoneme deafness or phonemic-sensory aphasia is actually present.

Wernicke's Aphasia

Symptomatology This is a combination of comprehension disorder, usually more severe than in patients with Broca's aphasia, and disturbance of expressive speech characterized by overabundance of small functional words, verbal paraphasia, and logorrhea with preserved fluency and prosodic structure of speech.

The main feature of comprehension disorder in Wernicke's aphasia is the disturbance of auditory word recognition, while single-phoneme recognition is usually preserved. But in more severe cases some difficulty of phoneme recognition, especially in more complicated conditions, is present. Alienation of word meaning, anomic aphasia, and sensory agrammatism may also be seen in such cases. Wernicke's aphasia exists quite often as a word-recognition aphasia combined to a greater or lesser extent with other types of posterior aphasia. Disorders of writing, reading, and calculation are usually associated with disturbances of comprehension and expressive speech in these patients. Movement and sensation are preserved, but transient right-sided hemiparesis and hemihypesthesia can be seen in some of the cases with Wernicke's aphasia in the first hours and days after the onset of a stroke. Right-sided hemianopia predominantly in the upper quadrant occurs more frequently and may be persistent in approximately one-fifth of the cases.

In the acute stage of stroke a loss of speech is combined with marked comprehension disorder in many cases of severe Wernicke's aphasia, and transient right-sided hemiparesis may also be seen in some of those patients. That loss of speech, however, is different from the complete loss of voice, or aphonia, in acute Broca's aphasia, and is characterized by the presence of unintelligible sound production or mumbling. Patients with severe Wernicke's aphasia answer the questions with a fluent flow of indistinguishable sounds pronounced loudly without slurring dys-arthria or hypophonic mumbling. These sounds somewhat resemble speech sounds, but it is impossible to recognize what phoneme has been pronounced. In some cases with acute Wernicke's aphasia, single vowels such as "a" or "o" emerge from the unintelligible flow of sounds, making the utterance resemble somewhat the flow of normal speech sounds.

In two or three days, sometimes seven or eight days after the onset of a stroke, the unintelligible flow of sounds usually becomes more and more distinguishable as a flow of speech sounds, and the classic picture of expressive speech in Wernicke's aphasia develops. In approximately half of the cases that picture may be seen from the beginning of the CVA. In it speech is well articulated with preserved prosody, but it is almost completely incomprehensible since most of the substantial words, predominantly nouns and verbs, are missed or replaced by verbal paraphasia, and speech consists of small functional words and verbal or less frequently literal paraphasias. This mixture of words may be called "word salad" or "jargonaphasia." Patients with "word salad" are often unaware that they have a language disorder and become very angry and agitated when someone fails to understand them.

Naming, repetition, recitation, and automatized speech are very much disturbed in patients with severe Wernicke's aphasia in the acute stage of CVA. The flow of unintelligible speechlike sounds and "word salad" or "jargonaphasia" usually occurs in response to various questions or commands, including testing of naming, repetition, etc., sometimes without any external stimulation, so that the term "logorrhea" appropriately describes this "nonstop" flow of words or speechlike sounds.

In less severe cases of Wernicke's aphasia, patients are able to name some of the objects, but not many, and they then produce a number of verbal and literal paraphasias while trying to formulate appropriate answers. Repetition is somewhat better but is still incorrect for many words and phrases. When asked to repeat vowels or especially consonants, patients produce a flow of speech sounds and words which sometimes include a requested phoneme that is hardly recognizable in the middle of this constant speech flow. Automatized speech and recitation are in general less disturbed than naming and repetition, but they often are interrupted by the unexpected intrusion of verbal and literal paraphasias.

Comprehension of conversational speech is markedly disturbed in the acute stage of stroke, especially in patients with an unintelliglble speech flow. Such patients cannot understand simple questions about their feelings or family. In many cases comprehension of gesture is also disturbed, and communication with the patient becomes extremely difficult in the first days after the onset of the stroke. Some patients with Wernicke's aphasia, therefore, who are in relatively good general condition resemble severe psychotic patients, since they produce a strange "salad" of words like the neologistic jargon of schizophrenic patients. They do not follow commands, and they show somewhat euphoric behavior quite inappropriate to recent stroke.

Reading, writing, and calculation are almost completely destroyed after a stroke in patients with severe Wenicke's aphasia. Five or six days later in the course of the CVA, however, patients start to read and follow some simple commands but still cannot write volitionally or on dictation, producing only some single, isolated letters. Copying is better for a limited number of letters and sometimes for short words. Calculation is impossible in most of the cases.

Tongue movement is preserved from the first hours of CVA, and buccofacial or limb apraxia may be seen in only a few cases, mostly as a result of comprehension difficulty in following commands. In most cases movement and sensation are completely preserved, but transient right hemiparesis with or without hypesthesia occurs for a few hours or one or two days in some cases. Right hemianopia that is more prominent in the upper quadrant may be persistent in every fourth or fifth patient with Wernicke's aphasia.

In the chronic stage of stroke the expressive speech of patients with severe Wernicke's aphasia is characterized by verbal paraphasias, omission of nouns and verbs, predominance of small functional words, and "word salad" or "jargonaphasia." The flow of speech is free and fluent, without effort and tension. The prosodic pattern is preserved and no distortion of articulation can be noted. Speech activity increases sometimes to the stage of logorrhea but the number of words used is limited, and the same word is often repeated in various situations with good articulation and prosody, so that impoverishment of language is overshadowed by the intact pronunciation, melodic line, rhythm, and intonation of speech. For example, one of our patients responded to the various questions without any delay or tension but always with the same phrases consisting largely of stereotyped phrases such as "Thank you," "I would like," "No problem at all," "Nothing could be done," "Take it easy," "With great pleasure . . . ," etc.

In spite of the numerous verbal paraphasias, the meaning of the patient's answer can often be recognized, although in some cases the literal paraphasias make the patient's speech completely unintelligible, but the patient remains convinced that his speech is normal.

Repetition and naming are strikingly disturbed in patients with severe Wernicke's aphasia. Patients cannot repeat consonants or even most vowels. Repetition and naming are often replaced by numerous literal and sometimes verbal paraphasias.

A tendency to logorrhea is manifested as an augmentation of the phonemes and words while the patient tries to repeat the speech sound or word or to name the object. Instead, he pronounces a stream of various phonemes or words, one of which may be what the patient is searching for. Prompting the first syllable or even the entire word often does not help in the patient's effort to find the correct name of the presented object. Sometimes after finding the correct name for the object, the patient then loses it, but then starts to use this word repeatedly in confrontation naming of new objects. The recitation and automatized recall of the days of the week and the names of the months is severely disturbed in many patients, but the automatized sequence of the digits from 1 to 10 may often be correctly recalled.

Comprehension of conversational speech is difficult. A patient may recognize that a conversation relates to his or her family or to his or her disease but still cannot comprehend the question completely.

Sometimes a patient will not pay any attention to the examiner's question and talks nonstop, listening only after the doctor has repeatedly touched his or her shoulders or hands in order to fix the patient's attention on the doctor's question. The patient may not understand most of the individual words or follow a simple command. He or she makes many mistakes in showing the body parts and objects in the room. Sometimes the patient correctly follows the first command, i.e., "Close your eyes," but then he or she develops a severe alienation of word meaning and cannot follow even simple commands. In some cases an involuntary gesture of the examiner may help the patient understand the command, e.g., fixing the doctor's gaze on the part of the body or the object which the patient has to point out, an unsatisfied expression on the examiner's face when the patient's performance is faulty, etc. In many cases, however, a disorder of gesture comprehension may also be seen.

Recognizing isolated vowels and consonants as well as phonemes in series is strikingly disturbed in patients with severe Wernicke's aphasia. A patient cannot correctly repeat the phonemes and fails at a simple test: "Raise your right hand when the examiner says 'a,' and do not raise the hand for 'o,' " so phoneme agnosia or phoneme deafness is evident in such cases.

In moderate Wernicke's aphasia the entire pattern of expressive speech remains unchanged compared with severe cases; "jargonaphasia" or "word salad" may be noted, but the number of paraphasias is lessened, and some substantive nouns and especially verbs appear in the fluent flow of speech. The proportion of small functional words declines, therefore, and the meaning of the patient's speech becomes clearer and more recognizable. Logorrhea is mild or does not appear at all in conversational speech, and increased speech activity is rarely noted.

The patient is rarely aware of his speech errors. Repetition disorder is less prominent and manifests itself mostly in numerous literal paraphasias in multisyllabic words and long or complicated phrases. Naming is markedly disturbed; the patient cannot find an appropriate name for most objects shown him, parts of the body, or actions. Attempts at naming are characterized by striking mispronunciation of the words, with literal paraphasias, or by the replacement of the right word with a series of verbal paraphasias. A prompting of the first one or two syllables of the name sometimes helps to find the appropriate word, but the examiner may often pronounce the entire word without enabling the patient to find it. Difficulty in automatized speech occurs for the enumeration of months and, to a lesser extent, the days of the week.

Comprehension of conversational speech, single words, and simple commands is mainly preserved in moderate Wernicke's aphasia. Patients follow most of the commands to show the parts of the body or objects. Severe disorder may be noted, however, when a patient is asked to follow the complicated instructions of Luria's or Head's tests, such as "With the index finger of the left hand show your right ear," or "Show with a pen or pencil," etc. Severe alienation of word meaning manifests itself in the "ear–nose–eye" test, not only with two components but also with one component: "Show your ear, then your nose, then eye . . . ear . . . nose . . . ear, ..."

The ability to distinguish single vowels is preserved in moderate Wernicke's aphasia, but a series of two or three vowels cannot be differentiated and the patient continues to raise his hand, indicating the same sequence even when the order of vowels has been changed in the series. Retention of word span is limited to one or two words, but if pictures of the objects are presented, the patient can sometimes correctly point to five or six of ten objects drawn on the cards placed in front of him.

Phonological analysis is severely disturbed in severe and moderate Wernicke's aphasia. Visual phonological analysis is possible only in some moderate cases in which the patients cannot analyze the spelling of the auditorially presented word but can indicate the cards with the correct phonemes and the pictures of objects with the corresponding phonemes in their names.

Reading and writing are almost impossible in severe cases. On dictation patients write some letters instead of the word, e.g., "p" or "h" or "a." Their writing is often so distorted that no letter is recognizable. The ability to copy is destroyed in many cases. In moderate cases, writing on dictation and reading are characterized by numerous literal paralexias and paragraphias; copying is performed correctly but slowly, with a tendency to "slavish" imitation.

No calculation can be performed in severe cases. Only single-digit calculations, such as $2 + 3, 3 + 4, 6 - 2$ can be done. The multiplication tables are completely erased from memory. Patients can read single digits in less severe cases, but figures such as 1050, 1005, 10,500 remain difficult to read.

Moderate buccofacial apraxia is seen only in individual cases with severe Wernicke's aphasia and usually is absent in moderate cases. In most cases with severe Wernicke's aphasia and in some moderate cases, construction and finger apraxia are seen. Patients cannot copy complex figures, such as a star, or objects, such as a house, a face, a table, etc. When trying to copy or draw from memory, patients lose many important parts of the objects. They draw a face with one eye and no nose, a house without windows; sometimes the drawing consists of one or two lines that have no resemblance to the requested figure.

Finger apraxia manifests itself when the patient is trying to stretch out his or her index and middle fingers or the index and the little fingers. Sometimes this task cannot be performed even with one finger and may be called finger agnosia.

Apraxia of hand position may also be seen. The patient follows successfully the simple commands in Head's tests when the examiner shows his right ear with the left hand or his left eye with the right hand but makes many mistakes in following more complex ones, such as to touch with his right index finger the inner corner of the right eye, left corner of the mouth, or to change the relative position of each hand.

The emotional status of a patient with Wernicke's aphasia is often characterized by euphoria, combined with "strange" behavior only partially related to communication difficulties. Movement and sensation are generally preserved. Transient right-sided hemiparesis in the first 24–48 hours of CVA completely disappears, or mild weakness of movement of the right hand may be seen in individual cases. More often the stretch reflexes in the right extremities increase in comparison with those of the left arm and leg. Right-sided hemihypesthesia to pinprick is seldom seen, but right upper quadrant hemianopia occurs in approximately 20–25% of cases.

Localization of the lesion in Wernicke's aphasia has been traditionally attributed to the posterior part of the first temporal gyrus in the dominant hemisphere. Wernicke (1874) first described ten cases with a disorder comprehension and a peculiar disturbance of expressive speech, reading, and writing. Three of those cases were studied at autopsy and had an area of lesion in the left posterior T_1, but in two of the cases a diffuse cerebral lesion was noted, and in one case, the lesion extended from the posterior T_1 to the adjacent part of T_2. The role of Wernicke's area has not been questioned for many years, however, in spite of the controversy about cases with an isolated lesion of Broca's area with transient aphasia or without any speech or language disorder at all. This may be partly related to Marie's original idea that the lesion of Wernicke's area (the posterior part of the first temporal gyrus) is responsible for the development of every aphasia syndrome, including Broca's aphasia, in which an additional lesion of the so-called lenticular zone connects with the lesion in Wernicke's area to produce an anarthric, nonlanguage component of a true aphasic syndrome. Later the focus of discussion turned to isolated lesions of Broca's area without aphasia, and no attempts were made to study the cases with isolated lesions of Wernicke's area, if any such cases had been reported. But in our own material we have one case with a small infarct restricted to Wernicke's area.

In this case severe transient Wernicke's aphasia occurred in the first hours following the onset of the stroke. On the second day expressive speech and comprehension remarkably improved, and a diagnosis of moderate anomic-sensory aphasia was made. The patient died on the forty-second day; an autopsy revealed a small area of infarction confined to the posterior part of the first temporal gyrus at the left hemisphere.

Case 9, KZ: A 65-year-old, right-handed woman with a long history of asthmatic bronchitis and COPD woke up one day with a language disorder. In answer to her daughter's questions the patient "mumbled something unintelligible" and could not understand a simple question. She had no problem with movement. Later on in the day the patient started to speak easily, without effort or tension, saying "Yes," "No," and "No problem," but her comprehension did not improve. The patient followed the first command to "Close your eyes," but then she started to close her eyes in response to every other command or did not make any attempt to follow commands, saying only "Yes" or "No problem," etc. She had trouble in understanding gestures; in order to make such simple gestures as closing and opening her mouth or raising her hand, she needed repeated instructions with gestures. A diagnosis of Wernicke's aphasia had been made by a general practitioner. The patient was admitted to the hospital with this diagnosis at 10:00 PM the same day. The next morning the clinical picture of Wernicke's aphasia in the acute stage of stroke was clear. The patient mumbled indistinguishable sounds and produced three or four words in response to questions or commands to repeat a word or syllable or to say the name of an object she was shown. She had great difficulty with comprehension.

The next day her language ability was remarkably improved, and a diagnosis of anomic-sensory aphasia was made. The patient started to speak fluently with quite long phrases but overused small functional words in favor of nouns and verbs. Only a few verbal and literal paraphasias were observed, but not "word salad." She had a slight tendency to logorrhea and augmentation, and her comprehension of conversational speech returned almost completely. She was able to follow most of the simple commands but had difficulty with the more complicated commands of Luria's and Head's tests. Differentiation and repetition were disturbed only for the series of three vowels. Retention of word series was limited, however, to the word span of one- or two-word series. Her comprehension of gesture recovered completely. The main sign of language disorder was a difficulty in naming presented objects and actions. She could not name more than approximately 80–85% of the objects and produced numerous verbal paraphasias in attempts to name the object or action. Buccofacial praxis and tongue movement were intact. A mild transient weakness in the right hand improved at the same time as her speech. During the next few days the patient's condition remained unstable, and the language disorder went from mild to moderate and back to mild anomic-sensory aphasia. Sometimes the clinical picture of language disorder resembled mild anterior aphasia, since her speech was simplified and impoverished but fluent, effortless, and without tension. There was no severe disorder of comprehension. Predominance of verbs and small functional words was noted as well as a tendency to logorrhea and augmentation in a repetition of phonemes, syllables, and words. These disturbances, together with mild difficulty in naming and in retention of word span, supported the diagnosis of mild anomic-sensory aphasia.

In the following weeks the patient's cardiac and pulmonary conditions continued to deteriorate without marked change in the language disorder. The patient died from cardiopulmonary insufficiency and cardiac arrest on the forty-second day following the onset of the stroke.

Anatomical Diagnosis COPD and hypertrophy of the cardiac ventricles were present. Ascites, bilateral hydrothorax, and hydropericardia were seen as well as a hemorrhagic infarction of the spleen. A gross anatomical examination did not reveal any sign of brain lesions. A histopathological examination was performed on the brain tissue taken from the following Brodmann's areas related to language function: 44 (posterior F_3), 43 (Rolandic operculum), 40 (supramarginal gyrus), 39 (angular gyrus), 22 (middle part of T_1), 22 (posterior T_1), 37 (posterior T_2), 41 and 42 (Heschl's gyri). The symmetrical parts of Brodmann's areas in the right and left hemispheres were studied. A small area of infarction was noted only in the gray matter of the posterior part of the first temporal gyrus on the borderline of the angular gyrus in the left hemisphere. No areas of infarction were seen in the other parts of the brain studied histopathologically. Moderate engorgement of the vessels and signs of brain edema were observed in the left hemisphere, however, especially in the vicinity of the area of infarction.

Severe Wernicke's aphasia in the first hours of CVA in this case may be related to the marked postictal edema of the brain tissue surrounding the small area of infarction in the posterior T_1. When the edema lessened in the course of the CVA, the only manifestation of this infarction was a mild anomic-sensory aphasia without clear signs of comprehension deficit, disorder of word recognition, "word salad," and logorrhea typical for Wernicke's aphasia. The transient character of Wernicke's aphasia in our case with a small infarction in Wernicke's area resembles the transient character of aphasia in cases with an isolated lesion of Broca's area. In many such published cases of Broca's aphasia, however, speech and language recovered completely in the course of CVA or did not show any sign of disorder at all. In our case the Wernicke's aphasia disappeared within hours, but mild anomic-sensory aphasia was present until the patient's death. No cases with complete recovery of language function and an isolated lesion of Wernicke's area seem to have been published. On the other hand, as in patients with Broca's aphasia, severe, stable Wernicke's aphasia occurs in cases with a more extended lesion of the posterior-superior part of the dominant temporal lobe, sometimes with extension to the adjacent area of the parietal lobe. Such lesions were revealed in our clinical-anatomical cases with Wernicke's aphasia. In all three cases the area of infarction spread from the medial-posterior T_1 to Heschl's gyri and adjacent areas of the parietal lobe in the left hemisphere.

Case 10, DD: A 63-year-old, right-handed woman with a long history of hypertension and atherosclerosis suddenly developed a mild weakness in the right hand and language disorder without loss of consciousness. The patient's speech consisted of indistinguishable, unintelligible sounds pronounced loudly but without modulation. Comprehension of speech was severely disturbed and repetition was impossible. The patient understood some simple gestures but not all. She did not say "ah" even during a larynx examination. She followed commands at first but showed alienation of word and often gesture meaning for the second and following commands. She could not read, write, or calculate. On the third day after the onset of the stroke she developed a transient hemiplegia of the right arm and leg. At the end of the same day she had mild weakness in the right extremities. That weakness completely disappeared on the eighth or ninth day. At that time her speech improved slightly, and the clinical picture of severe Wernicke's aphasia became evident. When the patient started to speak, her expressive speech became a stream of words with no apparent semantic or syntactical connection. Her speech was fluent, effortless, and without tension; normal prosody could be recognized, but innumerable paraphasias, predominantly verbal, and logorrhea turned it into true incomprehensible "word salad." The patient was unable to name 85–90% of the objects presented to her. Prompting of the first phonemes did not help in the naming, but stimulated a flow of verbal and literal paraphasias in the attempt to find the right word. Repetition was disturbed even for one or two syllables and words and series of two or three phonemes. At times the patient could not repeat a single vowel or consonant as in cases with "phoneme deafness." Later her comprehension improved somewhat, especially for conversational speech, but some questions had to be repeated two or three times and others remained incomprehensible to the patient. Her comprehension was easier if the conversation was restricted to one simple subject, e.g., her family or the history of her disease. The patient understood the examiner better if he spoke simply and pronounced his phrases clearly, slowly, and with a modulated voice. The patient followed commands much better but showed severe alienation of word meaning in the "eye–ear–nose" test. She had marked difficulty with the Head's test and Luria's complex logicogrammatical constructions. Gesture comprehension recovered completely. Alexia, agraphia, acalculia, constructional apraxia, and finger agnosia were noticeable and could be attributed to the additional parietal lobe lesion. During the next days and weeks the patient's condition stabilized, but her speech showed only slight improvement in the following months.

One and one-half years later the patient developed a new CVA with right-sided hemiplegia and a striking increase of the speech difficulty. The patient did not lose her ability to vocalize, but in response to questions, she answered only "Yes," "No," or "Ma." She could repeat only two words, "Mama" and "Papa." Comprehension of speech was disturbed, and the patient followed only simple commands, such as "Close your eyes" or "Raise your hand," showing severe alienation of word meaning for others. Because of this severe restriction of expressive speech to two or three words and the severe comprehension disorder, she was considered to have global aphasia. Movement in her right arm recovered only slightly during the following months, but her right leg regained its movement almost completely, and the patient was able to walk freely without the use of a cane or other support. The global aphasia remained unchanged in spite of an intensive course of speech therapy. Seventeen months later the patient became agitated and then drowsy on the next day. Communication with her became practically impossible. She made no sound and could not understand any simple command. She had mild weakness in the right leg and paralysis of the right arm. Her condition continued to deteriorate; she developed severe cardiac failure and died of cardiac arrest.

Anatomical Diagnosis Left ventricular hypertrophy and atherosclerotic nephrosclerosis were noted. Atherosclerosis of the aorta, cardiac arteries, magistral arteries of the neck, and cerebral arteries was present. A scar of the myocardium at the posterior wall of the left ventricle developed after infarction. Moderate enlargement, stretching, and tortuosity of the cervical parts of the internal carotid arteries, more prominent on the left, were revealed. Trifurcation of the internal carotid artery was seen on the right and hypoplasia of the left vertebral artery on the left.

Multiple old cysts after infarcts were present in the gray and white matter of the cerebral hemispheres (Fig. 4.1). The largest cyst in the territory supplied by the cortical branches of the left middle cerebral artery extended from posterior T_1 and the angular gyrus to the supramarginal gyrus and posterior lower third of the sensory strip. Three smaller additional cysts were present in the left hemisphere: in the

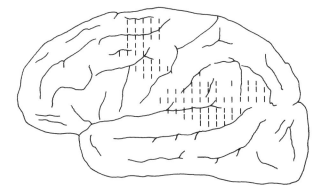

Figure 4.1
Case 10, DD, Severe Wernicke's aphasia after first CVA and global aphasia after subsequent strokes. Infarcts in the cortex of the left hemisphere (anatomical data).

middle part of the motor strip, in the posterior part of F_1 at the convexital surface of the hemisphere and posterior F_2, and in the lenticular nuclei. Two cysts in the right hemisphere involved the anterior portion of the thalamus and the lingual gyrus. The recent infarction was evident in the middle part of the first frontal gyrus on the convexital surface of the right hemisphere. There were fine cysts after hemorrhages in the left lateral thalamus and on the borderline between the right lenticular nuclei and the capsula extrema.

It is difficult to separate the exact role played in aphasia by the numerous cerebral cysts in this case. A comparison between the medical history and the site of the lesions may prove helpful, however. The severe Wernicke's aphasia and disorder of writing, reading, and calculation, as well as the construction praxis and finger agnosia after the first stroke seem to stem from the large left hemisphere infarction. This subsequently formed cysts in the posterior first temporal gyrus and angular gyrus and extended to the supramarginal gyrus and partly to the posterior part of the lower sensory strip. Development of the global aphasia and right-sided hemiplegia after the second stroke may be attributed to the left hemisphere lesion of the middle motor strip and posterior F_2 with possible microscopic involvement of the Rolandic operculum and posterior F_3, or Broca's area, as well as to the additional cyst of the lenticular nuclei characteristic of many cases of severe anterior aphasia. The role of the posterior F_1 lesion cannot be excluded, since the lesion was situated in the immediate vicinity of the supplementary motor area at the medial surface of posterior F_1. Multiple small cysts in the right hemisphere, especially in the thalamus and occipital lobes do not seem to be responsible for the aphasia syndrome in this case, but they evidently played an important role in the patient's general mental deterioration toward the end.

In this case global aphasia developed without any structural damage of Broca's area or the Rolandic operculum. The almost complete destruction of expressive speech, therefore, occurred without a lesion in the areas which are believed to have primary responsibility for severe expressive speech disorder in cases of anterior aphasia. Perhaps the severe expressive speech disorder in this case could be attributed to the extensive parietal and posterior-superior temporal lesion in combination with the lesions of such areas in the anterior language zone as posterior F_2, F_1, and the lenticular nuclei. Certainly histopathological examination of anatomically spared language areas in such cases is needed. That those areas may be completely spared in cases of global aphasia is evident from the famous case (Niessl von Mayendorf 1930) with global aphasia and an extended lesion of the inferior parietal-superior temporal region and Rolandic operculum. The histopathological examination showed no significant change in Broca's area in that case.

Case 11, NE: A 69-year-old, right-handed woman with a long history of hypertension and atherosclerosis lost consciousness for two or three minutes and developed a disorder of expressive speech and comprehension and mild weakness in the right hand. The patient answered all questions with the same speech sound, "d," and could not understand most of the commands and gestures addressed to her. The next morning she started to say individual words and in the afternoon answered simple questions with short phrases. Moderate anomia and predominance of small functional words in expressive speech were noted on the third day after the onset of the stroke, as well as right hemianopia and mild weakness in the right hand. Anomic-sensory aphasia was diagnosed, and the patient remained in relatively stable condition until the forty-sixth day, when a right-sided hemiplegia developed without loss of consciousness. Her speech disorder became much more severe during that episode. The patient's speech consisted of the "nonstop" flow of incomprehensible sounds, some of which resembled "a" and "o." Comprehension of simple commands and some gestures was greatly disturbed. A severe disorder of writing, reading, calculation, and constructional praxis was noted. Right-sided hemiplegia, hemi-hypesthesia, and hemianopia were present.

On the fifth day following that new episode the patient's speech improved somewhat. She was able to say clearly, "yes," "no," and "hi," but her comprehension remained poor. She quickly recovered movement in the right extremities and on the seventh day had only a mild weakness in the right hand. On the thirteenth day after a new

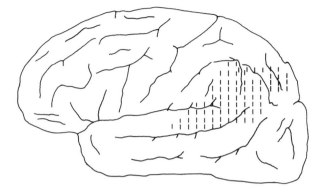

Figure 4.2
Case 11, NE, Severe Wernicke's aphasia. Infarction in the cortex of the left hemisphere (anatomical data).

CVA the patient died from a cardiac arrest due to acute myocardial insufficiency.

A large cerebral infarction, 10.0 × 8.0 cm, was seen in the cortical branches of the left middle cerebral artery at autopsy (Fig. 4.2). This infarction involved the posterior two-thirds of the first temporal gyrus, Heschl's gyri, angular and supramarginal gyri, the superior parietal lobule, and the small part of the lower occipital lobule.

The speech disorder after the second CVA could be considered a global aphasia. But preservation of sound production, the "nonstop" flow of these sounds, and the severe comprehension disorder supported the diagnosis of Wernicke's aphasia, since in cases with global aphasia or severe Broca's aphasia the acute stage of stroke is characterized by the complete loss of sound production; also, in these cases, the right-sided disorder of movement does not disappear in the first days of stroke.

Since only one cerebral infarction was demonstrated at autopsy, the exact site of the lesion related to anomic-sensory aphasia after the first CVA remains unclear, but the role played by the extended temporal-parietal lesion in the development of severe Wernicke's aphasia is evident.

Case 12, GV: A 60-year-old, right-handed male with many years' history of hypertension and atherosclerosis had transient episodes of speech disorder and right-sided hemiparesis lasting four to six hours. Such episodes took place four times without any sequelae until a fifth episode occurred two years after the first TIA. During this last episode the patient developed a right-sided hemiplegia and severe disorder of expressive speech, comprehension, reading, and writing. Movement in the right extremities improved dramatically in the three weeks after the onset of the stroke. Only a mild muscle weakness, predominantly in the right hand and foot, was noted then. No sensory loss or visual field defect was observed.

The patient's speech also improved, but to a lesser extent, and a diagnosis of moderate Wernicke's aphasia was made. The patient spoke fluently, without effort or tension or any tendency to logorrhea. His speech contained almost no nouns and consisted mostly of small functional words and verbs. It was somewhat impoverished; the patient often answered questions fluently without effort but using stereotyped phrases, e.g., "You are right," "No problem," "I don't know," etc. Repetition was disturbed for a series of three vowels and oppositional phonemes. The patient could not differentiate between gestures for "yes" and "no," or a series of three phonemes or three words. Repetition of one- or two-syllable words was preserved, but the patient repeated most of the three- or four-syllable words with severe literal paraphasias. Phrase repetition was noticeably disturbed, even for short, simple phrases consisting of two or three words. The patient produced a flow of literal paraphasias when attempting to name an object, a part of the body, or an action. He could not recall such automatized sequences as days of the week or months and could count only from 1 to 10.

Comprehension of conversational speech, gestures, single words, and simple commands was generally preserved. He made many mistakes, however, in following complicated commands from Luria's and Head's tests. He had mild alienation of word meaning in the "eye–ear–nose" test. He could recall no more than one or two words from a three- or four-word series.

Phonological analysis, reading, and writing were severely disturbed. The patient could not read or write on dictation most ideographs, although he read aloud some single letters correctly. He copied without mistakes, but used "slavish" imitation. Calculation could be performed only up to 10, e.g., $2 + 3$, $8 - 5$, $7 + 2$, but not $12 - 5$ or $7 + 6$.

Praxis, including buccofacial, limb, and constructional praxis, and visual gnosis were completely preserved.

Three months following the onset of the stroke the patient developed a myocardial infarction without evident change in the speech and movement disorder. Three days later he died from cardiac arrest.

Anatomical Diagnosis Left ventricular hypertrophy and arteriolonephrosclerosis were prominent. Marked atherosclerosis of the aorta, cardiac, and cerebral arteries was present. A recent infarction was seen in the posterior wall of the left ventricle.

Numerous foci of the cerebral infarction in the territory of the left middle cerebral artery were revealed (Fig. 4.3). In the temporal lobe a

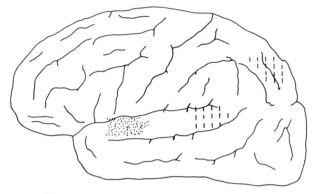

Figure 4.3
Case 12, GB, Severe Wernicke's aphasia. Infarcts in the cortical gray (dashed lines) and white (dotted lines) matter of the left hemisphere (anatomical data).

subarachnoid cyst, measuring 2.0 × 1.5 cm, involved the cortex in the posterior part of first temporal gyrus; a cerebral infarction, 2.0 × 1.0 cm, in the white matter of the anterior T_1 merged with the numerous fine infarctions in the insula. A large infarction, 4.0 × 3.5 × 2.0 cm, was present in the superior-posterior part of the parietal lobe at the borderline of the occipital lobe. Small areas of pseudocysts, 1.0 × 0.5 cm and 0.5 × 0.3 cm, were revealed in the putamen and globus pallidus in the territory of the lenticulostriate branches of the left middle cerebral artery.

The moderate Wernicke's aphasia in this case may stem from the extensive lesion of the anterior and posterior parts of the first temporal gyrus in the left hemisphere. The relatively moderate level of comprehension disorder, especially for conversational speech and simple commands, could be attributed to the anatomical sparing of the Heschl's gyri and the inferior parietal lobule. An additional small infarction in the insula and subcortical structures could be related in this case to the absence of logorrhea and to an episode of transient speech disorder with right-sided hemiplegia two years before the CVA resulting in Wernicke's aphasia.

Anatomical data of our four cases with Wernicke's aphasia are summarized in table 4.1.

It is clear that no final conclusion can be drawn from the autopsies of four single cases presented in table 4.1, but some tentative suggestions can be made. First of all, the connection between the size of the lesion and the severity of Wernicke's aphasia is seen. The number of involved cortical temporoparietal structures is three to six in the cases with severe

Table 4.1 Localization of the Left Hemisphere Infarction in Cases with Wernicke's Aphasia

Case Number and Initials	Severity of Wernicke's Aphasia	First Temporal Gyrus			Heschl's Gyri	Angular Gyrus	Supra-marginal Gyrus	Superior-Parietal Lobule	Insula	Subcortical Structures
		Posterior	Middle	Anterior						
Case 9, KZ	Mild transient	+	−	−	−	−	−	−	−	−
Case 10, DD	Severe	+	−	−	−	+	+	−	−	+
Case 11, NE	Severe	+	+	−	+	+	+	+	−	−
Case 12, GV	Moderate	+	−	+	−	−	−	+	+	+

Wernicke's aphasia, two in the moderate case, and one in the case with mild Wernicke's aphasia. The more extended lesion in both cases with severe aphasia involved the inferior parietal lobule, in the moderate case, the anterior and posterior parts of the first temporal gyrus as well as the superior-posterior part of the left parietal lobe, whereas in the mild case the lesion was confined to the posterior part of the first temporal gyrus and Wernicke's aphasia was transient. The lesion of the temporal lobe itself was most extensive in Case 11, with severe Wernicke's aphasia, and included the lesion of the posterior two-thirds of T_1 and Heschl's gyri. In Case 10, with severe Wernicke's aphasia, the lesion of the temporal lobe was confined to Wernicke's area. A histopathological examination of the anatomically preserved parts of T_1 and Heschl's gyri was not done in this case. On the other hand, Hopf (1957) made a serial histopathological examination of seventeen cases with various posterior aphasias and noted an extended lesion of posterior T_1, Heschl's transverse gyri, and the posterior part of the second and third temporal gyri of the left hemisphere in all of his four cases with what he called complete or almost complete Wernicke's aphasia. An additional lesion of the parietal lobe was also recorded by Hopf in these four cases. Certainly, the lesion of the posterior T_1 is crucial for the development of Wernicke's aphasia, since this lesion site has been noted in every published case of Wernicke's aphasia, including our four cases, as well as Hopf's four cases with Wernicke's aphasia. At the same time the exact clinical role of the more extensive lesion has yet to be clarified in such cases. Maybe the involvement of the inferior parietal lobule in cases with severe Wernicke's aphasia is responsible for the extreme difficulty in comprehension caused by sensory agrammatism, described in patients with a parietal lesion by Head (1926) and Luria (1947). Such extension of the lesion to the inferior parietal lobule was revealed in both of our cases with severe Wernicke's aphasia but was not present in Case 9 with mild and Case 12 with moderate Wernicke's aphasia. At the same time, in our clinical cases with moderate Wernicke's aphasia only three out of eleven had construction apraxia, apraxia of position of the hand, and other parietal signs. The role of the lesion extending from the left posterior T_1 to Heschl's gyri also should be considered a possible cause of the severe comprehension difficulties in patients with severe Wernicke's aphasia. The presence of the disorder of auditory word recognition or auditory word agnosia is essential to the diagnosis of Wernicke's aphasia; this symptom is mainly related to the lesion of the Wernicke's area in the posterior part of the first temporal gyrus in the dominant hemisphere.

Isolated hemorrhages in the posterior temporoparietal cortical area occur infrequently. We did not observe any case with Wernicke's aphasia due to cerebral hemorrhage. Some cases of thalamic hemorrhages with aphasia (Alexander and LoVerme 1980) have signs of Wernicke's aphasia, including logorrhea, paraphasia, and anomia, probably due to the extension of the edema and related pathological processes from the thalamus through the temporal isthmus to the posterior part of the T_1 and the adjacent parietal area.

Repetition Aphasia

Symptomatology Repetition aphasia is characterized by the disorder of repetition of words and phrases with relative preservation of expressive speech and comprehension, by literal paraphasia, and by anomia. Wernicke (1874) was the first to point out that an interrupted connection between the acoustical and motor centers of speech may lead to aphasia with a predominant disorder of repetition. Although this type of aphasia has been called "conduction aphasia," anatomical support for this conception is still not strong, so the term "repetition aphasia" seems preferable. Indeed, the very idea of this aphasia has long been controversial, with some authors denying its existence at all and others staunchly supporting it. Liepmann and Pappenheim (1914), Kleist (1934), and Hopf (1957) attributed this aphasia to a stage in the regression of Wernicke's aphasia, and Luria (1947) did not mention this type of aphasia at all. On the other hand, Goldstein (1927, 1934, 1948) considered it a "central" aphasia with an inner speech disturbance. Hécaen and Albert (1978) also mentioned that 12% of all aphasia patients seen on a large aphasia service had this type of aphasia. The relationship of repetition aphasia to expressive and sensory aphasia has been controversial for many years. Lichtheim (1884, 1885) described this type of aphasia as an expressive aphasia. Dubois *et al.* (1964) considered this disturbance an expressive aphasia with disorder of the emissive (encoding) system and difficulties in transposing or substitution phonemes. At the same time its relationship to sensory aphasia has been stressed by many authors, including Warrington and colleagues (1969, 1971), Tzortis and Albert (1974), and Albert *et al.* (1981). Attention should no longer be focused on a theoretical discussion but rather on the precise clinical description of this aphasia syndrome.

   In our own experience with hundreds of aphasia patients we have met only five patients with specific syndrome of repetition disorder. That syndrome differed from mild and moderate Wernicke's aphasia with regard to the predominance of literal instead of verbal paraphasias, preserved awareness of the errors in speech, and some peculiarity of anomia. Conversational speech in repetition aphasia is fluent, with moderate preservation of verbs and small functional words, and resembles the expressive speech of patients with Wernicke's or anomic-sensory aphasia. Literal paraphasias may be noted, however, especially when the patient is trying to tell a story. An excellent example of such paraphasias has been presented by Albert *et al.* (1981). Their patient, while intending to say "Nelson Rockefeller," said, "Nelson Nockenfellen, I mean Relso Rickenfollow, I mean Felso Knockerfelson." Such errors may be observed also in naming when the patient does not describe the use of the object as in Wernicke's or anomic-sensory aphasia but starts to produce similar sounding literal paraphasias. Prompting of the first phonemes of the word only enhances these paraphasias instead of helping to elicit the right name of the object as in ordinary anomic aphasia. For example, one patient with repetition aphasia intended to say "flower" but instead said, "flowing," "flying," "tower," "flushing."

Repetition is relatively more disturbed in comparison with expressive speech and comprehension. Patients recovering from Wernicke's aphasia may seem to have a relatively more prominent disorder of repetition, which may also lead to the diagnosis of repetition aphasia. Repetition difficulties, however, are different in both aphasia syndromes. In cases with Wernicke's aphasia, repetition is difficult, since the patient cannot pick up the auditory phonological pattern of the sequence of phonemes. Patients with repetition aphasia, on the other hand, experience difficulty in memorizing such sequences for the time of repetition processing. One of our patients who tried to repeat "pa-ba," said "a-a . . . remainder flew out"; then after a new presentation, "ba-ba-a . . . but the first disappeared." Retention of word span is also limited to one or two words, so that the patient can only repeat single phonemes, syllables, and short words. Series of vowels, syllables, and short and long phrases, however, are quite difficult for the patient to repeat, and in such attempts the patient produces numerous paraphasias, mainly literal with a tendency to augmentation. Sometimes this repetition disorder is quite difficult to distinguish from that in Wernicke's aphasia, but disturbances in the retention of phonemes and word span as well as literal paraphasias are much more noticeable in repetition aphasia. At the same time, patients with Wernicke's aphasia may repeat exactly the number of syllables in the series but distort their auditory pattern. For instance, "pa-ba" will be repeated as "da-ba," "ba-ba," "ba-da," or with augmentation, "ba-da-ta" or "pa-va-ba" instead of the "a-a-a . . . remainder flew out" typical of patients with repetition aphasia.

A comprehension disorder may be noted only in some of Head's "hand–ear–eye" and Luria's logicogrammatical tests. Alienation of word meaning is infrequent and may appear only in the "ear–eye–nose" test with two components.

Phonological analysis is slightly disturbed. Patients have problems in assessing the number of syllables only in words consisting of four or five syllables. The ability to read is usually preserved. Difficulty in writing on dictation, and volitional writing is characterized by moderate distortion of words with literal paragraphias, so that it is easy to understand most of the words written by patients with repetition aphasia. Calculation is mildly difficult, especially for oral subtraction of two or three digits.

Various forms of praxis, visual gnosis, right–left orientation, finger gnosis, and stereognosis are preserved.

Movement in the extremities is intact. Slight exaggeration of the stretch reflexes may be seen only in the right extremities, as well as right hemihypesthesia, and, more often, right-sided hemianopia.

Localization of the lesion in repetition aphasia remains controversial, especially because there are considerable differences between the clinical description and theoretic explanation of this aphasia syndrome. The more classical view of Wernicke (1874) and Lichtheim (1884) about interruption of the auditory-motor speech pathway has been recently supported by Geschwind (1965) and Kinsbourne (1972). Geschwind attributes the development of repetition aphasia to a lesion of the arcuate fasciculus in the deep white matter of the inferior parietal lobe. This pathway connects a large part of the temporoparietal cortex with the premotor frontal cortex. Kleist, Hopf, and other authors considered this type of aphasia a stage of recovery from Wernicke's aphasia and implicated a lesion of the middle first temporal gyrus anterior to the Wernicke's area (Kleist 1934) or partial damage of the caudal half of the superior temporal and Heschl's gyri (Hopf 1957). Green and Howes (1977), however, showed in their review of 25 such cases with postmortem or surgical confirmation that the lesion affected the supramarginal gyrus in 22 out of 25 cases, that the lesion extended to the posterior part of the first temporal gyrus in 13 cases, and that it was restricted to the temporal gyrus in the 3 remaining cases. Sixteen out of 25 cases, therefore, had a lesion at the superior-posterior temporal area, and the lesion extended to the supramarginal gyrus in 22 cases. The distinct differences in the localization of the lesion seem to depend on the differences in the definition and description of repetition aphasia. It seems likely that the same name has been applied to various aphasia syndromes in which a disorder of repetition was more noticeable and expressive speech and comprehension were less disturbed.

In our own two cases with repetition aphasia studied anatomically, the lesion had been restricted to the middle part of the left superior temporal gyrus, sparing the Wernicke's area and supramarginal gyrus. In one of those cases a focus of hemorrhage was revealed on autopsy, however, and the role of the pathological processes developing around the hemorrhagic foci had to be considered. The following is a description of this case.

Case 13, LE: A 57-year-old, right-handed male with a long history of hypertension and TIA with a transient left-sided hemiparesis developed a speech disorder without loss of consciousness six years after TIA. He produced jargonlike fluent speech with numerous paraphasias, mainly literal, and perseverations. His speech was impoverished, with no tendency to logorrhea. Repetition and naming ability were severely disturbed. His comprehension was almost completely absent. The patient did not even follow such simple commands as "Close your eyes," "Open your eyes," or "Open your mouth." He could not understand some gestures. His movements were completely preserved in the extremities. Stretch reflexes were slightly exaggerated in the right extremities. Mild hypesthesia of pain sensation on the left side was evident. He had marked ataxia in the left extremities in the finger-to-nose and heel-to-shin probe and right-sided hemianopia.

Three or four weeks after the stroke his speech noticeably improved and the clinical picture of a transient severe Wernicke's aphasia in the first hours and days of CVA eventually stabilized as a repetition aphasia one month after the stroke.

Conversational speech was fluent, without effort, tension, or arrest. Small functional words and verbs were somewhat predominant. No sign of jargonaphasia was recorded at that time. Paraphasias and perseverations were moderate but increased strikingly (especially literal paraphasias) when the patient tried to repeat some stories presented for repetition. Automatized speech was preserved.

Repetition was abnormal when the patient was tested for series of phonemes, syllables, words, and both short and long phrases. Numerous paraphasias, mainly literal, were noted during such attempts. Naming of presented objects, colors, or parts of the body was abnormal approximately 50% of the time. Prompting the first one or two syllables did not help in naming but rather made the patient produce more literal paraphasias. The patient often found the first syllable of a word without prompting, but then started to produce numerous literal paraphasias in his attempt to say the right word.

Comprehension improved noticeably, particularly in following the more complicated commands in Head's and Luria's logicogrammatical test. Alienation of word meaning in the "ear–nose–eye" test was mild even in the test with two components. However, retention of the syllables and word span was restricted to one or two syllables or words.

Phonological analysis, reading, and calculation were mildly disturbed.

A writing test showed some literal paragraphia and a reduced number of punctuation marks.

Various forms of praxis, including buccofacial and constructional praxis, visual and finger gnosis, and right–left orientation were preserved.

The patient's condition remained unchanged, but one morning two months after the stroke he suddenly fell and lost consciousness. Mild convulsions were recorded in the right and left extremities. Two hours later the patient, lying in bed, opened his eyes when he was asked questions by the doctor but could not speak or answer the questions. Right-sided complete hemiplegia and Babinski and Oppenheim's signs were noted, but sensation could not be tested. In the next few days the patient's general condition worsened, and he died from the increased cardiopulmonary insufficiency five days later.

Anatomical Diagnosis Hypertension was present with left ventricular hypertrophy and atherosclerosis of the coronary arteries, aorta, and cerebral arteries. Edema of the brain was noted. The recent hemorrhage in the subcortical region of the left hemisphere leaked to the ventricles and destroyed the lenticular nuclei, the lateral part of the thalamus in the posterior region, part of the thalamic pulvinar, and the posterior limb of the internal capsule.

An old hemorrhage (3.0 × 3.0 × 0.8 cm) was clearly outlined against the surrounding brain tissue and occupied the white matter of the middle part in the left first temporal gyrus, extending to the anterior portion of the posterior T_1. Multiple subarachnoid hemorrhages in the cerebral and cerebellar hemispheres and multiple fine cysts in the subcortical structures of both cerebral hemispheres were noted.

Severe Wernicke's aphasia in the first hours and days after the first stroke may be attributed to the severe edema around the focus of a hemorrhage in the middle part of the left first temporal gyrus. In three or four weeks the edema subsided and the hemorrhage in the middle T_1 resulted in a repetition aphasia with the following typical symptoms: (1) marked disorder of repetition with relatively well-preserved expressive speech and comprehension, (2) predominantly literal paraphasias, (3) anomic aphasia in which prompting increases the literal paraphasia, and (4) restricted retention of word span even though expressive speech and comprehension was only mildly disordered. The clinical data in this case did not point to parietal lobe pathology, since various forms of praxis, visuospatial and finger gnosis, and right–left orientation had been preserved after the first CVA.

One of the multiple fine cysts in the subcortical structures of both hemispheres in this patient may be attributed to the TIA with a transient left-sided hemiparesis six years before the first CVA.

The second CVA, with global aphasia and right-sided hemiplegia, developed five days before the patient's death and could be related to the recent large hemorrhage in the subcortical structures of the left hemisphere and left part of the thalamus. Similar cases with global aphasia and deep subcortical hemorrhages are described in the section on global aphasia in chapter 5.

The same type of repetition aphasia was noted in our clinical-anatomical Case 14, LR, after an initial stroke with cerebral infarction in the gray and white matter of the left first temporal gyrus and extension to the Heschl's gyri on the same side. After a second stroke in the symmetrical area of the left hemisphere, the patient developed a phonemic-sensory aphasia or "phoneme deafness." This case is described below.

In spite of the lesion localization in our two cases of repetition aphasia in the middle part of the left temporal lobe without extension to the parietal supramarginal gyrus, the role of that gyrus cannot be excluded, especially in cases of repetition aphasia with more severe literal paraphasia and articulation disorder.

Phonemic-Sensory Aphasia

Symptomatology Patients with phonemic-sensory aphasia cannot understand spoken language, but their expressive speech, reading, and writing abilities, as well as hearing, are almost completely preserved. Speech is fluent and grammatically correct, without logorrhea or augmentation. Literal and verbal paraphasia and sometimes difficulty in word-finding and naming may be observed occasionally, however. Auditory agnosia for nonverbal sounds may be accompanied by phonemic-sensory aphasia in some cases, but pure tone thresholds remain unaffected. The primary disturbance in phonemic-sensory aphasia is related to difficulty in auditory phoneme recognition. In patients with articulation aphasia the disorder of phoneme production forms the main manifestation of the aphasia syndrome, and the patient's speech often resembles that of a foreigner because of deformation and distortion in articulation. A mirror image of that phenomenon is seen in patients with phonemic-sensory aphasia, since they cannot recognize single phonemes and often complain that spoken language sounds like a foreign language, or in more severe cases, as mumbling or an indistinguishable noise. The difficulty in phoneme recognition leads to the disturbance in word comprehension.

Phonemic-sensory aphasia was first described by Kussmaul (1877) as *reinen Worttaubheit* ("pure word deafness") three years after Wernicke's famous description of sensory aphasia. The existence of this syndrome as an independent entity was doubted by many authors from the beginning. Some investigators, including Wernicke and Friedlander (1893), attributed it to incomplete sensory aphasia. More recently, Luria (1947, 1966) excluded "pure word deafness" from his classification of aphasia and described Wernicke's sensory aphasia as an acoustic-sensory aphasia with the chief difficulty in the auditory phonological analysis of words, combining both types of aphasia in one syndrome.

On the other hand, the role of peripheral hearing loss in the development of "word deafness" had been stressed by Freud (1891) and Freund (1895). In recent years a more complicated auditory processing disorder was demonstrated in patients with "pure word deafness" by Jerger (1964), Albert and Bear (1974), and Auerbach *et al.* (1982). These authors have stressed the role of central auditory nonverbal processing in the mechanism of "pure word deafness" and recognize that syndrome as an independent clinical entity.

We have encountered difficulty in phoneme recognition, or "phoneme deafness," in many of our patients with severe Wernicke's aphasia, but in six of our cases this syndrome was not accompanied by other signs of Wernicke's aphasia. Two out of six patients had a vascular lesion. In three cases phonemic-sensory aphasia developed after encephalitis, and in one case a brain trauma preceded its development.

In one of our cases we noted a marked change in prosody that we called "motor aprosody," since there was almost no fluctuation of intonation in the expressive speech. The patient spoke with a loud but completely toneless voice, and the emotional quality of his speech was indistinguishable. This aprosody was not as noticeable in our less severe cases, but some degree of motor aprosody could be noted in most of them.

The degree of comprehension disorder varies from case to case in patients with phonemic-sensory aphasia. Moderate cases, however, differ from those of Wernicke's aphasia with regard to the more noticeable comprehension disorder of conversational speech. When asked about well-known everyday events, a patient with phonemic-sensory aphasia looks at the examiner with a puzzled expression on his face, trying to listen carefully to the voice of the examiner just as a deaf person does. The term "word deaf" seems to be appropriate. Further analysis shows that the patient's actual disturbance is a severe disorder of phoneme recognition or "phoneme deafness." He cannot repeat even single phonemes, especially consonants, although if the illness is moderate he can often repeat vowels. He will also have difficulty in differentiating between two individual phonemes. Especially troublesome are voicing differences between phonemes, e.g., "p-b," "d-t," etc. These disturbances in phoneme recognition are responsible for difficulty both in repeating and in recognizing syllables, words, and phrases. Indeed, if the patient can correctly repeat a word of phrase, he does recognize it, and no sign of alienation of word meaning will be noted. A primary disorder of auditory word reocognition cannot be completely excluded in phonemic-sensory aphasia, however, since the disturbance in phoneme recognition makes assessing the level of comprehension risky. A clue is given by the fact that patients with less severe phonemic-sensory aphasia have less difficulty with auditory word recognition than with auditory phoneme recognition, which is borne out by the examiner's impression that the patient is somewhat deaf but partly understands spoken language.

On the other hand, the disorder of auditory word recognition in patients with Wernicke's aphasia may be accompanied by phonemic-sensory aphasia, especially in more severe cases. In these, however, the disorder of auditory word recognition is more prominent than the difficulty in phoneme recognition, and careful examination shows that the patient differentiates most of the phonemes after their repeated presentation. In some severe cases of phonemic-sensory aphasia a disorder of gesture comprehension or gesture agnosia may also appear. The patient does not understand a gesture inviting him to follow the examiner's pointing finger, to come into the examining room, to go out of the room, to raise his arm, to close his eyes, etc. This disorder of gesture comprehension is similar to that in patients with severe Wernicke's aphasia. Patients with phonemic-sensory aphasia, however, are usually in much better contact with their surroundings than are patients with Wernicke's aphasia. The patient does not understand some gestures and cannot recognize most words, but it is much easier to make contact with him or her or to help him or her get used to the everyday activity in the hospital ward. In our case with phonemic-sensory aphasia described below, gesture agnosia was accompanied by agnosia of facial expression without signs of prosopagnosia. The patient could not understand such facial expressions as a smile or a look of inquiry or surprise but recognized familiar faces and distinguished men from women and children from adults, so that he did not have typical facial agnosia. Isolated agnosia for facial expression in this case may be one of the manifestations of the more general syndrome of gesture agnosia. Further study and description of such cases is needed, however.

Reading, writing, and calculation abilities are preserved in patients with phonemic-sensory aphasia. Mild literal paragraphia and paralexia may be noted on occasion. There is no sign of finger agnosia, constructional apraxia, or right–left disorientation. Buccofacial and general praxis is also preserved. A disorder of nonverbal auditory comprehension may often be observed in these patients. Patients with normal auditory function for pure tone cannot recognize the sound of keys, applause, rubbing, rustling paper, bell ringing, etc. Especially difficult for some is recognizing the sound made by the wind, a train, a car, a cow, or a dog. Some patients with phonemic-sensory aphasia, however, do not have nonverbal auditory agnosia. Sensory amusia, the inability to recognize well-known melodies has often been reported in phonemic-sensory aphasia. In one of our cases comprehension of the rhythmic and melodic structure of speech was also disturbed. We call this disorder "sensory aprosody," since it is the equivalent of motor aprosody, a flattening of the rhythm of speech in patients with focal brain pathology. A patient with sensory aprosody or agnosia of voice expression cannot interpret the intonation of speech. He does not differentiate an interrogative intonation from that of surprise or excitement. He often cannot understand the inner meaning of a phrase as indicated by his intonation. Transient difficulty of this kind was described by Balonov and Deglin (1976) in patients with depression treated by limited right hemisphere electroshock. Blumstein and Cooper (1974) observed that dichotic listening revealed a greater preservation of intonation recognition for the left ear and therefore for the right hemisphere. A systematic study of sensory aprosody has still not been done in patients with focal brain lesion, however, and we could not find in the literature reports of such cases studied anatomically. Our clinical-anatomical case of phonemic-sensory aphasia and sensory aprosody or agnosia of voice expression seems to be the first such case ever reported. This case is described below. Transient right- or left-sided hemiparesis may be noted in some patients with phonemic-sensory aphasia immediately after stroke onset. Hemihypesthesia, left- or right-sided, may persist longer, as may right hemianopoia, predominantly for the upper quadrants of the visual field.

The lesion in phonemic-sensory aphasia is bilateral in most of the published cases studied anatomically and localized in the superior-medial part of the temporal lobe, sparing the cortex of Wernicke's area and partly involving Heschl's gyri or auditory radiation in this region (Henschen 1920–1922, Kleist 1934, Brain 1965). A unilateral lesion of the left temporal lobe was described by Schuster and Taterka (1926), but the relation of such cases to Wernicke's aphasia is still unclear. Lichtheim (1884) suggested that in patients with word deafness there is an interruption in the ascending auditory pathway to the cortical center where auditory word recognition takes place. This suggestion has survived many generations of aphasiologists and is generally respected by modern authors. There is still a lack of reliable anatomical confirmation of that theory, however, and in most cases, the lesion seems to occupy a large area of the cortical gray or white matter, as is usual in aphasia cases, since a small isolated gray- or white-matter lesion does not produce persistent aphasia. A bilateral lesion in the middle part of the first temporal gyri with extension to the adjacent Heschl's gyri seems to be crucial for the development of persistent phonemic-sensory aphasia. At least in our own severe case, anato-mohistolopathological study reveals such placement of the lesion.

Case 14, LR: A 65-year-old right-handed woman with a long history of angina pectoris and cardiac arrhythmia developed dizziness, right-sided paresthesia, and mild weakness in the right hand, and twenty minutes later lost consciousness. When the patient regained conscious-ness four hours later she had severe aphasia. She did not understand spoken language and produced a flow of indistinguishable sounds. These symptoms made the disturbance seem to be an instance of Wer-nicke's aphasia. No sign of paralysis or paresis was noted at that time. Three days later the patient started to speak, and her comprehension gradually improved in the following months.

Three months after the CVA the patient's expressive speech was fluent, without tension, articulation, or prosodic difficulties. Occasional literal paraphasia and mild word-finding and naming disturbances were noted. The patient found repetition of a multisyllable word series difficult and produced an increased number of literal paraphasias in attempting to repeat complicated words or series of syllables. Her retention of word span was restricted to two or three words and greatly exceeded in severity a slight difficulty in expressive speech and comprehension. The patient could not only understand the more complicated commands in Head's and Luria's tests, but she could comprehend without difficul-ty conversational speech and most simple commands. She had little alienation of word meaning even in the "ear–eye–nose" test with two components.

She maintained her ability to read. Her writing was characterized by occasional paragraphia, but she could do arithmetic. Her visual and finger gnosis and various forms of praxis, including constructional praxis, were intact.

Sensory amusia but not motor amusia was noted. The patient could not recognize most popular songs, but she sang them correctly without any difficulty.

The patient's nonverbal auditory gnosis was completely preserved. She easily reocognized sounds such as a key beating on a glass, wood, or iron, striking a match, etc. She easily recognized the number of beats and a simple rhythmic pattern and imitated them by tapping with a pencil on the table. Auditory thresholds for pure tones were charac-terized by age-related symmetrical hypoacusis on the high frequencies, with a hearing loss of 70–80 decibels comparable with the normal range for her age and moderate hypoacusis in the middle and lower frequencies. That hypoacusis became asymmetrical when pure tones against a background of white noise or short-duration tones were presented. The difference between the right and left ears reached 15 decibels for a pure tone of 1,000 Hz with white noise and 40 decibels over the absolute threshold due to the higher increase of the threshold of the right ear. Thresholds for short signals with duration of 10 msec and 1 msec differed by 6 decibels and 11 decibels, respectively, with more noticeable hearing loss on the right side. The ENT examination did not reveal any sign of peripheral ear, nose, or throat pathology. Motor function and sensation were preserved. No signs of hemianopia were noted.

A second CVA developed eight months after the first one. The patient suddenly fell down and lost consciousness. Two hours later signs of psychomotor agitation were noted, followed by prolonged sleep. When the patient regained consciousness several hours later, she could not understand spoken language but still retained expressive speech almost completely. She had no paresis or hypesthesia. Partial left-sided homonymous hemianopia with complete loss of vision in the upper quadrants was noted. The patient was cooperative, alert, polite, and gentle, without noticeable emotional or intellectual changes.

Her expressive speech was fluent and without grammatical errors or paraphasia. Her speech, however, almost completely lost its rhythmical pattern and intonation and became monotonous and aprosodic. Impoverishment of facial expression during speech was also observed. Her ability to name objects and actions was preserved, but her ability to repeat phonemes and words was greatly disturbed. The patient could not repeat, or repeated with many mistakes, consonants, syllables, and words, and some days she even made mistakes in repeating single vowels. The number of errors depended on the number and type of syllables. Fewer mistakes were noted in repetition of syllables consisting of two phonemes, especially a consonant followed by a vowel. Errors were characterized by missing phonemes and replacing them with incorrect vowels as well as consonants. Most often, "u" was replaced by "i" and voiced with voiceless consonants. The same difficulties occurred when the patient tried to differentiate vowels, consonants, syllables, or words. For example, she failed often to raise her hand when two presented items were the same, e.g., "a-a," "d-d," "pa-pa," "table-table," and raised her hand erroneously when the items were different, "a-o," "d-g," "pa-ba," "table–chair."

Comprehension of spoken language was greatly disturbed. Often the patient could not understand some very simple commands, e.g., "Put out your tongue," "Close your eyes," or the suggestion to point to well-known objects in a room, such as the window, the ceiling. the floor, a table, a lamp, a door, and so on. Sometimes her comprehension was better, especially when the command was repeated three or four times and the patient's selection was restricted to a small number of objects. For example, it was much easier for the patient to choose, after repeated verbal command, one of three presented objects. After some training trials the number of the presented objects could be increased to five, six, or even seven. When asked to show two of the objects, however, the patient only understood one of the words and shortly thereafter became totally confused in performing that task. Speaking louder did not improve her word comprehension, but speaking more slowly did help somewhat.

Conversational speech was also difficult for the patient to comprehend. She could not understand many simple questions about ordinary activities, including questions related to her sleep, meals, or speech therapy. Appropriate answers could be obtained only after repeating the same question two or three times.

Sensory aprosody was also noted after the second stroke. The patient could not interpret speech rhythms or intonation. This deficit was evaluated by presenting her with two short pseudosentences composed of nonsense words: "An ter fir sol" and "Ak mas sho zu." Each was uttered by an actor using various intonations to convey the states of anger, sadness, astonishment, and nervousness. He also modulated the expression of the pseudosentence to indicate the declarative, interrogative, and imperative grammatical mood. After hearing a sentence the patient was asked to identify the intonation. If she did not respond, she was shown cue cards with the words "anger," "sadness," "astonishment," or "nervousness." Each word was presented separately, and the patient had to indicate the right card. The same type of cue was presented for the different grammatical moods. After her first stroke this test did not present any difficulty for the patient, but after the second stroke she was unable to perform the test. Even after three or four trials and written explanations she was extremely doubtful about the appropriate choice and switched from one card to another, trying to find the correct answer. Eventually she refused to continue the examination.

The patient could not use gesture and facial expression as a clue to understanding spoken language. It was difficult for her to understand such simple gestures as "waving good-bye," "come here," "take it," put it on the table," etc. This agnosia of gesture was heightened by her inability to understand facial expressions. Ths patient could not recognize smiling, crying, or astonishment. Once, the patient did not understand that the speech examination was over for the day in spite of the lengthy explanation given by voice gesture and facial expression.

She went out of the doctor's office in the hospital to her room on the ward, returning with a new notebook in order to continue. She understood that the session was over only when the examiner wrote the phrase, "We finished today. See you tomorrow." Another time the patient could not understand that her friend was leaving her and asked with surprise, "Why are you moving your hand? What does that mean?"

In this case agnosia of facial expression was not accompanied by other signs of prosopagnosia. The patient recognized individual faces and pictures of celebrities and could tell male and female faces apart.

After the second stroke motor amusia developed in addition to the sensory amusia which had persisted after the first CVA. This disturbance of recognition of popular melodies was now combined with loss of the ability to sing the melodies of well-known songs. The test for nonverbal auditory gnosis showed a moderate deficit that was much less severe than the disorder of phoneme and word recognition. The patient had some difficulty in recognizing the sounds of animals or in imitating the sounds they make. Once she could not recognize the sound of applause. She recognized easily, however, most of the presented sounds, including the sound of keys, of rubbing paper, of tapping on a glass, of wind blowing, etc. Her disorder of rhythm recognition and imitation was also moderate, occurring only for rhythms consisting of four or more elements. Three-element rhythms were recognized without difficulty.

Auditory thresholds for pure tone without noise were asymmetric after the second CVA because the auditory function of the left ear had decreased more than that of the right ear. The patient's ability to detect a pure tone signal with noise of 40 decibels above the absolute thresholds did not show any change of asymmetry compared with the measurement of the auditory thresholds for pure tone without noise. The asymmetry for a short-duration signal became less prominent after the second stroke and did not exceed 2 decibels for signals of 10 msec and 1 msec duration; the thresholds were slightly higher in the right ear.

The disorder of auditory attention has to be considered in relation to the auditory-thresholds examination. As the testing began, the patient often did not understand that an auditory signal had been presented for recognition, or on identifying a signal she would lose the next signal, but after several trials she was able to perform the task reliably without a noticeable disorder of auditory attention.

Retention of pitch frequency was much disturbed after the second stroke. The patient was asked in writing to raise her hand when the tone of 200 Hz was presented. After ten trials, presentation of different pitch frequencies was started, including 205 Hz, 210 Hz, 300 Hz, 350 Hz, etc., with the written command, "Do *not* raise your hand." The patients with Broca's aphasia and anomic-sensory aphasia usually were able to differentiate the tone of 205–210 Hz from 200 Hz; some patients with Wernicke's aphasia showed an increase of this threshold to the 230 to 250 Hz in differentating from 200 Hz (Tonkonogy 1973). At first this patient started to differentiate tone 200 Hz from 300 Hz, but the differentiation ability for these two tones did not persist, and soon the patient raised her right hand for both of these tones. She could differentiate reliably only the tone 200 Hz from 400 Hz or 500 Hz, so that the steady threshold for pitch-frequency retention was around 200 Hz in comparison to 30–50 Hz in patients with Wernicke's aphasia and 5–10 Hz in the patients with Broca's and anomic-sensory aphasia.

Her retention of pure tone span was negative after the second CVA. A sequence of three tones: 200 Hz, 400 Hz, 800 Hz and four tones: 200 Hz, 400 Hz, 800 Hz, 2,000 Hz were presented as a signal for her to raise her right hand. After ten trials the order of the tones was changed to 1, 3, and 2 for the span of three tones and 1, 3, 2, and 4 for the four-tone span. The patient was asked not to raise her hand for these sequences. The patient could not perform this task at all even after repeated detailed instructions. She tried to imitate the frequency of the tone pitch with her voice or to name every presented tone as "loud," "not loud," etc., but those maneuvers did not help at all.

Following this, a series of visual signals were introduced. Three or four colors were presented in the same order, e.g., red, white, green, and yellow, and the patient was asked to raise her hand for this sequence. Then the position of the two middle components was changed, just as in the auditory-signals sequences. The patient learned to do this task after three or four attempts as did the normal control group. Nonetheless, further efforts to generalize the correct performance from the visual to the auditory signals failed. The patient continued to manifest a retention deficit for the pure-tone series.

A new, third CVA developed three months after the second one. In the morning the patient complained of paresthesia in her right arm and at 3 PM she suddenly lost consciousness after vomiting and becoming agitated. Several hours later she regained consciousness but was lethargic. She had ptosis of the left eyelid with a right deviation of the left eyeball and external deviation of the right eyeball. She was able, however, to move her extremities. Sensation was difficult to evaluate, but no clear hypesthesia was noted. The patient's condition fluctuated, and she developed pneumonia, which led to her death thirteen days after the beginning of the third CVA.

Anatomical Diagnosis Hypertension was present. Atherosclerosis of the aorta with numerous atherosclerotic plaques was noted. Carotid and vertebral arteries of the neck and cerebral vessels contained only single atherosclerotic plaques.

There were symmetrical cortical infarcts in the temporal lobes (Fig. 4.4). The infarction in the left hemisphere destroyed the anterior two-thirds and some of the posterior part of the first temporal gyrus, the middle portion of the second temporal gyrus, and the anterior part of Heschl's gyri. The right hemisphere infarction was much more extensive and completely destroyed Heschl's gyri, the first temporal gyrus, the middle and posterior portions of the second temporal gyrus, the posterior part of the supramarginal gyrus, and part of the insula at the level of the sensory strip. Old small infarcts were revealed in the left parahippocampal gyrus and the left cerebellar hemisphere. The most recent infarction was situated in the left thalamus.

The histopathological examination showed an additional microscopic zone of infarction in the lower motor strip of the right hemisphere and in the insula of the left hemisphere. No sign of infarction was seen in the occipital lobes or the angular gyri of either hemisphere.

Thus repeated cerebral emboli were related to the persistent atrial fibrillation in this case. After the first CVA the patient developed a moderate repetition aphasia that could be attributed to the left hemisphere infarction in the anterior-middle part of the first temporal gyrus and probably to the partly damaged Heschl's gyri. The second CVA produced many symptoms, including severe phonemic-sensory aphasia, sensory amusia, and moderate nonverbal auditory agnosia. All these phenomena have been repeatedly described in cases with a bilateral lesion in the middle part of the first temporal gyri or a bilateral lesion of the auditory pathway in the white matter of the temporal lobes. In this case, both of these lesions were present, including the complete destruction of Heschl's gyri in the right hemisphere and their partial damage in the left hemisphere.

Sensory aprosody also developed after the second CVA and might be attributed to the right temporal infarction in Heschl's gyri and the medial portion of the first temporal gyrus. The possibility may be supported by the data of Blumstein and Cooper (1974), which showed the dominant role of the right hemisphere in the dichotic recognition of intonation. Balonov and Deglin (1976) described a transient sensory aprosody during right-hemisphere electroshock therapy for depression. Heilman et al. (1975) noted disturbed comprehension of affective speech in patients with right-hemisphere lesions confirmed by radioisotope brain scan, and Ross and Mesulam (1979) attributed prosody and associated expressive gesturing to the language functions of the right hemisphere. Detailed analyses of ten cases with aprosodies were presented by Ross (1981). In all the cases the lesion was localized by CT

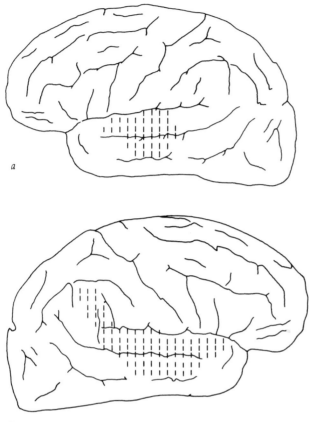

Figure 4.4
Case 14, LR, Phonemic-sensory aphasia. *a*, Infarction in the cortex of the left hemisphere (anatomical and histopathological data). *b*, Infarction in the cortex of the right hemisphere (anatomical and histopathological data).

scan. The author reported a lesion of the right posterior-superior temporal lobe and the adjacent area of the inferior parietal lobe in one of the cases with sensory aprosody. Our case is the first case of sensory aprosody to be studied anatomically. The choice has to be made between a lesion of Heschl's gyri and a lesion of the medial T_1 of the right hemisphere as the one responsible in this case. The existence of an additional symmetrical lesion of the left hemisphere cannot be excluded, although no clear indication of sensory aprosody was revealed in patients with various types of anterior and posterior aphasia that developed after unilateral left hemisphere lesions. Boller *et al.* (1979) reported that sentences with an emotional component produced a greater number of correct responses from patients with global or Wernicke's aphasia than did their neutral counterparts.

Motor aprosody as well as motor amusia in this case may be related to the anterior extension of the right hemisphere lesion with involvement of the supramarginal gyrus and the insula. In three cases of motor aprosody described by Ross (1981), the CT scans showed right fronto-parietal infarctions. The clinicopathological data in this present case serve to point out the possible crucial role of a lesion of the left supramarginal gyrus in the development of motor aprosody.

Facial expression agnosia without signs of prosopagnosia has not been previously reported. The fact that there was no occipital lesion in our case is important, since a bilateral, largely right occipital lesion is responsible for the development of the difficulty in facial recognition, including facial-expression agnosia. No additional or extensive lesion in the superior part of the temporal lobe has been described in the published cases of prosopagnosia studied anatomically. Since, on the other hand, great difficulty in gesture comprehension was noted in our case, facial-expression agnosia could be a part of this syndrome. A similar disturbance in the comprehension of emotional gesturing was also observed in patients with sensory aprosody by Ross (1981). Gesture agnosia is regularly noted in patients with severe Wernicke's aphasia caused by a left superior-posterior temporal lesion. No careful study of facial expression gnosis has been performed in such cases.

There was no direct correlation between the degree of severity of the verbal nonauditory agnosia, which was moderate, and the sensory aprosody, which was almost complete, in our case. Recognition of speech prosody, therefore, seems to be relatively independent of gnosis of objects or sounds.

In our case severe disorders of auditory nonverbal processing were revealed. They include difficulty in filtration of a signal from noise, in detection of a signal of short duration, and in recent memory of tone pitches and their series. A similar disorder at the prephonemic level of auditory processing was found in patients with pure word deafness by Albert and Bear (1974) and Auerbach *et al.* (1982). These authors described a large increase of the click-fusion threshold and diminution of the number of clicks counted per second in their patients. A close association was also noted (Tallal and Newcombe 1978) between disorders of verbal and nonverbal auditory processing in patients with dysphasia. When Tonkonogy and Kaidanova (1963) observed that patients with Wernicke's aphasia showed increased thresholds for tone detection to white noise, this seemed likely. Routine comparison of the auditory thresholds of the left and right ears unexpectedly revealed an asymmetry caused by the greater increase of the threshold of tone detection for white noise on the right ear opposite the side of the lesion in the temporal lobe of the left hemisphere. This asymmetrical increase of the thresholds was also obtained in patients with preserved speech who had lesions of the right temporal lobe. Thresholds for tone in white noise were shown to be higher at the left ear, opposite the lesion of the right hemisphere. Therefore no direct correlation between Wernicke's aphasia and disorders in the testing of auditory-signal masking was found.

Further experiments with signals of short duration, including clicks, showed similar results. Baru *et al.* (1964) studied thirteen patients with Wernicke's aphasia without any sign of aphasia due to cerebral infarction in the temporal lobe of the left and right hemispheres. A greater increase in thresholds for clicks of 1 msec and 10 msec duration was obtained for the ear opposite the damaged hemisphere. Baru and Karaseva (1972) confirmed the presence of asymmetry, describing the patients with tumors of the left and right temporal lobes. Experiments with steady-state (unvarying) vowels, the slow rate of change in format transitions (Tallal and Newcombe 1978), and the discrimination of pure tones with minimal pitch differences of 200 Hz (Chedru *et al.* 1978) also did not show any significant impairment in aphasia patients with left-hemisphere lesions.

On the other hand, a close association was found in disturbances of auditory short-term memory in patients with both Wernicke's and phonemic-sensory aphasia (Tonkonogy 1973). Patients were asked to discriminate between tone pitches as frequency differences between the two pure tones were gradually reduced from 100 Hz to 5 Hz. Patients were asked to respond to a pure tone pitch of 200 Hz by pushing a panel on a box, whereas in response to a tone of 300 Hz, 250 Hz, or 205 Hz, patients were not supposed to push the panel. In this experiment, the differential thresholds between two pure tones were significantly increased in patients with Wernicke's aphasia and was in the normal range in patients with anomic-sensory aphasia and Broca's aphasia. Our patient with phonemic-sensory aphasia had extraordinary difficulty with this test. She could discriminate pitch only at the level of frequency differences of 200 Hz, whereas patients with Wernicke's aphasia started to have difficulty with differences of 30 Hz to 50 Hz, and all patients with Broca's aphasia could discriminate at the 10 Hz level. A special experiment was designed to reveal an impairment of auditory filtration. Of the patients with Wernicke's aphasia, 53.8% could perform the test when the tones of 200 Hz and 300 Hz were preceded and followed by a masking white noise. At the level of 210 Hz and 200 Hz, not one patient with Wernicke's aphasia was able to discriminate these two pitches, although all patients with Broca's aphasia and 77.8% of patients with anomic-sensory aphasia did so. Thus the deficit in nonverbal auditory processing noted in patients with Wernicke's aphasia and phonemic-sensory aphasia may be attributed to disturbances of phoneme perception, since no deficit in this test performance was found in patients with Broca's and anomic-sensory aphasia and since phoneme recognition was preserved.

Anomic-Sensory Aphasia

Symptomatology Patients with anomic-sensory aphasia have pronounced disorder of naming as well as alienation of word meaning. This type of posterior aphasia resembles the transcortical sensory aphasia of Wernicke-Lichtheim in that repetition ability is better preserved than expressive speech and comprehension. However, this is true in patients with moderate and especially mild Wernicke's aphasia or patients with semantic anomic-spatial aphasia; it is more accurate to use the clinically descriptive term "anomic-sensory aphasia" for this type of posterior aphasia rather than "transcortical sensory aphasia."

Conversational speech in anomic-sensory aphasia is fluent with good retention of intonation and articulation ability but marked by impoverishment and hesitation in searching for an appropriate word. In this way it is similar to the speech of a patient with dynamic aphasia or mild Broca's aphasia; this may lead to mistakes in the differential diagnosis, especially in the acute stage of stroke. Anomic-sensory aphasia may be recognized by the following features: predominance of the small functional words in conversational speech, presence of paraphasias, mainly verbal, and inability to recognize one's own errors. Especially noticeable is the disorder of naming. The patient cannot give the name of 40–50% or even 70–80% of the presented objects, parts of the body, or actions. Particularly difficult are relatively low-frequency words, such as eyelash, handle, knuckle, hangnail, etc. Attempts to find a requested word often lead to verbal and literal paraphasias. In trying to find a proper name, the patient produces a series of verbal paraphasias with some acoustical or semantic relation to the word he or she is seeking, as well as literal paraphasias. Sometimes the patient indicates the use of the presented object, such as comb or pencil, but still cannot say its name. In most cases anomia for object, action, and body part is equally distributed, with object-naming perhaps most difficult. Prompting of the first two or three phonemes of the word usually helps these patients name the presented item. Some patients must have most of the phonemes prompted before they can find the appropriate word.

Repetition ability is disturbed in paired opposite phonemes ("pa-ba," "ba-pa," "da-ta," or "ta-da"); in series of three vowels, syllables, or words; in more complicated, longer phrases; and in phrases mainly composed of small functional words. Augmentation of syllables may often accompany the correct repetition of the phonemes, syllables, or words. Automatized speech is preserved in most patients. Comprehension of conversational speech, isolated words, simple commands, differentation of phonemes, and series of two or three vowels is usually preserved. Patients with anomic-sensory aphasia, however, cannot follow the more complicated commands of Head's test, e.g., "Show your right ear with your left index finger," or most of Luria's logicogrammatical commands, such as "Show the pencil with the pen," "the pen with the pencil," "the pencil with the pen," "the tiger had been killed by the lion; who was dead?", etc. Especially notable is the alienation of word meaning. Severe alienation may usually be noted in the "eye–ear–nose" test with two components, "Show your ear; your nose," "your nose, your eye," "your eye, your ear," "your ear, your nose," as well as in the series with one component: "Show your ear," "your nose," "eye," "nose," "ear," "eye," etc. Word-span retention is restricted to two or three words from the spoken series of words. Written presentation of the words or pictures of the objects lifts the upper limit to five or six objects out of ten. Patients with anomic-sensory aphasia, therefore, have correct comprehension, differentiation, and repetition of single phonemes, syllables, and words, as well as short series of words, as contrasted with patients with Wernicke's aphasia, who have a disorder of acoustical recognition. The main comprehension problems in anomic-sensory aphasia are the alienation of word meaning, difficulties in following complicated logicogrammatical commands, and word-span retention.

Phonological analysis is preserved or slightly disturbed in anomic-sensory aphasia. Reading, writing on dictation, and volitional writing usually reveal only mild literal paralexia, paragraphia, and verbal paralexia. Sometimes there is moderate slowness in reading and writing.

Calculation is greatly disturbed in approximately half the cases, especially in subtraction over 10, 20, and 30; e.g., 25 − 17, 36 − 19, 15 − 8. Some patients have difficulty with all four arithmetic operations under ten; e.g., 4 + 3, 8 − 5, etc. Errors in multiplication of digits over 5 (e.g., 6 × 7, 8 × 9, 7 × 8) also occur frequently. In some cases the multiplication table almost completely disappears from the patient's memory. In other cases, however, the disorder of calculation is mild and patients may be able to subtract orally 123 − 47 or to divide 325 by 5. No clear differences in the severity of anomic-sensory aphasia have been observed between the groups with noticeable or mild calculation disorder. Probably the severe calculation disorder arises when the lesion extends to the parietal structures.

Buccofacial praxis is preserved in all cases with anomic-sensory aphasia. Disordered constructional praxis, finger gnosis, and praxis are noted only occasionally.

In the acute stage of stroke anomia, alienation of word meaning, oversimplification, impoverishment of speech, and difficulty in following commands are more frequent and severe, but in general the clinical syndrome of anomic-sensory aphasia is not different from that noted in the chronic stage.

Mild transient right-sided hemiparesis may be noted in the first days of the CVA. In some cases slight weakness in the right hand persists through the chronic stage. Right-sided hemihypesthesia occurs only in a few cases in both acute and chronic periods. In many cases persistent complete right hemianopia or a defect in the right upper quadrants is noted.

Dating from Lichtheim's famous paper (1885), *the lesion* in anomic-sensory aphasia has often been considered to be the interruption of the connection between the intact speech area and the cognitive and memory areas of the brain. Geschwind *et al.* (1968), Benson and Geschwind (1976), Whitaker (1976), Albert *et al.* (1981), and Goodglass and Kaplan (1983) have all emphasized that in transcortical sensory aphasia the anatomic separation of the intact perisylvian language zone from the rest of the brain interferes with the association necessary for comprehension but permits repetition, since information may be forwarded within the intact language zone from Wernicke's to Broca's area. Evidence supporting this view has come from cases with a relatively generalized lesion that have been studied anatomically. On the other hand, some authors have pointed out that anomic-sensory aphasia or a similar aphasia syndrome occur when the lesion is restricted to the posterior part of the second and third temporal gyri in the dominant hemisphere without direct involvement of the first temporal gyrus. In a detailed anatomohistopathological study of four cases with what he called "naming deafness," equivalent to anomic-sensory aphasia, Hopf (1957) found the most severe damage in the posterior part of the left middle and inferior temporal gyri. Luria (1947, 1966) related the site of the lesion in what he calls amnestic-sensory aphasia to the middle segments of the convex part of the temporal region in the dominant hemisphere, corresponding to areas 21 and 37. Recently, the lesion in this type of aphasia was localized in the superior-posterior watershed area between the middle and posterior cerebral arteries according to CT and isotope scans in 15 patients by Kertesz *et al.* (1982). These authors also mentioned that in some of their cases the lesion was more medial and inferior, corresponding to the territory of the posterior cerebral artery. A similar site of the lesion was described by Kleist (1934), who postulated that a lesion of the middle part of the third temporal gyrus of the left hemisphere may be responsible for the naming disorder.

Our own experience has shown that a more complete picture of anomic-sensory aphasia with noticeable comprehension disorder occurs in cases with a lesion localized in the cortical area adjacent to Wernicke's area or in a small cortical lesion in that area itself. Such a case has been described above in the section on Wernicke's aphasia; in this case the patient had a clinical picture of Wernicke's aphasia in the acute stage of stroke. Later on in the course of the stroke, the disorder evolved into anomic-sensory aphasia. The autopsy revealed a microscopic infarction in Wernicke's area alone. The autopsy in our other case of anomic-sensory aphasia showed a relatively large area of infarction in the white matter of the left posterior first and second temporal gyri, in the white matter, and partly in the cortex of the angular gyrus. Small microscopic infarcts or scattered infarcts in the cortex of the posterior T_1 and T_2 cannot be excluded. The following is the clinical-anatomical description of this case.

Case 15, RR: A 73-year-old, right-handed man with a long history of hypertension and atherosclerosis developed a language disorder without loss of consciousness. The patient had difficulty in comprehension and his speech was hard to understand because of multiple verbal paraphasias. Hs also had some weakness in his right hand. His speech slowly improved, and four months later he had moderate anomic-sensory aphasia as well as mild weakness of the right hand. His conversational speech consisted of two- or three-word phrases. His speech was fluent and included many low-frequency words, but verbs and small functional words predominated, and occasional verbal paraphasias were noted. His speech activity was somewhat decreased.

His ability to repeat phonemes, syllables, words, and short phrases was preserved. Errors occurred only in the repetition of series of three words, pairs of opposed phonemes, and long, complicated phrases or

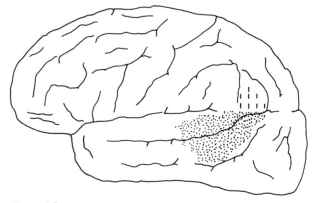

Figure 4.5
Case 15, RR, Anomic-sensory aphasia. Infarction in the cortical gray (dashed lines) and white (dotted lines) matter of the left hemisphere (anatomical data).

phrases in which there were many small functional words. Automatized speech was mainly preserved.

The patient's naming ability was greatly disturbed. No presented object could be named without prompting of the first and second syllables of the word. His comprehension of conversational speech, single words, and simple short phrases was preserved. Differentiation of the vowels and naming the vowels in sequence was performed without error. Alienation of word meaning, however, was noted in the "eye–nose–ear" test with one component. Errors were also noted in following more complicated commands from Head's and Luria's tests, such as "Show your right ear," "with your left hand, your left ear."

Phonological analysis, reading, writing, and calculation were severely disturbed, although stereognosis, finger gnosis, praxis, and right–left orientation were preserved.

Nine months after the stroke, acute heart failure and pneumonia developed, and the patient died with no sign of a new CVA.

Anatomical Diagnosis Atherosclerosis of the cerebral arteries was present. There were two large areas of cerebral infarction in the left hemisphere. The first one, measuring 4.5 × 2.5 × 1.5 cm was situated in the territory of the cortical branches of the left middle cerebral artery occupying the white matter of the posterior part of the first and second temporal gyri with partial extension to the cortex of the angular gyrus (Fig. 4.5). The second large focus measured 4.2 × 1.1 × 0.4 cm and was located in the territory of the lenticulostriate branches of the left middle cerebral artery destroying the putamen, the head of the caudate nucleus, and the adjacent part of the anterior limb of the internal capsule.

The site of the lesion was adjacent to and perhaps partly involved with the cortex of the posterior first temporal gyrus. Nonetheless, no sign of auditory verbal agnosia or difficulty in the differentiation and repetition of phonemes and words was noted. A combination of severe anomia and marked alienation of word meaning was evident, which is typical for anomic-sensory aphasia. The severe disorder of phonological analysis, reading, writing, and calculation may be related to the involvement of the cortex in the left angular gyrus. The role of the second large focus of infarction in the subcortical structures is difficult to evaluate in this case, but absence of logorrhea may be related to the presence of this additional lesion.

In some cases, anomic-sensory aphasia results from a lesion in the middle-posterior part of the hippocampal and fusiform gyri with occasional extension of edema to the middle-posterior part of the third temporal gyrus in the acute stage of stroke.

Case 16, GN: The patient was an 84-year-old, right-handed man with a long history of hypertension, atherosclerosis, and myocardial infarction six years before the CVA. He tried to get up from his bed at 4 AM and noticed numbness in his right eye. He returned to bed and slept quietly, but in the morning he awoke with weakness in the right extremities and incomprehensible speech.

Neurological examination two days later showed the patient to be alert, oriented in three spheres, and able to recognize his relatives.

The patient's expressive speech was fluent, but he had frequent paraphasias and perseveration. At times he was quite talkative, producing an incomprehensible "word salad." At other times he spoke correctly, without marked paraphasia, but his speech was simplified and impoverished, and its activity was diminished. On testing, repetition of both simple and complicated syllables and words was preserved, but phrases were difficult, probably because of his restricted word-span retention. His comprehension of conversational speech was mainly preserved, but alienation of word meaning was noticeable. The patient could not follow the command "Close your eyes" even after he performed successfully such commands as "Open your mouth," "Stick out your tongue," and "Give me your hand." After a short rest he regained his ability to follow some simple commands, but then his performance worsened and he could not point to a glass when shown a glass and a spoon and asked to select a glass. Alienation of word meaning was especially apparent in the "ear–eye–nose" test, and his ability to name objects was severely disturbed. A reading test elicited numerous literal paralexias. Moderate right-sided hemihypesthesia and complete right hemianopia were also evident.

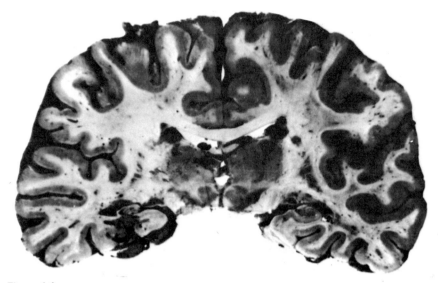

Figure 4.6
Case 16, GN, Anomic-sensory aphasia. Coronal section at the level of the mamillary bodies. Infarction in the white matter of the hippocampal and parahippocampal gyri. Multiple small infarcts in the left thalamus and in the rentrolenticular part of the internal capsule.

Anatomical Diagnosis There was atherosclerosis of the cerebral vessels at the base of the brain, with thrombus in the left posterior cerebral artery and cerebral infarction in the territory of this artery destroying gray and white matter of the fusiform, parahippocampal, and lingual gyri (Fig. 4.6). Multiple small infarcts in the thalamus and the retrolenticular part of the internal capsule in the left half of the pons were present.

The histopathological examination showed only a slight change in the upper part of the motor strip and Wernicke's area of both hemispheres.

Our clinical diagnosis in this case was incorrect, since anomic-sensory aphasia was confused with dynamic aphasia because the clinical pictures of both these forms of aphasia are similar, especially in the acute stage of stroke. Confusion was multiplied by the presence of the right-sided hemiparesis, more noticeable in the leg. A lesion in the superior-posterior and medial parts of the frontal lobe, which is common in dynamic aphasia, had been suspected. The right hemihypesthesia and hemianopia were explained by the extension of the lesion to the posterior limb of the internal capsule from the territory of the anterior to the middle cerebral artery. Autopsy showed that the right-sided neurological motor and sensory deficit was due to the lesion in the left half of the pons, as well as to the thalamic and occipital lobe infarction, the latter being responsible for the hemianopia of the right visual field. The suspected dynamic aphasia, therefore, turned out to be anomic-sensory aphasia, and a more careful retrospective reevaluation of the patient's language performance supported that diagnosis. In this case, alienation of word meaning and anomia were much more severe than they would be in a patient with dynamic aphasia. Paraphasia was more prominent, and there was actually a tendency toward logorrhea. This case showed clearly that right-sided hemiparesis in patients without severe Broca's or Wernicke's aphasia may be misleading and indicate the wrong diagnosis of an aphasia type.

Anomia aphasia may appear as a symptom not only in anomic-sensory aphasia, but also in other aphasia syndromes, including anomic-spatial aphasia, dynamic aphasia, and a speech disorder related to a lesion of a subcortical structure. Attempts to describe anomic aphasia as an isolated aphasic syndrome led in the past to the recognition of the various sites of lesion localization within the peri-Sylvian language zone. Goldstein (1948) attributed anomic aphasia to a disorder of categoric thinking that was caused by a lesion within the large parietemporal language zone in the dominant hemisphere. Albert *et al.* (1981) pointed out that anomia is present in diffuse or multifocal brain damage, e.g., in Alzheimer's dementia or as an early sign of brain tumor, regardless of the localization. Anomic aphasia was attributed to a lesion of the left temporal or temporoparietal region by Pitres (1898), Nielsen (1946), Brain (1965) and Newcombe *et al.* (1971). It seems preferable, however, to consider anomia one of the various aphasia symptoms, such as comprehension disorder, alienation of word meaning, or agrammatism, that can be caused by damage to one of a number of areas within a language zone in the brain. Peculiar combinations of such symptoms appear in the aphasia syndromes related to lesions in the better defined cortical areas, including Broca's, Wernicke's, and dynamic aphasia as well as anomic-sensory aphasia.

Anomic-Spatial Aphasia

Symptomatology The language disorder related to a parietal lesion in the dominant hemisphere has been a subject of occasional interest during decades of aphasia study. Such authors as Geschwind (1965) and Green and Howes (1977) pointed out the role of the parietal lobe in conduction aphasia. Others noted a lesion of the temporoparietal region in anomic aphasia (Nielsen 1946; Goldstein 1927, 1948; Brain

1965; Benson 1979; Albert *et al.* 1981). Head (1926) was possibly the first to try to describe an unusual type of aphasia attributed to the foci in the supramarginal gyrus of the dominant hemisphere. He proposed the name "semantic aphasia" for this syndrome and developed a special test battery for its evaluation. This included a series of tests intended to study language performance with regard to spatial orientation (including body image), spatial relationship in the real surrounding space and in the concept of space, mathematical operation, drawing, retelling of complex stories that required describing a spatial relationship, etc. Head believed that a "semantic defect" in the language function underlay disturbances in this area. He attributed this semantic defect to an inability to combine the details mentally into a whole. It may be because this definition is imprecise that "semantic aphasia" has been generally abandoned as an aphasia syndrome.

However, Luria (1940) helped focus attention on "semantic aphasia" as a special aphasia syndrome. The second volume of his doctoral thesis for a degree in Medical Sciences was devoted to the study of "semantic aphasia," which he considered a manifestation of language disturbance in the area of complex spatial orientation and synthesis. Luria (1940, 1947, 1966) developed a series of tests for this disturbance, including logicogrammatical structures examining the spatial relationship between single objects or figures and the inverted spatial order of words in a phrase compared to their semantic sequence. He showed that such a language disorder occurs in patients with a lesion of the left parieto-occipital region and included anomic aphasia as a part of "semantic aphasia."

It seems better to call this type of aphasia "anomic-spatial aphasia," since this term reflects more closely its main abnormalities.

Conversational speech in patients with anomic-spatial aphasia is only slightly disturbed. Speech is fluent and well articulated with normal prosody and preserved grammatical structure of words and phrases. The free flow of conversation may be interrupted sometimes, however, by the need to search for the correct word. There is moderate simplification and shortening of phrases, probably in order to avoid the use of a complicated logicogrammatical structure. Paraphasias, verbal or literal, are noted occasionally. There is no indication of augmentation or logorrhea.

Although the difficulty in conversational speech is minor, anomia is noticeable; patients cannot find the appropriate names for 20–30% of objects presented to them. Their difficulties are perceptibly increased if they are asked to name parts of the body, when difficulty in naming may reach 40–50% of the presented body parts.

Repetition ability is mainly preserved, but difficulty may occur when phrases with complex logicogrammatical construction are presented for repetition.

Comprehension of conversational speech, single words, and simple phrases is preserved. There is no indication of alienation of word meaning or of disturbed retention of syllable and word span of three to five items. Patients usually have difficulty following commands when given Head's body-part test or Luria's logicogrammatical tests. They tend to make errors in following such commands as, "Touch your right ear with your left hand," "Touch your right ear with the index finger of your right hand," "Touch the right corner of your left eye," and "Touch the left corner of your mouth." Patients have similar difficulty imitating the spatial relationship of body parts, as when the examiner touches his or her left ear with the index finger of the right hand; the right ear with the middle finger of the left hand; the outside corner of the left eye with the left hand; or when the examiner uses his or her hands in various spatial relationships.

Logicogrammatical structures have no direct connection with the spatial relationship of parts of the body, but reflect this relationship as well as the space-time relationship. Patients with anomic-spatial aphasia cannot point to an object "below" or "above," "behind" or "ahead," "to the right of" or "to the left of." They make mistakes when trying to "place a pen above a key," "a key below a pen," or "a key above a pen but below a pencil." They have difficulty in assessing the correctness of such time sequences as "after" and "before" as in the phrases "Fall before winter," "Winter after spring," or "I had dinner before breakfast." Such patients have special difficulty when the order of the objects in a phrase is reversed, e.g., "Touch a pencil with a pen," "A key with a pen," "Touch with a key, a pen," "Touch a pen with a key," or "A tiger was killed by a lion. Who is dead?" or "The sun is lit by the earth. The earth is lit by the sun. Which is correct?" Difficulty is also encountered when comparing two objects or persons, as, "Ann is shorter than Kate. Who is taller?" or a more complicated additional phrase, "Kate is shorter than Sophie. Who is the taller of these three women?"

It is difficult for patients with anomic-spatial aphasia to express the relationship between two persons, such as "My brother's sister: Is that a man or a woman?" "My mother's father crossed the road. Who crossed the road—a male or a female?" Such expressions may be better understood if the phrase is fuller and contains more direct, detailed description of the relationship: "I have a mother. My mother has a father. My mother's father crossed the road. Who crossed the road, a male or a female?" The logical difficulty still exists, but the grammatical structure has become simpler and thus more comprehensible.

Patients with anomic-spatial aphasia have special difficulty in distinguishing between their own body parts and those of other persons. When asked to "Show your arm," a patient may show an arm of the examiner, or when told to "Touch my nose," he or she will touch his or her own nose.

Retention of syllable and word span is mainly preserved for a series of three or four or even five or six items. Anomic-spatial aphasia is usually accompanied by various signs of left parietal lobe syndrome, including astereognosis, disorder of topographic memory, constructive apraxia, apraxia for body-part position, symbolic apraxia, finger agnosia, acalculia, pure agraphia, and right–left disorientation.

Transient, right-sided hemiparesis has been noted in only a few of our cases. Persistent right hemihypesthesia to pinprick may appear as well as right hemianopia, predominantly in the inferior quadrant. Usually, however, there is no sign of motor or sensory disorder or visual field loss.

The lesion in patients with anomic-spatial aphasia seems to be in the inferior parietal region of the left hemisphere. Head (1926) attributed what he called semantic aphasia to trauma in the left supramarginal gyrus. Luria stressed the role of lesions of the left parieto-occipital areas. My own experience consists of clinical cases with only anomic-spatial aphasia. Clinical-neuropsychological signs of a lesion in the inferior parietal areas of the left hemisphere were noted in all of our six cases.

The essential signs of anomic-spatial aphasia may be observed in almost every patient with some form of anterior or posterior aphasia. Most of the aphasia symptoms can be noted in the various syndromes, but they differ greatly in severity and frequency. In patients with anomic-spatial aphasia, however, this syndrome is the only one that is strikingly evident. In cases of Broca's or Wernicke's aphasia, the disorders of spatial-temporal relationship are secondary to the more general aphasic disorder, but in patients with anomic-spatial aphasia this is a primary disorder by which the lesion can be localized in the left inferior parietal area.

5

Mixed Anterior–Posterior Aphasia

An aphasia syndrome often results from a lesion involving both parts of the language zone, anterior and posterior. A typical example is global aphasia, a combination of severe Broca's and Wernicke's aphasia caused by an extensive lesion of the anterior and posterior language zones. Other types of anterior–posterior aphasia have not been well studied in the past and have often been attributed to a single form of anterior or posterior aphasia. Nonetheless, at least two types of mixed anterior–posterior aphasia exist in addition to global aphasia. One type is an articulation aphasia combined with moderate repetition aphasia. Another type is a combination of severe or moderate Broca's aphasia with anomic-sensory aphasia. Both of these are characterized by a syndrome different from the "pure" form of anterior and posterior aphasia.

Global Aphasia

Symptomatology This syndrome is characterized by an almost complete loss of expressive speech that occurs at the same time as a noticeable disorder of comprehension, often including gesture comprehension. A severe disturbance of reading, writing, and calculation is a feature of patients with global aphasia. Construction apraxia, finger agnosia, buccofacial, and often ideomotor apraxia, positional apraxia of the hands, disorder of topographic memory, and other "parietal" symptoms may also be noted in such patients. Most patients have hemiplegia or marked right-sided hemiparesis with right hemihypesthesia along with the severe language disorder, and some also have constriction of the right visual field.

Acute Stage of Stroke An absence of sound production is combined with a severe disorder of speech and gesture comprehension. The patient is completely mute, unable to produce any sound when attempting to answer questions or to repeat words. Sometimes a patient tries to move his or her tongue and open and close his or her mouth but cannot make any sound. Occasionally a patient may cough or moan loudly but is unable to cough when asked to repeat the cough of the examiner. Patients' tongue movement is slow and restricted inside the mouth, and they cannot protrude their tongues on verbal command or in response to a gesture. Swallowing is not disturbed, and there is no other sign of pseudobulbar disorder. Aphonia usually lasts 10 to 20 days after the stroke onset. The first sounds to be produced are "a," "da," "ta-ta-ta," "pa-pa-pa," "ma-ma-ma."

Comprehension of speech and gesture is severely disturbed in the acute stage of stroke. Patients cannot follow simple commands. They may sometimes close and open their eyes and even raise a hand, but after one successful performance a patient will start to perseverate in the first command: He or she will close and open his or her eyes in response to every command, showing severe alienation of word and phrase meaning. Comprehension of conversational speech concerning familiar events is also greatly disturbed. Within three or four days the initial drowsiness has largely disappeared, but a patient with global aphasia still cannot understand simple questions about family, work, or surroundings. The examiner may attempt to improve the patient's comprehension by means of gestures, but to no avail.

Reading, writing, and calculation are severely impaired. Patients cannot read or write even one or two syllables or high-frequency words. Buccofacial and ideomotor apraxia are noticeable as well as construction apraxia, finger agnosia, and positional apraxia of the hands. Improvement of comprehension, including understanding gestures, begins from one to three weeks after the onset of the CVA. Conversational speech is better understood, and there is less alienation of word meaning. The first speech sound is usually made at the same time. Nonetheless, the general picture of severe language disorder remains unchanged for months, and patients' speech is often restricted to the pronunciation of three or four "embolophasic" syllables or short words and their comprehension to only a few simple commands and conversational phrases.

In the acute stage of stroke all patients with global aphasia have a persistent right-sided hemiplegia, or plegia of the right hand and marked paresis of the right leg, and right hemihypesthesia, and some patients have a right hemianopia.

Chronic Stage of Stroke Expressive speech is restricted to the pronunciation of one or two words, or syllables called "speech embolus" or "embolophasia." Patients answer every question with "yes" or "no"; "no-no"; "ta-ta"; "tu-tu-tu-tu"; "a-la-la"; or "okay." The intonation of the word or syllables often reveals the patient's meaning; the word "yes" may be said with an intonation indicating "yes," "no," or surprise.

Some patients may correctly say two or three names, usually the names of their husbands, wives, or children.

Repetition, naming, and automatized speech are greatly disturbed. Patients produce a "speech embolus" in almost every attempt to repeat a speech sound, syllable, or word, to name a presented object, or to recite a series of numbers, days of the week, or months. Some patients may repeat single vowels, isolated short syllables ("ma," "pa," "la"), or short words ("cat," "dog," "house"), often with numerous literal paraphasias. Occasionally they may be able to name objects after prompting of the first phoneme, as in anomic aphasia, but most patients' ability to do so is completely destroyed and replaced by the embolophasia.

Comprehension remains severely disturbed in all patients with global aphasia. Some cases are also characterized by a disorder of gesture comprehension. Patients have difficulty in following most simple commands. The first command is often performed correctly, but the next one will indicate severe alienation of word meaning: instead of an ear, the patient will show a table, or he or she will show a window when asked to point to his or her nose. Comprehension of conversational speech is also disturbed. Patients often cannot understand such simple questions as, "Do you have children?" "How long have you been sick?" Auditory recognition and differentiation of words, syllables, and phonemes are also extremely disturbed.

Phonological analysis, reading, and writing are severely impaired. Few patients can recognize their printed last name. Patients cannot even match three printed words to the pictures of the corresponding three objects. When asked to write on dictation they will draw a figure somewhat resembling the corresponding letter, or print one of the same few letters ("A," "B," "P") in response to every task. Patients cannot even write their last name or such well-known ideographs as "U.S.A." or "O.K." A few patients can copy with "slavish" imitation of the letters instead of writing. They cannot do even simple arithmetic.

Buccofacial apraxia is noticeable. Movement of the tongue is regained in the chronic stage of stroke, but patients cannot follow oral commands or perform most of the tests for buccofacial praxis. They cannot whistle, cough, suck through a straw, or blow out a match. Symbolic praxis of the limbs is also disturbed; patients cannot show how to flip a coin, make a fist, salute like a soldier, or comb their hair. Position apraxia of limbs is another manifestation of apraxia in patients with global aphasia as well as finger agnosia, disorder of topographic memory and right-left orientation. In some cases astereognosis occurs in the right hand or in both hands, which is further evidence of damage to the left inferior parietal lobe. Patients with global aphasia preserve their topographic orientation in the hospital and do not make errors in finding their room, bed, bathroom, or dining room. They readily adjust to the everyday schedule of hospital life. Such patients, however, show extreme difficulty in working with a series of pictures telling some simple story or when faced with a new condition.

Additional neurological signs are quite prominent. Right-sided spastic hemiplegia or severe spastic hemiparesis are regular features of patients with global aphasia. However, in a few cases the severe disorder of movement exists only in the acute stage of stroke, and movement is normal in the subsequent period of recovery. Right-sided hemihypesthesia is noted in all patients, and right hemianopia, predominantly for the upper quadrant, may be revealed in some patients if their comprehension is well enough preserved for them to understand the test.

Lesion Localization An extensive cerebral infarction in the left hemisphere may be observed in cases of global aphasia. This infarction is mainly situated in the territory of the cortical and lenticulostriate branches of the left middle cerebral artery and occupies the cortical gray and white matter around the Sylvian fissure, destroying anterior and posterior language zones extending from Broca's area, the Rolandic operculum, and the insula through the supramarginal gyrus and the anterior and middle parts of the first temporal gyrus to the angular and posterior first temporal gyri on the surface of the left hemisphere. The infarction usually extends in depth to the caudate nucleus, the putamen, and the internal capsule (Fig. 5.1). Some of the crucial language areas are preserved in most cases of global aphasia, however, in spite of the severe disorder of expressive speech and comprehension. For instance, in the following case with prominent and persistent global aphasia, autopsy revealed in the left hemisphere a lesion of Broca's area, the Rolandic operculum, the insula, the supramarginal gyrus, and part of the angular gyrus, and the anterior part of T_1. Wernicke's area and the rest of the left temporal lobe were spared.

Case 17, VN: A 53-year-old right-handed man with a long history of hypertension and atherosclerosis had a transient right-sided hemiparesis and diplopia five years before the CVA. A stroke developed without loss of consciousness; suddenly the patient was unable to pronounce any sound and could not understand speech or gesture. He developed plegia of the right arm and leg at the same time. Three weeks later he could say only "va-va." Eighteen months later he continued to have right-sided hemiparesis, more prominent in the arm, and walked with his right arm flexed and his right leg extended, with marked circumduction. He showed right hemihypesthesia to pinprick. His position and vibration senses could not be examined because of poor comprehension. Blinking in response to a threatening movement

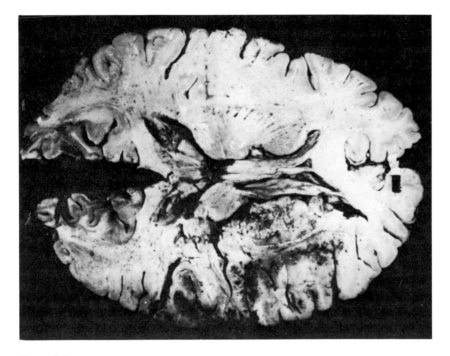

Figure 5.1
Case 23, KC, Global aphasia. Large infarction in the cortical and subcortical structures of the left hemisphere.

of the examiner's hand was weaker on the right, perhaps indicating right hemianopia.

The patient produced the speech embolus "va-va" in answer to any question. He tried to say the numbers 1 to 10 but was dysarthric and produced literal paraphasia, omitting many phonemes, but pronounced the numbers 2 and 5 quite clearly and correctly. He could not say the days of the week or the months. He repeated one or two lines from some popular songs, sometimes completing a word which had been started by the examiner. He was able to repeat several vowels and some syllables (a, o, ba, da). All other vowels, consonants, syllables, and words were repeated as "va-va," as were attempts to name certain objects.

The patient's comprehension of speech and certain gestures was severely disturbed. He sometimes could not follow such simple commands as "Close your eyes," or "Raise your hand." He was unable to read, write, or do simple arithmetic. Buccofacial apraxia and apraxia for symbolic gestures were noted, but his orientation on the ward was preserved. The patient could find his room and bed, feed himself, and put on his clothes. Construction praxis and finger gnosis were impossible to examine because of poor comprehension.

One week later the patient developed acute heart failure and bilateral pneumonia and died after three days of cardiac arrest.

Anatomical Diagnosis Hypertonia with moderate hypertrophy of the left ventricle was present. Marked atherosclerosis of the aorta, the coronary arteries, the common and internal carotid arteries, and the cerebral arteries was revealed. Complete atherosclerotic obturation of the intracranial part of the left internal carotid artery was present. Thrombi closed the lumen of the left carotid artery and the right external carotid artery at the bifurcations.

A large white cerebral infarction in the left hemisphere was located in the territories of the anterior and middle cerebral arteries and destroyed (Fig. 5.2) the caudal part of the first frontal gyrus on the convesital and medial surface of the hemisphere, the posterior parts of the second and third frontal gyri, the lower half of the motor and sensory strips, the Rolandic operculum, the insula, the supramarginal and angular gyri, and the anterior part of the first temporal gyrus. A small infarction was revealed in the territory of the right anterior cerebral artery at the external end of the corpus callosum dorsolaterally from the anterior limb of the internal capsule. A small cyst was noted in the basis of the peduncle and three small cysts in the pons. The cysts were located in the paramedian region of the pons basis, two on the left and one on the right.

Global aphasia in this case resulted from the large cerebral infarction in the territory of the left anterior and middle cerebral arteries. Infarction destroyed all areas of the anterior language zone, including Broca's area, the Rolandic operculum, the insula, and the supplementary motor area of Penfield, as well as the inferior parietal lobule and the anterior part of T_1. The main areas of the posterior language zone, Wernicke's area, Heschl's gyri, and the middle part of the first temporal gyrus, were preserved in spite of the severe disorder of speech and gesture comprehension in this case. Some moderate histopathological changes might be seen in the posterior language areas. More severe lesions and destruction of these areas seems doubtful, however, since the patient lived more than eighteen months after stroke onset and marked histopathological changes could become anatomical, visible in such a long period of time after CVA. It is noteworthy that global aphasia developed in this case without any lesion in the semi-oval center and the subcortical structures. In all our other anatomically confirmed cases of global aphasia, however, a lesion was observed in the subcortical structures.

Global aphasia may also occur in cases with a spared Broca's area

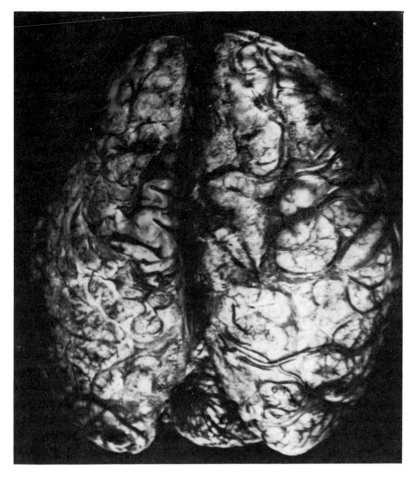

Figure 5.2
Case 17, VN, Global aphasia. Marked diminution of the size of left hemisphere due to a large cortico–subcortical infarction in the territory of the anterior and middle cerebral arteries.

and a destroyed Wernicke's area. In our Case 10, DD, described in the section on Wernicke's aphasia in chapter 4, a severe global aphasia developed 15 months after the first stroke, which had led to severe Wernicke's aphasia. Autopsy revealed that infarction in the left hemisphere had destroyed the posterior part of the first temporal gyrus, the angular gyrus and part of the supramarginal gyrus, and the lower sensory strip. Cysts from the old infarcts were noted in the middle motor strip, the posterior first and the second frontal gyri. Since Broca's area, the Rolandic operculum, and the insula were preserved, the lesion mainly destroyed the posterior language zone, but the anterior language zone had been only partly damaged, and thus what have been called crucial areas in the anterior zone had been spared. As shown in table 5.1, only seven out of our eleven cases of global aphasia studied anatomically had total destruction of Broca's area. Of the remaining four cases, damage was incomplete in three cases and was absent in one case. In five cases, Broca's area appeared to be spared, and a severe or moderate lesion had been revealed only on histopathological examination in four of those cases. A lesion in Wernicke's area, the posterior part of the first temporal gyrus, occurred less frequently than damage in Broca's area. Four out of eleven patients had a severe lesion of Wernicke's area. The lesion was partial in three cases. In four cases the autopsy showed a preserved or only slightly damaged Wernicke's area.

Broca's and Wernicke's areas were anatomically intact in two cases with global aphasia persisting for a long time in the chronic stage of stroke (Case 10, DD, with a spared Broca's area and Case 17, VN, with a preserved Wernicke's area). The development of global aphasia in these cases, therefore, cannot be attributed only to the edema and other pathological processes in the brain tissue adjacent to the area of infarction. On the other nand, in almost all cases of global aphasia an anatomical lesion was present at the intermediate zone connecting Broca's and Wernicke's areas. In approximately half of the cases of global aphasia there was no visible lesion of Broca's and Wernicke's areas. In one out of eleven cases, Broca's area was completely spared and in five out of eleven cases Wernicke's area was preserved so that the large lesion occupying anterior and posterior language zones may produce a syndrome of global aphasia. A lesion of both Broca's and Wernicke's areas is not crucial for the development of such a syndrome, however, and the size of the infarction within the language zone seems to be more important in producing expressive speech and comprehension disturbances than involvement of both the main language zones of Broca's and Wernicke's areas.

On the other hand, in some cases total destruction of most of the

Table 5.1 Localization of the Left Hemisphere Infarction in Patients with Global Aphasia

Case Number and Initials	Posterior F₃		Rolandic Operculum		Insula		Anterior Middle T₁		Posterior T₁		Supramarginal and Angular Gyri		Corona Radiata, Subcortical Structures, Internal Capsule		Left Internal Carotid Artery	
	A	H	A	H	A	H	A	H	A	H	A	H	A	H	A	H
Case 18, VM*	0	2	3	–	3	–	2	–	2	–	2	–	3	–	1	–
Case 19, BA*	0	3	3	–	3	–	2	–	0	1	0	–	2	–	3	–
Case 20, SM*	0	3	3	–	3	–	3	–	0	3	2	–	2	–	3	–
Case 21, LL*	0	3	3	–	0	3	0	–	0	–	3	–	2	–	0	–
Case 10, DD**	0	–	2	–	0	–	0	–	3	–	3	–	2	–	2	–
Case 22, CA*	2	–	2	–	3	–	2	–	2	–	2	–	2	–	3	–
Case 23, KC*	2	–	2	–	3	–	2	–	2	–	2	–	2	–	3	–
Case 24, KL*	3	–	3	–	3	–	3	–	3	–	2	–	2	–	3	–
Case 25, EM*	3	–	3	–	3	–	3	–	0	–	2	–	2	–	3	–
Case 17, VN***	3	–	3	–	3	–	3	–	0	–	3	–	0	–	3	–
Case 26, BI**	3	–	3	–	3	–	3	–	3	–	2	–	2	–	2	–

*Patient died in acute stage of stroke.
**Patient died in chronic stage of stroke.
Anatomical (A) and Histopathological (H) data: 3, complete destruction; 2, moderate changes; 1, mild stages; 0, intact.
Lumen of the vessel: 3, complete obliteration; 2, severe stenosis; 1, mild stenosis; 0, normal.

anterior and posterior language zones, including Broca's and Wernicke's areas, may produce only transient global aphasia, with slow recovery to the stage of severe Broca's aphasia and a moderate disorder of comprehension. Such cases have been traditionally attributed to covert left-handedness. In one such case, described below, the patient was right-handed without any sign of ambidexterity. However, he was much younger than the usual patient with stroke, and relative sparing of speech could be attributed to the compensatory role of the right hemisphere, which was not affected by the aging process.

Case 26, BI: A 30-year-old right-handed man suffered a myocardial infarction (MI) at the age of 29. On the fourteenth day after the MI the patient had a CVA with loss of consciousness and convulsions. The patient regained consciousness in five or six hours but had global aphasia and right hemiplegia. Within five weeks he completely recovered movement in the right extremities. His speech then started to improve, and three months after the stroke the patient had a severe Broca's aphasia with a lesser disturbance of comprehension.

The patient answered any questions with speech emboli: "Yes," "No," "Okay," "Sure." His main mode of communication was facial expression and gesture. Trying to answer questions, the patient sometimes produced several nonembolic words but employed numerous literal paraphasias, e.g., "So . . . yes . . . not titing (eating) . . . so . . . so . . . Sonya also . . . drying (crying) . . . drying . . . she . . . drying." Speech activity was markedly decreased, the patient made attempts to speak only in answer to questions.

The patient could not repeat vowels, consonants, syllables, or short words without severe paraphasias. He could not repeat words of two or more syllables, phrases, series of syllables, etc. He had no ability to name objects, saying only "Yes," "No," "a-a," in attempting to do so. He could say when prompted automatized sequences of numbers, days of the week, and months; his pronunciation was slurred with literal paraphasia and omission of phonemes and syllables, mostly at the beginning of a word.

The patient retained limited comprehension of conversational speech. He followed commands and showed most of the objects in the room with only a few errors. In the "eye–ear–nose" test, however, severe alienation of word meaning was noted. Numerous errors were also observed in Head's test using commands to show a right or left ear or eye with the right or left hand. The logicogrammatical constructions of Luria were also difficult for the patient. Auditory word recognition was relatively preserved, and the patient could distinguish isolated vowels, series of two or three vowels, or single words as being identical or different. Nonetheless, an increase of the delay between presented sounds or words led to difficulty in their differentiation.

Phonological analysis, reading, and writing were severely disturbed. Reading aloud produced the same speech emboli "a," "o," "u," but when given the picture-word test the patient could connect the correct word strip to the corresponding picture of the object. The patient wrote on dictation only his first and last name and the letters "A" and "U." Copying consisted of "slavish imitation," redrawing of the letters. He could not do even simple arithmetic.

Buccofacial apraxia was severe. The patient could not show on command or imitate the gesture of sucking, coughing, blowing, or whistling. Apraxia of symbolic gesture was also noted. Astereognosis was noted only in the right hand. The patient showed a striking constructional apraxia and finger agnosia.

Orientation on the ward and in its everyday activity was completely preserved. The patient could easily get the point of the test he was given and understand events of ordinary life. He could not put in correct order a relatively complicated story in the picture series, however.

Fifteen months after suffering an MI and CVA the patient developed severe chest pain and died several hours later of cardiac arrest.

Anatomical Diagnosis The left ventricle was hypertrophied. A large scar with aneurismatic bulging in the apex of the left ventricle was related to the old MI. Severe atherosclerosis of the aorta and coronary arteries was revealed. Notable atherosclerosis of the carotid arteries was characterized by plaques, especially prominent at the bifurcations.

A large cystic cerebral infarction (Fig. 5.3) in the territory of the middle cerebral artery destroyed the gray and white matter of the pars orbitalis and pars opercularis of the third frontal gyrus, part of the posterior part of the second frontal gyrus, the lower portion of the motor and sensory strip, the Rolandic operculum, the insula, the lower third of the supramarginal and angular gyri, and the first and second temporal gyri, including Wernicke's area. Cerebral infarction extended in depth to the corona radiata at the border of the anterior limb of the internal capsule and to the dorsolateral part of the caudate nucleus and putamen.

The clinical diagnosis in this case was severe Broca's aphasia. The more prominent disorder of comprehension was considered unusual for a patient with anterior aphasia. Extension of the lesion far back to Wernicke's area was unexpected since many cases with global aphasia have limited lesion of the temporal lobe with preservation of Wernicke's area. Repeated questioning of the patient's family did not reveal any left-handedness in the family or in the patient. Therefore the role of the age factor has to be stressed, since the patient was only 30 years

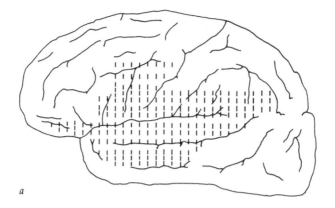

a

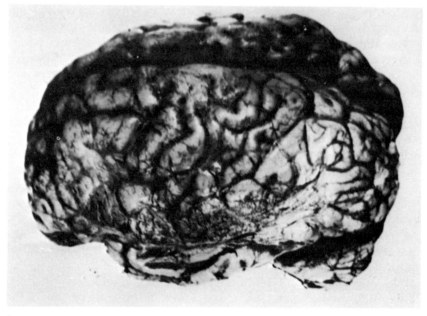

b

Figure 5.3
Case 26, BI, Global aphasia. *a*, Infarction in the cortex of the left hemisphere. *b*, Massive cystic infarction on the convexital surface of the left hemisphere. Infarction extends as a wide strip from the posterior F_2 and F_3 to the anterior border of the occipital lobe.

old and the usual age of patients with stroke is 50 to 60 years or more. In those older patients, the preserved areas of the brain have undergone subtle changes due to the aging process and atherosclerosis of the cerebral vessels.

The additional subcortical lesion also played a part in creating an unusual clinical picture. A lesion of the subcortical structures has been found in only one of our eleven cases with global aphasia. In ten cases an infarction occupied a large part of the putamen and globus pallidus with extension to the caudate nucleus, the internal capsule, and the corona radiata. It is still not clear, however, what responsibility if any the subcortical structures have in language processing. For many years any infarction in this region had been considered as a cause of some speech disorder (not language disorder), including disturbances in speech loudness, speed, and rhythmical–melodic structure. Such speech disorders may greatly increase the language disturbances in patients with global aphasia and make it more difficult to compensate for the language disorder. The role of a subcortical lesion in aphasia, especially in so-called subcortical aphasia, has yet to be clarified, since no reliable cases with a pure subcortical infarction and aphasia studied anatomically have been published, and all the recently published cases have only CT scan confirmation of the subcortical infarction (Damasio et al. 1982; Naeser et al. 1982).

There is no doubt that subcortical hemorrhage may produce various types of aphasia, including global aphasia. In those cases mass effect plays a major role in the development of aphasia, since marked brain edema and other pathological processes are extended from the sub-cortical site of hemorrhage in the left hemisphere to the cortical language areas. More detailed analysis of such cases is presented in the last section of chapter 6.

Mixed Nonglobal Anterior–Posterior Aphasia

In four of our cases the clinical picture in the stage of recovery resembled global aphasia, with a lesser disturbance of expressive speech and com-prehension. All these cases differed from cases of global aphasia, how-ever, by the markedly better ability to repeat phonemes, syllables, and words, including multisyllable words. Patients were classified as having transcortical aphasia, therefore. This type of mixed aphasia has been described mainly in patients with multifocal or diffuse brain pathology in degenerative dementia (Whitaker 1976) or hypoxic encephalopathy in carbon monoxide poisoning (Geschwind et al. 1968). In some cases this syndrome has also been found with cerebral infarction in the ter-ritory of the left middle cerebral artery (Stengel 1936, 1947).

Conversational speech is noticeably disturbed, but patients speak better than do patients with global aphasia, and embolophasia is usually absent. Patients have a tendency toward echolalic repetition of single words of the question or the entire questions, at times adding an appropriate word. For example, they answer the question "How are you feeling?" "feeling good!" Patients have no spontaneous speech and when asked their first and last names cannot answer.

Repetition is strikingly better. Patients may correctly repeat single phonemes, syllables, or words, including four- or five-syllable words, and short simple phrases. Literal paraphasia and omission of the phonemes appear only in repetition of multisyllabic uncommon words, series of three-vowel syllables or words, oppositional phonemes (such as p − b, c − d) and longer or more complicated phrases.

The patient's ability to recite automatized sequences is preserved only for pronunciation of numbers from 1 to 10. Naming is impossible without clues. Prompting of the first one or two syllables leads to correct naming, often with numerous literal paraphasias, so that prompting has to include most of the syllables of the word.

Comprehension of conversational speech is somewhat difficult. Patients follow commands to show the objects in a room but often demonstrate alienation of word meaning. Severe alienation of word meaning is observed in the "eye–ear–nose" test. Patients cannot follow commands from Head's "hand–ear–eye" test and Luria's logicogrammatical constructions.

Phonological analysis, reading, and writing ability are noticeably destroyed. Patients may only be able to read two or three well-known ideographs, such as "U.S.," "N.Y.," or to read or write their own last names. Some patients can copy short words but with "slavish imitation," drawing the letters but not being able to rewrite them.

The ability to calculate using numbers up to 10 is preserved. Buccofacial apraxia and apraxia for symbolic gesture as well as constructional apraxia and finger agnosia are present in all cases.

Severity of right-sided hemiparesis varies from mild to severe. Right-sided hemianopia was revealed in one case, but presence of hypesthesia was difficult to confirm.

We have not had any cases with mixed Broca's and moderate posterior aphasia studied anatomically. A large cerebral infarction in the territory around the Sylvian fissure has to be supposed, since patients have a severe disorder of expressive speech and comprehension, reading, writing, and calculation, various forms of apraxia, and finger agnosia. Their markedly better repetition ability may be related to a smaller area of infarction than that in cases of global aphasia. Another possibility is that this type of anterior and posterior aphasias is different from global aphasia, i.e., the combination of dynamic or moderate Broca's aphasia with anomic-sensory aphasia may produce a severe expressive speech and comprehension disorder with preserved repetition. The existence of a parietal lesion in such cases is unquestionable, since various types of apraxia and finger agnosia were noted in all our patients with mixed nonglobal anterior–posterior aphasia.

Mixed Repetition–Articulation Aphasia

The syndrome of repetition–articulation aphasia has been noted in eight of our cases. This peculiar language disorder resembles a repetition aphasia, since these patients cannot repeat series of single phonemes and their comprehension is relatively mildly disturbed. They also produce literal paraphasias and have anomia, just like patients with repetition aphasia. The disorder of expressive speech including anomia, however, is much more pronounced than in repetition aphasia. Patients produce an almost indistinguishable string of speech sounds with wrong articulation and deformation of phonemes resembling the speech of patients with articulation aphasia. Sometimes the pronunciation becomes clearer and simple speech sounds may be recognized, but their sequence is disrupted by the numerous literal paraphasias. A patient speaks fluently without tension and with speech prosody resembling the normal one, but deformation of articulation and literal paraphasias give the impression that the patient is speaking a foreign language, often one of the Scandinavian languages, since the almost complete absence of voicing is an outstanding feature of such speech. Logorrhea and increased speed of speech are also typical. The patient may sometimes slow down his or her speech activity and start to pronounce clearly and correctly certain words, especially after repeated stimulation to do so by the examiner. These words are usually verbs or small functional words, rarely nouns, another indication of posterior aphasia in addition to the logorrhea.

The patient's ability to repeat, name, and use automatized speech is markedly disturbed by the numerous literal paraphasias and severe deformation of the units of articulation, making speech production almost completely indistinguishable. Prompting of the first syllable does not significantly help to improve naming, as it does for patients with "pure" repetition aphasia.

The comprehension of conversational speech and single words, the ability to follow simple commands, and the differentiation of vowels and series of two vowels are preserved. Severe disorder is revealed in following commands from Head's "hand–ear–eye" test and Luria's logicogrammatical tests. Marked alienation of word meaning is observed in the "ear–eye–nose" tests with two components and in many cases with one component. Retention of word span is restricted to two or three words pronounced by the examiner and to four or five words when pictures of the various objects are shown.

Phonological analysis, reading, writing, and calculation are severely disturbed much more than in patients with pure repetition aphasia. Reading aloud consists of numerous literal paraphasias and a string of indistinguishable speech sounds. Some patients may silently read a simple command, however, and then they can correctly follow that command. Writing on dictation is completely impossible. The patient is able to write one or two occasional letters and then refuses to write at all. The ability to copy is preserved in some cases but is actually "slavish imitation." Calculation can be performed only if the task is presented in written form, and only simple arithmetic. The multiplication table is almost completely forgotten by the patients.

Buccofacial apraxia and apraxia for symbolic gesture are noticeable. Constructional praxis and finger gnosis are spared in most cases, and only slight disturbances may be revealed in some cases.

Plegia or severe paresis of the right arm and moderate paresis of the right leg are often present. In some cases only a slight weakness in the right extremities is revealed. Right-sided hemihypesthesia to pinprick is noted in most patients. Right-sided hemianopia is also present in some cases. This syndrome has often been considered a "conduction aphasia." Therefore at least two types of "conduction aphasia" may exist. One type is a pure repetition aphasia with moderate literal paraphasia and unusual anomia described under "repetition aphasia." The second type is actually a combination of repetition and articulation aphasia.

A syndrome similar to the second type has been described as "undifferentiated jargon" by Alajouanine *et al.* (1952) and Alajouanine and Lhermitte (1964). In this syndrome speech consists of strings of phonemes without meaning or grammatical organization. There is a tendency to stereotypy and perseveration. Repetition and reading are disturbed, but oral and written comprehension are retained. Brown (1979) made a detailed analysis of such cases, presenting his own case with what he called severe "phonemic jargon." Brown notes that this term is used by the French to describe cases of conduction aphasia, but since such cases can hardly be said to have jargon, he used the term "phonemic jargon" instead of "undifferentiated jargon." Undifferentiated or phonemic jargon differs from that in our cases with mixed articulation–repetition aphasia by the undistorted articulation and the fact that there is no deformation of articulatory units or sign of articulation aphasia in those cases. Brown also discussed the appearance of stereotyped jargon in cases of undifferentiated phonemic jargon, and he pointed out its presence in a patient with severe motor aphasia. Further study must be made of new cases with these two somewhat similar syndromes of undifferentiated or phonemic jargon and mixed articulation–repetition aphasia.

Articulation–repetition aphasia results from both lesions that are seen in patients with articulation aphasia or repetition aphasia. This lesion in patients with articulation–repetition aphasia probably involves the superior-middle part of the left temporal lobe and the adjacent area of the supramarginal gyrus and the Rolandic operculum. A similar lesion site was noted by Brown (1979) in his case of "phonemic jargon." CT scan revealed infarcts in the temporoparietal region of the left as well as the right hemisphere. The right hemisphere infarction did not seem to play any substantial role in the development of "phonemic jargon," so that the extensive lesion of the left temporoparietal region is probably responsible for the development of the mixed articulation–repetition aphasia. This extensive lesion may explain the relative severity of aphasia in such cases, including severe disturbances of articulation, reading, writing, phonological analysis, and calculation.

6

Subcortical Lesion and Vascular Aphasia

The term "subcortical aphasia" has been used from the very beginning of aphasia study. In the Wernicke-Lichtheim classification this term was applied to the syndromes in which reading and writing were preserved but expressive speech was disturbed (patients with subcortical motor aphasia) or to syndromes in which there was a comprehension deficit (patients with subcortical sensory aphasia). The site of the lesion was postulated in the subcortical white matter of Broca's or Wernicke's area. It was believed that subcortical motor aphasia resulted from the interruption of the pathway to the lower center regulating movement of the muscles participating in speech production and subcortical sensory aphasia from the interruption of the pathway from the auditory nuclei to the higher language auditory center.

A subcortical lesion was present in Leborgne's brain, the first of Broca's two famous cases. In that case the lesion extended from the posterior part of the third frontal gyrus through the lower part of the central gyri to the anterior part of the first temporal gyrus. The wall of the lateral ventricle was also seen through the cavity in the frontal part of the lesion, so that a lesion of the subcortical structures could be assumed. But Broca did not cut Leborgne's brain and paid no attention to the parts of the lesion outside of the posterior part of the third frontal gyrus in the left hemisphere. Leborgne's brain was fixed in alcohol by Broca and has been maintained in satisfactory condition at the Dupuytren Museum in Paris since Broca's time. Recently, Castaigne *et al.* (1980) and Signoret *et al.* (1984) studied this brain with a CT scan and showed that the lesion involved the posterior part of the third frontal gyrus, the precentral and postcentral gyri, the anterior part of the first temporal gyrus, extended through the insula to the lenticular nuclei, and communicated with the ventricular system in the left hemisphere. The extension of the lesion to the subcortical structures in Leborgne's brain was commented on by Marie (1906a–c). He and his colleague Moutier (1908) collected most of the cases of aphasia described in the literature at that time that had been studied anatomically, including the two famous Broca's cases, and added some of their own cases to show the role of a subcortical lesion in the development of a peculiar aphasia syndrome. That syndrome was called "anarthria" by Marie, and its development was attributed to a lesion of the "lenticular zone" which included, according to Marie, the caudate nucleus, the putamen, the globus pallidus, the internal and external capsule, the insula, the Rolandic operculum, and the supramarginal gyrus on the inner side of the Sylvian fissure. Marie did not give a precise clinical description of his anarthria but stated that patients with anarthria "do not know how to speak" and that patients with dysarthria "cannot speak." According to Marie, however, true aphasia includes a comprehension disorder and may only be noted if an additional lesion of Wernicke's area is present. No single case of pure subcortical infarction and anarthria was presented in the Marie–Moutier collection, and many of their so-called pure cases had a subcortical hemorrhage; distance mass effect on the cortical language areas was obvious in those cases. Heated discussion between Marie and Déjerine accompanied these publications. Déjerine (1908) disagreed completely with Marie and drew a map of the cortical language zone with a detour around the Rolandic operculum from Broca's area to the temporal lobe, since the Rolandic operculum had been included by Marie mainly in his subcortical "lenticular zone." Their dispute was soon forgotten, and Marie's "lenticular zone" became a feature of many books on aphasia in spite of the fact that no one actually accepted Marie's point of view. Authors continued to describe localization in various types of aphasia as mainly cortical, with possible involvement of the white matter adjacent to the cortex of the language areas.

Subcortical Infarction and Aphasia

Foix and Levy, in their famous 1927 paper on "Sylvian softening," stated that global aphasia resulted "from global Sylvian infarction" occupying almost all the territory of the cortical and lenticulostriate branches of the left middle cerebral artery. In severe Broca's aphasia the lesion extends from the foot of the third frontal gyrus to the motor strip, the Rolandic operculum, the lower part of the second frontal gyrus, and the anterior part of the insula. The additional involvement of the corona radiata and subcortical structures leads to a form of Broca's aphasia in which the "anarthric" component is prominent, with at most a mild comprehension deficit. If destruction spreads to the temporal lobe, the comprehension disorder is increased. Although the role of the subcortical lesion was noticed by these authors, they did not single out subcortical infarction as the only cause of aphasia.

New anatomically demonstrated data on subcortical lesions in aphasia patients were obtained in the early 1960s and 1970s by Tonkonogy (1964, 1968) and Stolyarova (1964, 1973). Extension of the cerebral infarction from the cortical language areas to the subcortical structures was revealed (Tonkonogy 1964, 1968) in most of the cases of global aphasia, Broca's and dynamic aphasia, and Wernicke's aphasia. In cases with subcortical hemorrhages in the left hemisphere, global aphasia had been noted in the acute stage of stroke (Tonkonogy 1968, Stolyarova 1973). No direct involvement of the cortical language area was observed, and the role of the mass effect was invoked since the severity of the aphasia decreased with increased distance from the cortical language area.

Nonetheless, the exact role of subcortical lesions in the formation of aphasia still has to be clarified. Anatomically studied cases of various types of aphasia have been described in this book, and in most of the cases lesions of the subcortical structures were present. In a few cases aphasia developed without a subcortical lesion. This included Case 17, VN, with global aphasia; Case 3, GA, with severe Broca's aphasia; Case 11, NE, with severe Wernicke's aphasia; Case 9, KE, with transient Wernicke's aphasia; and Case 14, LR, with phonemic-sensory aphasia. Two of these five patients, VN and LR, died in the chronic stage of stroke; therefore the influence of brain edema in the acute stage of CVA may be ruled out in at least these two patients. The number of aphasia cases without a subcortical lesion would sharply increase if more patients with mild and transient aphasia were included in our data. Such anatomically studied cases are less frequently obtained, however, since the course of stroke is, in general, more benign in such cases. Extension of cerebral infarction from the cortical language areas to the subcortical structures has also been described in articles using anatomical or CT scan data in patients with aphasia syndromes (Mohr 1973, Mohr et al. 1978, Kertesz 1979). The importance of this extension in the development of severe and persistent aphasia has been suggested. Some authors have used these data to promote a new conception of "putaminal aphasia." Naeser et al. (1982) described eight clinical cases of aphasia with CT scan examination showing a predominantly subcortical lesion site. They believed that more anterior capsular-putaminal infarction produced an aphasia syndrome resembling Broca's aphasia but with "more grammatical speech," that Wernicke's aphasia occurred in cases with more posterior capsular-putaminal infarction, and that large anterior-posterior capsular-putaminal infarction resulted in global aphasia. The authors stressed that the aphasia in their cases was not identical to the aphasias in Broca's and Wernicke's aphasia. Damasio et al. (1982) published 11 cases with various types of what they considered atypical aphasia, using CT scan images of relatively small and deep subcortical infarction without any CT-scan sign of cortical involvement in the left hemisphere. The authors described semantic paraphasia and disorders of comprehension in their cases. The types of speech and language disorders vary in those cases from Broca-like to Wernicke-like aphasia, and from slurring dysarthria to severe hypophonia and hoarseness typical for voice disorders usually associated with additional brain-stem lesions. Anatomical and CT-scan data have clearly shown the involvement not only of the cortical but also of the subcortical structures in many cases with aphasia. The role of this involvement in the development of aphasia remains obscure, however, since no anatomically studied case of persistent aphasia with isolated subcortical infarction has been described in more than 100 years of aphasia study. Further clarification is also needed for the aphasia cases that are purely subcortical according to the CT-scan data, because in some cases of aphasia (DeWitt et al. 1984), magnetic resonance-imaging (MRI) reveals involvement of the cortex when only a purely subcortical lesion has been detected by the still imperfect CT-scan technique.

Dysarthria and Unilateral Subcortical Infarction

Aphonia, hypophonia, and slurring dysarthria were more severe and more frequent in our cases with left-hemisphere lesions than in those with right-hemisphere lesions. The difference was especially noticeable in cases with aphonia, an almost complete loss of sound production. Aphonia occurred in three out of five anatomically studied cases with a lesion restricted to the lenticulostriate branches of the left middle cerebral arteries. The aphonia lasted one to two weeks. Our patients were mute and could not make any sound except by moaning or coughing, especially during sleep. They had good comprehension and preserved reading, writing, and calculation. They could follow simple as well as complex commands from Head's and Luria's tests, including, "With the index finger of your left hand show your right eye" or "Show the pencil with the pen," "With the pencil show the pen." Good performance of these tests differentiates patients with aphonia from those with aphasia, especially in the acute stage of stroke when general drowsiness makes both groups appear to have difficulty in comprehending. Patients with aphonia, however, are able to perform correctly most of the complicated tests related to body image. At the same time, aphasia in the acute stage of stroke is characterized by disturbances in following simple commands and by marked alienation of word meaning. In the process of recovery, aphonia is followed by hypophonia and slurring dysarthria, with diminished volume and hypernasality of the voice. Hypophonia is characterized by a gentle, quiet voice and usually occurs concurrently with slurring dysarthria. Sometimes the patient only whispers. Hypernasality and unintelligibility of speech is typical for patients with slurring dysarthria. Aphonia, hypophonia, and slurring dysarthria in our cases with a unilateral brain hemisphere lesion had some important differences from dysarthria secondary to bulbar and pseudobulbar lesions in the brain stem. In patients with severe dysarthria or "anarthria" due to brain-stem lesion, no complete loss of phonation was noted. A patient produces some sounds resembling the vowels "a" or "o," but the voice is dysphonic and coarse with too high or too low pitch. A disorder of swallowing, especially of solid food, is also present in patients with a brain-stem lesion. Patients with a unilateral hemisphere lesion do not show any marked sign of dysphonia. Their tongue movement is often restricted and slow, and they cannot protrude it from the mouth in response to command or gesture, especially in the first three or four weeks after stroke onset. Swallowing is completely preserved, however, and transient difficulty in swallowing may be noticed only in the first 24 to 48 hours of stroke.

The cerebral infarction was restricted to the lenticulostriate branches of the left middle cerebral artery in our three anatomically studied cases with pure aphonia without aphasia. The lesion occupied the caudate nucleus and the anterior limb of the internal capsule and extended back to the lenticular nucleus. In one of these three cases an additional small infarction was revealed in the pons.

The following is the description of a case of aphonia and unilateral subcortical infarction in the left hemisphere.

Case 27, GP: A 68-year-old right-handed woman had a long history of hypertension and atherosclerosis. She developed right-sided hemiplegia without loss of consciousness and a speech disorder with complete loss of phonation. The patient moved her lips in trying to answer a question, but she could make no sound. Her comprehension was comletely preserved, and she even followed the complicated commands of Head's and Luria's tests, including, "Show your left eye with your left hand," "Show your right ear with the index finger of your left hand," "Show the pencil with the pen," "With the pen show the pencil," etc. The patient could also follow these commands when they were written. Nonetheless, central paresis of the right facial nerve was present. Her tongue movement was slow, and the patient could not protrude her tongue from her mouth, although she could swallow liquids and solid food. Right-sided hemiplegia accompanied right-sided hemihypesthesia. The aphonia did not change until the patient died of cardiac arrest on the eleventh day after the stroke onset.

Anatomical Diagnosis A large cerebral infarction was present in the

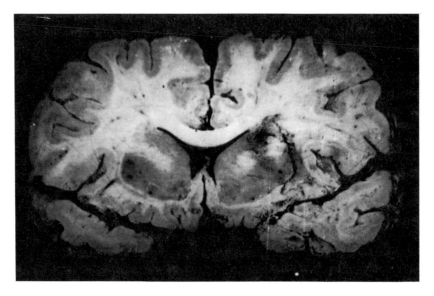

Figure 6.1
Case 27, GP, Aphonia without aphasia. Coronal section at the level of chiasm. The infarction is seen as a fine line in the lateral portion of the putamen.

lenticulostriate branches of the left middle cerebral artery. The infarction destroyed the head of the caudate nucleus, the anterior limb of the internal capsule, and the dorsal part of the putamen.

A coronal section at the level of the temporal poles showed the infarction placed laterally to the anterior horn of the lateral ventricle with extension to the head of the caudate nucleus. The next section at the level between the temporal poles and the chiasm revealed the extension of the infarction to the anterior limb of the internal capsule and to the dorsal part of the putamen (Fig. 6.1). At the level of the chiasm, the infarction diminished and appeared at the external side of the putamen as a narrow gap, 10 cm in length. At the level of the mammillary bodies no sign of infarction was noted.

On the other hand, neither aphonia nor hypophonia was noted in any of our six anatomically studied cases with cerebral infarction confined to the deep branches of the right middle cerebral artery. The following is a description of one such case.

Case 28, PA: A 65-year-old right-handed man with a long history of hypertension and atherosclerosis developed left hemiplegia without loss of consciousness. He had moderate central paresis of the left facial nerve. His tongue protruded from his mouth with deviation to the left

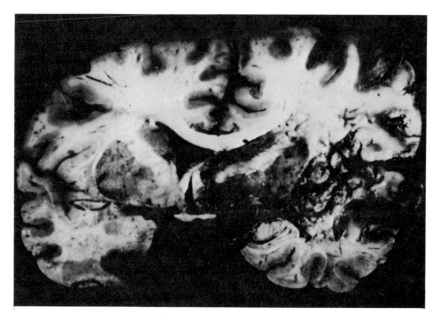

Figure 6.2
Case 28, PB, No speech disorder. Coronal section at the level of the chiasm. A large infarction in the right hemisphere has destroyed the caudate nucleus, the anterior part of the putamen, the adjacent white matter of the corona radiata and the insula.

side. Left-sided hemihypesthesia to pinprick and a disorder of the vibration and position senses in the left fingers and toes were present. The patient did not speak of his own accord, but he answered questions with full, grammatically correct phrases, and his speech was clear and without any sign of dysarthria or hypophonia. Comprehension, naming, and repetition abilities, as well as reading and writing, were preserved. Death occurred on the third day after stroke onset because of sudden cardiac arrest.

Anatomical Diagnosis A thrombus completely obturated the right internal carotid artery at the level of bifurcation. A large infarction was revealed in the territory of the lenticulostriate branches of the right middle cerebral artery. It destroyed the caudate nucleus, the anterior part of the putamen, and white matter in the depth of the frontal–central–parietal region and the insula (Fig. 6.2). A small subarachnoid hemorrhage was revealed at the angular gyrus. There was a small hemorrhage in the medial part of the substantia nigra on the right, as well as small perivascular hemorrhages in the middle part and at the base of the pons.

To compare these two cases, in Case 28, PA, without a speech disorder, a large cerebral infarction existed in the subcortical region of the right hemisphere. That infarction was accompanied by small hemorrhages in the brain stem. In Case 27, GP, with persistent aphonia, the cerebral infarction was less extensive and confined to the subcortical structures of the left hemisphere. Thus a subcortical lesion in the left hemisphere may be responsible for the development of aphonia without aphasia in cases with cerebral infarction.

Hypophonia also resulted from a unilateral subcortical lesion of the left hemisphere more often than from a lesion of the right hemisphere. Moderate and mild slurring dysarthria was revealed in our 110 cases with predominantly unilateral hemisphere lesion in approximately the same proportion of cases with right and left hemisphere lesion. Such dysarthria probably stems from the difficulty of the muscle movement related to speech production caused by the central paresis of the facial and hypoglossus nerves. For this reason, primary slurring dysarthria due to failure in the left-hemisphere control mechanism of speech may be difficult to distinguish in such cases from the secondary dysarthria.

The normal speed of speech is often altered in patients with a lesion of the subcortical structures. Knowledge in this field is sparse, but some general remarks have to be made. Festinating speech has often been observed in patients with slurring dysarthria secondary to Parkinson's disease (Adams and Victor 1981). The patient's speech resembles his movement when he walks with increasing speed. Such increasingly fast speech is slurred and unintelligible. The patient may try to slow down his speech and make it clearer, but this effort lasts only a short time, and soon he starts to speak with increasing speed and slurring. Speech activity is not increased in patients with festinating dysarthria, however. Festinating dysarthria often occurs without any other sign of Parkinsonian syndrome or with a mild nonprogressive extrapyramidal disorder and is probably related to the putaminal lesion. Nonetheless, the site and laterality of the striatal lesion in festinating dysarthria still has to be clarified.

In some patients with dysarthria, palilalia may be noted. The patient repeats one word of the phrase three or four times, e.g., "I am going to a movie-movie-movie-movie"; "My daughter-daughter-daughter-daughter will visit this-this-this-this hospital today." The speed of speech is quite fast and slurring is increased when the patient repeats a word. Palilalia differs from perseveration in patients with anterior aphasia and frontal lobe lesion, since perseveration usually includes the repetition of a word or phrase from the previous task or test. For example, a patient with perseveration will correctly say "I am going to a movie," but on being asked to say a new phrase, "I am going to the shopping center," he will perseverate in the previous one, "I am going to a movie." In cases of perseveration, delay and effort between words is noted instead of the fast repetition in patients with palilalia. Palilalia has been ascribed to striatal lesion. Precise localization of the lesion in the subcortical structures, probably in the thalamus, still has to be made.

The development of dysprosody characterized by slow, laborious, effortful speech without aphasia has not been described in anatomically studied cases with a single subcortical infarction. A cortical lesion in the anterior language zone usually results in motor dysprosody. The possible role of a Rolandic operculum lesion in the development of motor dysprosody is discussed in chapter 3. The role of a subcortical lesion, however, especially in cases of motor dysprosody without aphasia, cannot be completely excluded. A lesion of the caudate nucleus in the left hemisphere may play a part in the development of the decreased level of speech initiation and activity in cases with dynamic aphasia partly resulting from a lesion of the posterior first frontal and the cingular gyri on the mesial surface of the left hemisphere. Such a lesion often extends to the adjacent part of the caudate nucleus. Better understanding of this condition will occur when more cases are studied anatomically.

Lesions of the subcortical structures may produce various types of speech disorders, including aphonia, hypophonia, festinating and slurring dysarthria, and palilalia. It is probable that a more anterior subcortical lesion plays a part in the development of decreased speech initiation and dysprosodic slowness of speech. These speech disorders differ from slurring pseudobulbar and bulbar dysarthria by the disturbances of the prosodic components of speech. There is also no direct correlation between these speech disorders and paresis of the muscles participating in speech production. In cases with pseudobulbar or bulbar dysarthria, slurring and hypernasality of speech occur secondary to the paresis of the corresponding muscles. More noticeable difficulty in tongue movement in patients with aphonia usually subsides before the aphonia and does not cause a swallowing disorder accompanying pseudobulbar and bulbar dysarthria.

A subcortical lesion may produce a primary disorder of speech-regulating mechanisms, especially disturbance of certain prosodic components of speech. Our data have shown that these speech disorders often occur in cases with a unilateral subcortical lesion in the dominant left hemisphere. Speech prosody is deeply involved in language processing, forming the emotional background of language communication expressed through intonation. The subcortical speech disorder, therefore, may substantially modify the manifestation and course of aphasia language disturbances resulting from the lesion of the cortical language areas. Aphonia, hypophonia, or slurring dysarthria increases the difficulty of expressive speech in cases with Broca's aphasia and prolongs and makes less complete the process of speech and language recovery. Severe aprosody secondary to festinating dysarthria makes language processing and speech prosody impossible to use for compensation and recovery in aphasia. It is well known that in some patients with severe Broca's aphasia, a blocked speech output may be freed when the patient sings a familiar tune, producing the words and phrases of the song with little difficulty. The melodic line of the song helps in releasing his or her verbal output. This mechanism unfortunately cannot be used when speech prosody is impaired.

Marie's original theory (1906a–c) suggested that anterior aphasia developed as a concurrent manifestation of subcortical anarthria and Wernicke's aphasia. New data have shown, in addition to the cortical lesion of the traditional language zone, an extended lesion in the subcortical structures of the left hemisphere in cases with persistent global, anterior, and partly posterior aphasia. For this reason it seems better to modify Marie's theory and to consider the more permanent and persistent types of aphasia as a result of cortical and subcortical lesions manifested as a combination of the various types of subcortical dysarthria and dysprosody with different types of language disorders varying in accordance with the site and size of lesions within the large language zone in the dominant (usually left) hemisphere. The combination of subcortical dysarthria and dysprosody with a cortical disorder of language may result in the persistent, more severe forms of global, anterior, and/or posterior aphasia.

Thalamic Infarction and Speech Disorders

Focal thalamic infarcts have been repeatedly described in cases with pure sensory stroke or sensorimotor stroke. Aphasia was not reported in previously published cases (Mills and Swanson 1978; Caplan 1980; Fisher 1965, 1978; Mohr et al. 1977), but hypersomnia, apathy, and amnesia occurred in certain cases in which autopsy revealed bilateral paramedian thalamic infarcts (Shuster 1936–37, Castaigne et al. 1966, Castaigne et al. 1981). Recently, the description of "thalamic aphasia" in cases with thalamic hemorrhages and dysphasia following thalamotomy (Mohr 1983) has drawn attention to speech disorders in patients with thalamic infarctions. Guberman and Stuss (1983) mentioned "mild aphasia disturbances" in one of their two patients with bilateral paramedian thalamic infarcts demonstrated on CT scan. Both patients were disoriented, somnolent, and hypokinetic, with prominent retro- and anterograde amnesia. The first patient, with a more prominent left thalamic lesion, had a low volume and monotonous but fluent speech and a great deal of perseveration and naming difficulty for less common items on the Boston Naming Test. Repetition and comprehension problems occurred only with long phrases and complicated material.

Graff-Radford *et al.* (1984) described disorientation, memory loss, and a fluctuating level of attention in three patients with left thalamic infarction and in two patients with right thalamic nonhemorrhagic infarction demonstrated by CT scan. The patients were withdrawn and somnolent, especially for the first five or six weeks after the acute cerebrovascular episodes, differing little from the previously described cases with thalamic infarcts. However, these patients developed poorly articulated speech, soft voice, paraphasias, and naming and comprehension defects similar to the disturbances described by Guberman and Stuss (1983) in their first patient. The paraphasias in these cases should probably be better termed incoherent speech. This phrase was used by Graff-Radford *et al.* (1984) in describing the speech disturbances in their Patient #3. This incoherent speech seems to represent the salient feature of the described disorder and may be related to the confusion frequent in the acute stage of stroke. This kind of confusion, characterized by incoherent speech and naming difficulties as well as disorientation, amnesia, and sometimes apathy, resembles what is known in the older psychiatric literature as "amentia." Amentia may occur in cases with left thalamic infarction, and careful psychopathological evaluation would be of great help in the future study of similar cases.

Subcortical Hemorrhage and Aphasia

The most reliable data about the direct development of aphasia due to a subcortical lesion are in cases with cerebral hemorrhage. The usefulness of such cases in studying language localization is doubtful, since subcortical structures are the most frequent site of cerebral hemorrhages, and aphasia usually develops as a result of a marked mass effect extending from the hemorrhage to the cortical language areas. From the clinical-neurological and especially from the neurosurgical point of view, the study of such cases is important, since a cerebral hemorrhage occurs some distance from the cortical language areas in patients with aphasia.

For many years aphasia in the chronic stage of stroke was a focus of study in language localization. Many of the well-known and widely discussed cases of aphasia had resulted from cerebral infarction, including Broca's and Wernicke's cases. Most patients with cerebral hemorrhage simply did not survive the acute stage of stroke and therefore could not be studied in the chronic stage of CVA. Aphasia in patients with cerebral hemorrhages has only been brought to attention in the last 20 years, when interest in studying the acute CVA increased because of striking improvements in the pharmacological, neurosurgical, and nursing treatment of stroke. The recent advent of the use of CT-scan technique made evaluating brain pathology in living patients with aphasia due to cerebral hemorrhage possible.

Tonkonogy (1964, 1968) and Stolyarova (1973) were probably the first authors to stress the unusual subcortical localization of hemorrhage in patients with aphasia. These authors studied aphasic syndromes in the acute stage of stroke and described a series of clinical-anatomical cases with aphasia resulting from lateral, mainly striatal and medial, mostly thalamic hemorrhages. A new series of aphasia cases caused by thalamic hemorrhage shown by means of the CT-scan was published (Ciemens 1970, Mohr, Watters, and Duncan 1975, Reynolds *et al.* 1979, Alexander and LoVerme 1980). Nonetheless, few cases of aphasia due to striatal hemorrhage proven by CT scan have been published and discussed (Hier *et al.* 1977, Benson 1979, Alexander and LoVerme 1980). According to the literature (Adams and Victor 1981), cerebral hemorrhage may develop in the white matter of the cerebral hemisphere, usually due to the rupture of an aneurysm or AV malformation of the cerebral vessels. Much more often cerebral hemorrhage occurs in the subcortical structures as a complication of hypertension and cerebral atherosclerosis. These subcortical hemorrhages may be divided into three major groups:

(1) Lateral or striatal hemorrhages are placed outside, laterally to the internal capsule occupying the putamen, the globus pallidus, the claustrum, the external and extreme capsules, and the white matter of the semioval center; hemorrhages often have a spindlelike shape and largely extend in the anterior–posterior direction.
(2) Medial or thalamic hemorrhages are placed medially to the internal capsule, mainly in the thalamus, sometimes extending to the head of the caudate nucleus or cerebral pedunculi.
(3) Mixed lateral–medial hemorrhages destroy subcortical structures medially and laterally to the internal capsule as well as in the adjacent white matter, i.e., both striatum and thalamus are involved by the hemorrhage.

The distance from the cortical language areas increased in the thalamic hemorrhages compared with the striatal hemorrhages. In cases with mixed striatal–thalamic hemorrhage, this distance is not different from the cases with pure lateral hemorrhage. Most subcortical hemorrhages are lateral or lateral medial. Pure medial or thalamic hemorrhages occur less often. Of the 25 clinical-anatomical cases of aphasia due to sub-cortical hemorrhages in the left hemisphere, Stolyarova (1973) described only medial, mainly thalamic hemorrhages in four cases.

Lateral Striatal Hemorrhage and Aphasia
Global aphasia with aphonia and a severe comprehension disorder of speech and gesture occurs in the first one to ten days after stroke onset in almost all cases with lateral hemorrhage in the left hemisphere. Stolyarova (1973) noticed the development of global aphasia in 10 out of 11 anatomical cases with striatal hemorrhage in the left hemisphere. Both of our two patients with lateral hemorrhage also developed global aphasia. However, nonglobal mixed aphasia may be noted in the first hours of stroke onset in some cases with more limited and less severe striatal hemorrhage. Death occurred in most of the anatomically studied cases five to ten days after onset of the lateral hemorrhage, and global aphasia usually remained unchanged during this time. If the patient survives, speech starts to recover within the first two weeks, and global aphasia is observed in a few cases eight to ten weeks later. The language syndrome at the stage of the acute CVA is characterized by slowness and impoverishment of speech, word-finding and naming difficulties, sometimes paraphasia, agraphia, alexia, marked hypophonia, dysarthria, and short phrase length, but no dysprosody or effort in speech. A disorder of comprehension of complex phrases and moderate alienation of word meaning may be noted. Repetition ability is preserved for one- or two-syllable words. Therefore the clinical picture resembles that in nonglobal mixed aphasia. Most patients tend to recover language ability completely but may have some hypophonia and dysarthria in the later stage of stroke. Since there are no similar cases in the chronic stage of CVA that have been anatomically studied, knowledge of speech disorder in such patients is scanty, and further collection of data, including CT-scan evaluation, from living patients with striatal hemorrhage should be helpful.

The lesion in cases of global aphasia and lateral hemorrhage is confined to the subcortical striatal structures in the left hemisphere without direct destruction of the cortical language areas. Brain edema, however, is usually prominent on such cases and extends from the deep white matter to the cortex of the left hemisphere.

In our two anatomical cases with global aphasia Case 29, KE, and Case 30, KM, large lateral subcortical hemorrhages were revealed in the territory of the lenticulostriate branches of the left middle cerebral artery. In both cases hemorrhages destroyed the caudate nucleus, the putamen, the globus pallidus, the internal capsule and part of the corona radiata adjacent to the striatum. Cortical anterior and posterior language areas were preserved in both cases, and the distance from the hemorrhagic foci to these areas was 3 to 5 cm. Severe brain edema, however, extended from the immediate vicinity of the cerebral hemorrhage to the cortical gray and white matter of the left hemisphere, including the cortical language areas. The following is a description of one of these two cases.

Case 29, KE: A 54-year-old right-handed woman with a long history of hypertension developed weakness in the right extremities and loss of speech. About ten minutes later she lost consciousness and remained unconscious for 12–14 hours. When the patient regained consciousness she could not make any sound and had a severe disorder of comprehension. In attempting to answer questions, she moved her lips and made an obvious effort to speak but could make no sound except moaning. She followed only some simple commands ("Close your eyes," "Raise your hand"). She manifested severe alienation of word meaning and of gesture comprehension after following correctly one or two commands. Her right nasolabial fold was effaced. She could not protrude her tongue from her mouth, and the movement of the tongue in the mouth was slow, with some deviation to the right, but she could swallow. Her gaze was directed to the left. She had plegia of the right arm and severe paresis of the right leg, as well as right-sided hemihypesthesia to pinprick. The visual fields were impossible to evaluate.

On the fifth day after stroke onset a trepanation of the skull in the left frontal–parietal–temporal region was performed and a hematoma was partially removed. After surgery the patient developed pneumonia and died on the ninth day following her stroke.

Anatomical Diagnosis Hypertonia was present. Hypertrophy of the left cardiac ventricle and moderate arteriolonephrosclerosis were revealed. Severe brain edema was present in the right and left hemispheres. A large subcortical hemorrhage was revealed in the territory of the lenticulostriate branches of the left middle cerebral artery. The hemorrhage destroyed the caudate nucleus, the putamen, the globus pallidus, and the anterior and posterior limbs of the internal capsule and extended through the corona radiata to the white matter of the motor strip.

In the right hemisphere an old, small infarction measuring 1.5 × 2.5 cm was noted in the white matter of the angular gyrus. Tiny pseudocysts were present in the right thalamic pulvinar and in the left cerebral pedunculus. The pseudocysts measured 0.6 × 0.3 cm and 0.2 × 0.1 cm. It is evident that in this case a massive striatal hemorrhage in the left hemisphere led to the development of the global aphasia. The hemorrhage extended at one point to the white matter of the left motor strip, but the cortical language area was not directly involved by the hemorrhage, and severe bilateral brain edema was noted.

In both of our cases (Case 29 and Case 30), a massive striatal hemorrhage was present just as in most of the anatomical cases with global aphasia described by Stolyarova (1973). In one of Stolyarova's cases, however, a relatively small striatal hemorrhage produced global aphasia. The aphasia was transient and changed to nonglobal mixed aphasia two weeks after the stroke onset. The hemorrhage in this case destroyed the putamen, the external and extreme capsule, the claustrum, and part of the posterior limb of the internal capsule. The caudate nucleus, the globus pallidus, and the corona radiata as well as most of the anterior and posterior limb of the internal capsule were free of hemorrhage.

Medial Thalamic Hemorrhage and Aphasia
Substantial differences exist in the syndromes of aphasia or speech disorders, depending on the size of the thalamic hemorrhage. Massive hemorrhages in the left thalamus often spread to the adjacent areas of the subcortical structures, especially to the posterior limb of the internal capsule and internal parts of the putamen. Brain edema is usually noticeable in such cases and involves the cortical structures in the left hemisphere. The development of aphasia may be considered a result of these extended pathological processes in the left hemisphere. In cases with massive thalamic hemorrhage, however, aphasia is less severe than in cases with massive striatal hemorrhage, because the distance from the cortical language zones, in thalamic hemorrhage reduces the role of edema in these zones, with corresponding lessening of the aphasia manifestations. Stolyarova (1973) presented two cases of aphasia with thalamic hemorrhages documented on autopsy. In these cases the hemorrhages were massive and occupied almost all the left thalamus, spreading to the adjacent areas of the left hemisphere.

In the first case the left thalamus had a 2 × 5 cm hemorrhage that extended to the internal part of the putamen and to the central part of the internal capsule. In the second case a hemorrhage in the left thalamus spread to the posterior part of the internal capsule. A nonglobal mixed aphasia was recorded in both cases. In the first hours and days after the stroke onset, the patients did not develop the aphonia and severe comprehension disorders observed in cases with global aphasia in the acute stage of CVA. They did not speak voluntarily, however, but answered questions with a single word or with short phrases. Repetition also stimulated speech production, and patients repeated one- or two-syllable words ("table," "chair," "house") and some simple phrases. They were unable to name objects in the first hours after the stroke onset but soon regained the ability to name certain things ("spoon," "watches," "finger"). Moderate paraphasias were noted, and speech was often hypophonic and slurred. Comprehension of simple instructions was preserved, but following more complicated commands was disturbed, as well as writing and calculation. The patients could read only short words. Language function started to improve on the fourth day, but both patients died on the seventh day after stroke onset, so that the process of recovery could not be followed.

Both patients described by Stolyarova (1973) had some important features of so-called thalamic aphasia reported in cases with less extensive left thalamic hemorrhages documented on CT scan. Those features particularly include extreme expressive inertia, decreased speech activity, paraphasias, and anomia, but preserved ability to repeat words and phrases. Nonetheless, the entire picture remains much more characteristic in cases of massive left thalamic hemorrhage, probably related to the spread of the brain edema to the cortical language areas in the left hemisphere. On the other hand, as has been pointed out by Mohr (1983), dysnomia, paraphasia, and comprehension disorders occur in cases with small left thalamic hemorrhages characterized by a "fluctuating level of alertness" as well as by disorientation, apathy, and confusion, and hypophonic, barely intelligible, mumbled speech, perseveration, and bursts of jargon intermittent with normal speech. Mohr (1983) summarized the cases in the literature with speech or language disorders due to small left thalamic hemorrhages documented mainly by the CT scan, including cases described by Mohr, Watters, and Duncan (1975), Reynolds et al. (1979), Walshe et al. (1977), and Alexander and LoVerme (1980). Mohr added 11 personally reviewed cases of thalamic hemorrhage from a survey of 16,000 autopsies performed over 15 years up to 1975 at the Massachusetts General Hospital. He stressed that these speech and language disorders cannot be classified in the traditional terms of aphasia (Broca's, Wernicke's, conduction, or transcortical) and related these disturbances to the peculiar type of delirial fluctuation in alertness with unusual paraphasias that he suggested calling "aphasic delirium." Mohr believes that the paraphasic speech in these cases "runs beyond the level of simple phonemic or semantic alteration," and that the old psychiatric term "incoherent or rambling speech" more properly describes their clinical peculiarities. Probably the term "amentia" may be used to describe this type of "aphasic delirium," since "amentia" was characterized in the older psychiatric literature by the presence of disorientation, amnesia, apathy, and incoherent speech with naming difficulties. Further study of the relationship between "aphasic delirium" or "amentia" and left thalamic lesion may be rewarding.

Thalamic hemorrhage often spreads to the adjacent areas of the subcortical structures, especially to the internal parts of the putamen, and the posterior limb of the internal capsule, as well as to the cerebral pedunculi. However, the left thalamus remains the major site of such medial hemorrhages in aphasia cases. Brain edema is usually evident. Edema is less severe than in striatal hemorrhage, and distance from the cortical language areas reduces the force of the brain edema and other pathological processes caused by the intracerebral hemorrhage. That is why aphasia may be less severe and the speech disorder fluctuates in patients with thalamic hemorrhage.

Mixed striatal-thalamic hemorrhages in the left hemisphere produce aphasic syndromes similar to aphasia in striatal hemorrhage. Global aphasia occurs in most cases after the stroke onset. Subsequent recovery through a stage of nonglobal mixed aphasia usually occurs. In some of the patients with deeper but less extensive lesions, the aphasia syndrome is manifested as a nonglobal mixed aphasia from the beginning.

These striatal-thalamic hemorrhages destroy the left thalamus, the putamen, the globus pallidus, and in some cases the caudate nucleus and part of the internal capsule and often spread to the coronal radiata in the left hemisphere.

In the following case a global aphasia developed after striatal–thalamic hemorrhage in the right hemisphere. This is probably the first published anatomical case of aphasia in a left-handed patient with subcortical hemorrhage in the right hemisphere.

Case 31, KC: A 59-year-old left-handed woman with a long history of hypertension and atherosclerosis suddenly developed loss of consciousness. After three hours, consciousness returned, and slurring dysarthria, as well as severe right-sided hemiparesis, were noted. She gradually recovered speech and movement, and six months later in the chronic stage of stroke she had a moderate slurring of speech and mild, right-sided weakness, mainly in the right hand. Three years later the patient developed a new CVA with transient loss of consciousness for three hours. She had a severe speech disorder and left-sided hemiplegia. She remained conscious but could not produce any sound other than a sort of moan. She retained comprehension of a simple command but could not follow a second command immediately thereafter, nor could she understand gestures. She could not stick out her tongue and could swallow only soft food. Left-sided hemiplegia, hemihypesthesia, and hemianopia were noted together with mild right-sided hemiparesis, mostly in the right hand. On the fourth day the patient deteriorated further and died of cardiac arrest on the sixth day after the onset of the second stroke.

Anatomical Diagnosis Hypertonia was present. Hypertrophy of the left cardiac ventricle was revealed, and moderate atherosclerosis of the

Figure 6.3
Case 31, KC, Global aphasia and left-handedness. Large hemorrhage in the subcortical structures of the right hemisphere.

aorta and carotid arteries. In the territory of the lenticulostriate branches of the right middle cerebral artery, hemorrhage destroyed the putamen, the globus pallidus, the anterior and posterior limb of the internal capsule, and the thalamus. The hemorrhage extended to the lower part of the insula (Fig. 6.3). In the left hemisphere three old, small infarcts were revealed in the territory of the lenticulostriate branches of the middle cerebral artery. One infarction measuring 0.7 × 0.6 cm was placed in the anterior limb of the internal capsule. A pseudocyst of the second infarction, measuring 0.5 × 0.3 cm, was present in the external and basal parts of the putamen. A pseudocyst measuring 2.5 × 0.9 cm was revealed in the medial nuclei of the thalamus.

Aphonia in this case cannot be explained by the bilateral pseudobulbar disorder alone, since a severe comprehension disturbance is characteristic of aphasia, and aphonia with severe comprehension disorder has to be considered a global aphasia. Probably the severity of aphasia in this case is related to the extension of the intracerebral lesion from the thalamostriatal region to the insula close to the cortical language areas. Thus the disorder is manifested as a global or mixed nonglobal aphasia in most cases with striatal, thalamic, and striatal–thalamic hemorrhages. Further collection of similar data is needed, since the site of the thalamic hemorrhage is more posterior than in striatal hemorrhage, and therefore the left thalamic hemorrhage is situated closer to Wernicke's area than is the left striatal hemorrhage. Benson (1979) reported some similarity of the aphasic syndrome to Wernicke's aphasia in certain patients with thalamic hemorrhage and jargon output with verbal paraphasia. This jargon aphasia could be explained by extensive brain edema in the posterior cortical language areas because of the relatively shorter distance to them from the site of the thalamic hemorrhage compared with the striatal hemorrhage. Analysis of our and Stolyarova's anatomically studied cases, however, does not show any clear distinction between the types of aphasic syndromes resulting from striatal and thalamic hemorrhages. Alexander and LoVerme (1980) and Albert *et al.* (1981) also noted no substantial difference in aphasia due to left thalamic or putaminal hemorrhage.

Differences have been noted only in the severity of aphasia, since left striatal hemorrhage tends to produce global aphasia in the first hours of stroke and thalamic hemorrhage usually produces a nonglobal mixed aphasia. If a patient with aphasia caused by a hemorrhagic stroke survives the first days, his or her speech recovery is better than that of a patient with aphasia resulting from a cerebral infarction, but that recovery is faster and more complete in patients with aphasia resulting from thalamic hemorrhage than striatal hemorrhage.

The development of aphasic syndromes after subcortical hemorrhages often was not observed in the past, since the question of the cortical localization of language areas was easily confused with the problem of localization of the main focus of the pathological process. Indeed, aphasia in patients with left subcortical hemorrhage can be explained as resulting from the extension of severe brain edema to the cortical language areas in the left hemisphere. Therefore the localization of the lesion is the subcortical structures, although the main site of the language areas is the cortical structures. Nonetheless, dysarthria, aphonia, and dysprosody in patients with left subcortical infarction probably play a special role in the persistent and prominent aphasic syndromes resulting from a cortical–subcortical cerebral infarction. Therefore a left subcortical hemorrhage may not only be responsible for the development and extension of brain edema to the cortical language areas, but also participates in the formation of the dysprosodic and dysarthric subcortical component of the cortical language disorder. The mechanism of aphasia formation is similar in cerebral infarction and hemorrhage, since involvement of the left cortical language and subcortical speech areas is probable in both of these types of cerebral pathology. Prominent brain edema is less frequent in cases with cerebral infarction, and that is why softening has to be cortico–subcortical to produce marked and persistent aphasia. In patients with subcortical cerebral hemorrhage a severe, extensive brain edema involves the cortical language areas, and an aphasic syndrome develops because of the cortico–subcortical pathologic processes. Cortical involvement is less persistent and aphasia usually clears after the first days and weeks of stroke as soon as the subcortical cerebral hemorrhage stabilizes and severe brain edema subsides. Further reporting of cases of aphasia and small subcortical hemorrhages should be fruitful.

III

Localization of Lesions and Vascular Aphasia

7

Localization of Cerebral Infarction and Aphasia Syndromes

Various mechanisms reduce or eliminate the disturbances of brain functioning that result from cerebral infarction, hemorrhage, or other causes. These mechanisms seem to be especially successful in protecting brain functioning from relatively small lesions. A limited lesion of Broca's area, Wernicke's area, or the Rolandic operculum does not produce a persistent aphasia syndrome. On the other hand, an extensive lesion of the language zone in the dominant hemisphere results in permanent and often severe aphasia, since great damage to the language zone destroys the protective mechanisms of language processing in the brain. That is why localization diagnosis has to take into account the size of the lesion. At the same time, the brain does not function as a simple equipotential entity, and the site of the lesion remains an important factor, probably the main one in the question of the localization problem in aphasia. The site and size of the lesion is discussed in this chapter in relation to the cerebral infarction, since cerebral hemorrhage presents additional difficulty in localization because of the role of mass effect. The problem of localization in aphasia caused by cerebral hemorrhage is discussed in chapter 8 as well as in chapter 6.

Infarction in the Anterior Language Zone and Aphasia

The cortical areas of the anterior part of the language zone in the dominant left hemisphere include the posterior part, the pars opercularis, of the third frontal gyrus (also known as Broca's area), the Rolandic operculum, and the insula. This zone extends on the left hemisphere surface to the posterior part of the first and second frontal gyri with a supplementary motor area, described by Penfield and Rasmussen (1950) and Penfield and Roberts (1959) on the mesial surface of the posterior F_1. The function of the subcortical structures as part of the language zone has also been discussed since Marie's famous publications (Marie

1906a–c). It has been shown that the caudate nucleus, the putamen, and the globus pallidus can be destroyed in anterior aphasia, especially in cases with severe and persistent language disorder (Tonkonogy 1968, Mohr *et al.* 1978, Naeser and Hayward 1978, Levine and Mohr 1979, Kertesz 1979, Kertesz *et al.* 1979). The relationship of a subcortical lesion to the language component in aphasia disorders remains obscure and is discussed separately in chapter 6. The involvement of the cortical lesion in the development of anterior aphasia is clearer, although many questions are still unresolved.

The Posterior Part of F_3 (Brodmann's Area 44)
The role of a lesion in this area of the left hemisphere in the development of aphasia was first suggested by Broca (1861a,b), whose name has been given to this type of anterior aphasia. Later on, Marie (1906b) criticized the "dogma of the third frontal convolution," and one of his three papers regarding aphasia was titled, "The third frontal convolution does not play any special role in language function." In support of this point of view, Marie (1906b) and Moutier (1908) presented three anatomically studied cases in which no aphasia had developed despite the infarction situated in the posterior part of the third frontal gyrus in the left hemisphere. For instance, in Moutier's Case 1 (the patient named Berlin) the infarction involved the pars opercularis and the pars triangularis of the left F_3. In his Case 2 (patient Prudhomme) there was mild right-sided hemiparesis but no speech disorder. Autopsy revealed a small infarction in the gray and white matter of the upper part of the pars opercularis in the third frontal gyrus with extension to the central part of the second frontal gyrus of the left hemisphere. In Case 3 (patient Jacquet) a neurological examination only revealed dementia without a speech disorder and a slight numbness in the right extremities. Autopsy showed a general senile atrophy of the brain with an infarction in the pars triangularis and in the upper part of the pars opercularis of the left F_3.

Niessl von Mayendorf (1926) discussed twelve similar cases from the literature, including three of Moutier's cases. There was no aphasia in seven out of twelve cases, but in one of the seven cases there was no information concerning the speech condition immediately after the stroke began. In the remaining five cases a transient aphasia occurred directly after the CVA. The autopsy showed complete destruction of the pars opercularis of the left F_3 in seven cases and incomplete destruction in five cases. In four cases the infarction extended to the pars triangularis of the same gyrus. A lesion of the insula was revealed only in one case. The lower parts of the central gyrus were intact in all 12 cases. Microscopic examination of this area, however, was not performed in most of the cases. Victoria (1937) noted that there was no persistent language disorder in ten cases with an isolated lesion of the posterior part of the third frontal gyrus in the dominant hemisphere. Six of these cases had been included in the collection of Niessl von Mayendorf (1926). Victoria added three cases from the literature and one case of his own. Two of those cases had a complete destruction of the pars opercularis of the left F_3, and two had a partial destruction. The lesion extended to the pars triangularis in two out of the four cases. Therefore aphasia was absent (11 cases) or transient (5 cases) in at least 16 published cases with limited lesion of posterior F_3 (the 12 cases collected by Niessl von Mayendorf and an additional four cases in Victoria's review). In recent years an isolated lesion of the posterior F_3 has been described in one case with transient aphasia (Tonkonogy and Goodglass 1981), summarized in chapter 3. Out of the 17 aforementioned cases, complete destruction of the pars opercularis of the left F_3 was noted in 10 cases, and partial destruction was seen in 7 cases. Extension of the infarction to the pars triangularis occurred in 8 out of 17 cases. The Rolandic operculum and the lower part of the motor and sensory strips were preserved in all 17 cases, at least according to the result of macroscopic examination. A partial lesion of the insula of the left hemisphere was revealed in one case and of the orbital gyrus in another case.

The data presented noting the complete absence of any speech disorder in 11 out of 17 described cases may not be totally trustworthy, because transient aphasia could have been missed in some of those cases. Since the patients' speech had been first examined in detail two or three months after the stroke took place, a retrospective clinical description of the speech status was made in cases in which autopsy showed an unusual isolated lesion in the posterior F_3.

Similar data were presented by Mohr (1973, 1976), Mohr et al. (1978), and Levine and Mohr (1979). Mohr et al. analyzed 22 personal cases documented by autopsy in 4 cases, by CT scan in 11 cases, and by radionucleide brain scan or arteriography in the remaining 7 cases. Limited infarcts in the left inferior frontal region were revealed in all 22 cases. The authors stressed that interruption of speech lasted from hours to days in all 22 cases. Mohr et al. also reviewed the autopsy records of the Massachusetts General Hospital from 1963 to 1973 and noted 10 cases with infarcts limited to Broca's area alone or within one additional gyral width. No mention of persisting aphasia was made in these 10 cases. The authors suggested that the limited lesion in Broca's area and its immediate environs did not lead to a persistent or significant disturbance in language function. The absence or the transient character of the language disorder may also be attributed to the compensatory role of the right hemisphere in some cases, especially in left-handed patients, and to a corresponding shift of language dominance to the right hemisphere. Nonetheless, persistent aphasia was not manifested in certain cases with a bilateral lesion of the posterior part of the third frontal gyrus. Moutier (1908) described a 75-year-old woman (his case 41) who at age 73 developed right hemiplegia and transient aphasia after a stroke but whose speech recovered completely. She suffered a new stroke at age 75 which resulted in left hemiplegia without any speech disorder. The autopsy showed bilateral softening in the posterior parts of F_3 without any other lesions. Comte (1900) and Nielsen (1946) described bilateral lesions of the posterior F_3 and adjacent cortical areas with dysarthria in Comte's case and mutism without aphasia in Nielsen's case. Pool et al. (1949) performed bilateral surgical removal of posterior F_3 without post-operative speech disturbances. In our own Case 1, RA (see chapter 3), a moderate and transient Broca's aphasia of one month's duration developed after the first stroke. A transient mild right hemiparesis was observed, predominantly in the right hand. According to the anatomical and histopathological data, the stroke was associated with an infarction in the posterior part of the left F_3, including the pars triangularis and the pars opercularis, with partial extension to the orbital gyrus. Left hemiplegia and left hemihypesthesia with dysarthria developed after a second stroke 10 months later; no indication of aphasia was observed. Anatomical and histopathological examination revealed a lesion of the right posterior F_3 with extension to the insula and to the anterior part of the temporal lobe. Bilateral destruction of the third frontal gyri did not necessarily produce persistent global or severe Broca's aphasia in the four cases described by Levine and Mohr (1979). The authors documented the localization of the lesion by a CT scan in all cases. They came to the conclusion that extensive frontoparietal lesion of the minor hemisphere may impair articulation, but the disorder is mild and often transient. A lesion of posterior F_3 in the nondominant hemisphere, therefore, may lead to more prominent dysarthria of the pseudobulbar type in cases with a symmetrical lesion of the dominant hemisphere. Involvement of the minor hemisphere, however, does not increase the severity of global or Broca's aphasia resulting from the lesion of the left, dominant hemisphere.

Absence of language disorder or transient aphasia in cases with an isolated lesion of the pars opercularis of F_3 cannot be considered as a confirmation of the postulate that the third frontal gyrus does not play any role in language function, because a small cortical lesion usually produces a mild and transient neurological deficit. This has been repeatedly observed in cases with movement and sensory disorders caused by a small cortical lesion of the motor and sensory strip, and there is no reason to reject such a possibility for language disorder.

A small lesion in any other part of the language zone also does not produce a persistent aphasia, so that in Case 6, DC, a transient articulation aphasia was attributed to the limited infarction of the lower motor strip and the Rolandic operculum in the left hemisphere, and Wernicke's aphasia was transient in Case 9, KZ, with a small infarction in the left posterior T_1. The role of the posterior part of the left third frontal gyrus in language disorder has found additional support in the data obtained by electrical stimulation of this region by Penfield and Roberts (1959). The aphasic type of reaction was especially prominent when the authors stimulated various points at the left posterior F_3. Some authors (Henschen 1920–1922, Nielsen 1946, Hécaen and Consoli 1973) presented cases with more severe and stable aphasia and lesions of the left posterior F_3. But the lesion usually extended in such cases to the Rolandic operculum, the anterior temporal lobe, and the insula, and deep in the white matter. For instance, not one of the 25 cases described by Nielsen from Henschen's original book (1920–1922) may be considered sufficient confirmation that the aphasia persisted because of an isolated lesion of the left posterior F_3. In one out of 25 cases, death occurred within the first 10 days after the stroke onset, so that persistence of the aphasia remained unclear. The lesion extended to the Rolandic operculum, the insula, and anterior T_1 in 12 other cases. In one case, the infarction also involved the subcortical structures and in another case (the case of Lelong, Broca's second case) isolated infarction of the pars opercularis of the third frontal gyrus accompanied diffuse senile atrophy of the brain. In three cases a mild speech disorder was considered an aphasia by the authors who originally described those cases. In one case, aphasia was transient.

It is evident that an isolated lesion of the pars opercularis of the third frontal gyrus in the left, dominant hemisphere may produce a transient aphasia (Fig. 7.1) resembling a mild Broca's aphasia. At the same time, the development of severe and persistent Broca's aphasia stems from a large lesion not limited to Broca's area (Fig. 7.2) alone. Foix and Levy (1927) were perhaps the first to stress the lesion size in Broca's aphasia. They clearly showed that in cases of severe Broca's aphasia, the lesion involved the posterior part of the third frontal gyrus extending to the Rolandic operculum, the lower part of the second frontal gyrus, and the anterior part of the insula. In the 15 cases with marked Broca's aphasia reported by Mohr et al. (1978), all had large infarcts involving the left inferior frontal, opercular, and insular regions with extension of the lesion to the adjacent subcortical structures or to the supra-Sylvial convexital region in the territory of the cortical branches of the middle cerebral artery. In the acute phase of the stroke, those patients' speech was characterized as "total aphasia," "severe

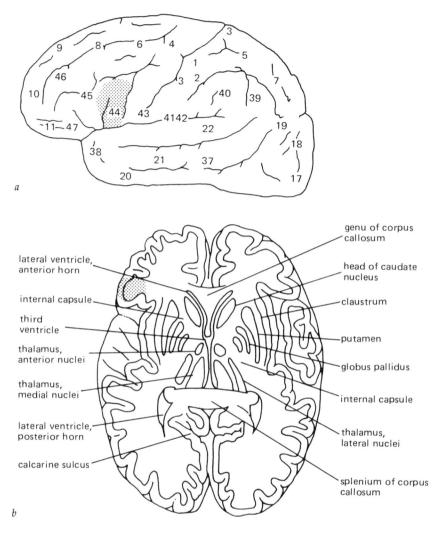

Figure 7.1

Transient Broca's aphasia. Localization of the small cerebral infarcts in the left hemisphere. *a*, Diagram of the small cortical infarction in the posterior F₃. The numbers indicate Brodmann's cytoarchitectonic areas. *b*, Diagram of the horizontal section. Cortical infarction spreads only to the adjacent subcortical white matter of the opercular part of the third frontal gyrus.

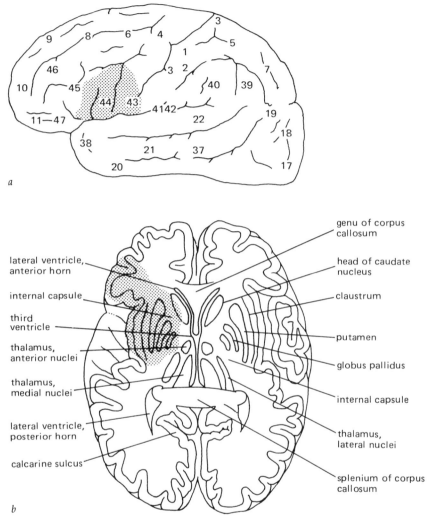

Figure 7.2
Severe Broca's aphasia. Localization of the large cerebral infarction in the cortical and subcortical structures of the left hemisphere. *a,* Diagram of the cortical infarction with destruction of the posterior part of the third frontal gyrus and the lower parts of the motor and sensory strips. *b,* Diagram of the horizontal section. Lesion spreads from the cortex to the striatum.

aphasia," "severe expressive aphasia," or "the total inability to speak."
Difficulty in speaking has been mentioned in follow-up of such patients
for months and even years, in one case up to 26 years after the stroke.
Using CT scan, Mohr *et al.* (1978), Naeser and Hayward (1978), Levine
and Mohr (1979), and Kertesz (1979) demonstrated that in cases with
severe Broca's aphasia, lesions extended beyond F_3 to adjacent cortical
and subcortical areas. In our four anatomically studied cases with severe
Broca's aphasia, cerebral infarction occupied a large portion of the
anterior language zone of the dominant left hemisphere involving the
posterior part of the third frontal gyrus and the insula in all four cases
and the Rolandic operculum in two. Subcortical structures and the
adjacent part of the corona radiata were also involved in all four cases.

A lesion of Broca's area extended to the adjacent cortical and the
deep subcortical structures in cases with severe Broca's aphasia. The
persistence of aphasia in such cases, as opposed to its transient character
in cases with an isolated lesion of Broca's area, may be explained by
the lack of compensatory function of the other structures in the language
zone, since those structures are damaged by the extended cerebral
lesion in the same hemisphere. Symmetrical parts of the opposite hemisphere do not seem to play a substantial role in language compensation
and recovery, since bilateral lesion of the Broca's area does not produce
a persistent aphasia (see Case 1, RA). This was also shown by Levine
and Mohr (1979) in the analysis of their four cases with bilateral destruction of Broca's area and the immediate environs. The severity of
the language disorder depended on the size of the frontoparietal lesion
in the dominant left hemisphere. A symmetrical lesion in the minor
hemisphere did not change the manifestation of the language disorder
and produced only a prominent dysarthria of pseudobulbar type.

On the other hand, destruction of the non-Broca's area in the anterior
language zone may result in a clinical picture of Broca's aphasia without
a lesion of the posterior F_3, especially if the cerebral infarct extends to
the posterior language zone, resulting in global aphasia, a combination
of severe Broca's and Wernicke's aphasia. Niessl von Mayendorf (1930)
described one such case. Severe Broca's aphasia was manifested by
embolophasia and deeply disturbed comprehension. A detailed, serial
anatomohistopathological examination revealed that although all the
frontal gyri in the left hemisphere were preserved, the infarction destroyed the gray and white matter of the Rolandic operculum, the
supramarginal and angular gyri, and almost all the first, second, and
third temporal gyri. In five of our eleven cases of global aphasia, Broca's
area was anatomically preserved. Histopathological examination of this
area revealed moderate changes in three cases and slight changes in
one case. Broca's area was completely preserved in our Case 10, DD,

with global aphasia. The autopsy showed (Fig. 4.1) that Broca's area, the Rolandic operculum, and the insula were preserved; two cerebral infarcts were revealed in the left hemisphere. One infarction destroyed the posterior first temporal gyrus, the angular gyrus, and part of the supramarginal gyrus with extension of the lesion to the lower sensory strip; another area of an old infarction with cyst formation was found in the middle motor strip, the posterior first and second frontal gyri. These data support the important role of non-Broca's areas of the anterior and posterior parts of the language zone in processing expressive speech. Therefore localization diagnosis has to take into account that Broca's area may sometimes be spared or only partially destroyed in patients with severe Broca's aphasia or global aphasia. On the other hand, isolated lesions of the pars opercularis in the third frontal gyrus of the dominant left hemisphere usually produces a transient, mild Broca's aphasia, mainly characterized by the disorder of word-finding, particularly finding the small functional words, and word-production disturbance; articulation ability is usually preserved in these cases.

The Rolandic Operculum (Area 43)
The important role played by the lesion in this area in the development of aphasia was postulated by Marie (1906a–c). He considered the Rolandic operculum a part of the "lenticular zone" (quadrilateral space) and included in this zone the corpus striatum, the internal capsule, and all the cortex of the insula, together with adjacent noninsular cortex, including the Rolandic operculum and the intra-Sylvian part of the supramarginal gyrus. According to Marie, lesions in this zone lead to "anarthria," characterized by articulatory disturbances. The clinical description of "anarthria" was vague, and clinical differentiation of slurring dysarthria from anarthria was not made. Marie stated that anarthria corresponded to the "subcortical motor aphasia" of Wernicke-Lichtheim, saying that a patient with anarthria "did not know how to speak," whereas a patient with pseudobulbar dysarthria "could not speak."

Niessl von Mayendorf (1911, 1930) stressed the importance of the Rolandic operculum in the development of articulatory disorder in his case of global aphasia with a large infarction in the anterior and posterior language zones in the left hemisphere. One of the destroyed areas was the Rolandic operculum; Broca's area was intact. A lesion of the Rolandic operculum was suggested by Kleist (1934) as a factor in what he termed "aphasic dysarthria." Luria (1947, 1966) stressed the role of the lesion in the lower part of the sensory strip and adjacent areas of the supramarginal gyrus in cases of what he called "afferent motor aphasia" with a predominant disorder of articulation. The first anatomically studied cases of aphasia with an isolated lesion of the Rolandic operculum were published only recently, however, by LeCours and Lhermitte (1976) and Tonkonogy and Goodglass (1981). LeCours and Lhermitte described a patient as having a "phonetic disintegration syndrome." The anatomohistopathological examination in this case revealed an infarction that destroyed the cortex of the middle and lower parts of the left motor strip as well as its immediate subcortex, including U-fibers to and from the second and third frontal gyri. The infarction extended to the insular cortex. The microscopic examination showed that the posterior part of F_3 was spared. Our case was characterized by dysprosody, slowness, and some deformation of articulation. An ischemic necrotic lesion of the lower part of the left motor strip and the anterior part of the Rolandic operculum was revealed at autopsy. In both cases, speech disorders related to the lesion of the Rolandic operculum were transient, just as in patients with an isolated lesion of the left Broca's area. The clinical picture of these speech disturbances was described as a nonslurring articulation disorder. Our patient (Case 6, DC) had altered speech sounds with omission of some distinctive features (predominantly voicing), as well as moderate word-finding difficulties. Both patients stuttered and had poor control of pitch, indications of motor dysprosody.

It is evident, therefore, that isolated destruction of the Rolandic operculum leads to the development of the transient articulation disorder that may be called articulation aphasia accompanied by motor dysprosody.

A lesion of the Rolandic operculum in the left hemisphere may be revealed in many cases with more severe Broca's and global aphasia. Such a lesion was present in all our eleven anatomically studied cases of global aphasia and in two of the four cases of severe Broca's aphasia. A lesion of the left Rolandic operculum is probably responsible for the development of the articulation disorder and the motor dysprosody in patients with Broca's or global aphasia, although this suggestion must be substantiated by further research.

Insula (Area 13 and Area 14)
Lesions of the insula have been recorded in many aphasia cases (Moutier 1908, Henshen 1920–22, Niessl von Mayendorf 1930, Goldstein 1948, Mohr *et al.* 1978, Levine and Mohr 1979, Brown 1979). The role of this lesion in the development of aphasia remains unclear; however, Wernicke (1874) and Lichtheim (1884) suggested that it is responsible for the development of conduction aphasia. More recently this type of aphasia has been attributed to a lesion of the middle-posterior region of the first temporal gyrus and supramarginal gyrus (Green and Howes 1977). Marie (1906c) included the insula in his "lenticular zone." Ac-

cording to Marie, a lesion of this zone leads to anarthria, an articulation disorder resembling the subcortical motor aphasia of Wernicke-Lichtheim. Niessl von Mayendorf (1930) considered the anterior insula a part of Broca's area, and Pick (1931) considered the posterior insular part of Wernicke's area. Goldstein (1948) raised the insula to central stage in "thought–speech transition" and attributed what he called "central aphasia," which resembles conduction or repetition aphasia, to a lesion of the insula. Nonetheless, there are no reliable anatomically studied cases of persistent or transient aphasia due to an insula lesion found in the literature. Brown, who reviewed this subject in 1979, noted only Rasmussen's personal communication about the development of a transient aphasia after surgical ablation of the left insula. He believed, however, that post-operative edema played an important part in such cases. Electrical stimulation of the insula did not cause speech arrest (Penfield and Roberts 1959), but Ojemann and Whitaker (1978) reported the development of dysphasia in a patient during stimulation of the left anterior insula.

It should be stressed that the insula is often involved in aphasia cases, and a lesion of the insula may well increase the severity and persistence of Broca's and possibly articulation aphasia. In all our four cases of severe Broca's aphasia, the insula was destroyed. A lesion of the Rolandic operculum was seen in two of the four cases, and Broca's area was spared in one case. In eleven cases of global aphasia, anatomical examination showed destruction of the insula in nine cases, of Broca's area in six cases, and of the Rolandic operculum in all eleven cases. A lesion of the insula in the left hemisphere occurred more often than did a lesion of Broca's area and as often as a lesion of the Rolandic operculum in our cases with severe Broca's and global aphasia. The insula was destroyed in one out of four of our anatomically studied cases of severe Wernicke's aphasia.

Posterior Part of the F_1 (Area 6, Including Supplementary Motor Area)
Cases of aphasia with lesions outside the posterior F_3 and posterior T_1 were described soon after the famous publications of Broca and Wernicke. In some cases the lesion occupied the superior-posterior part of the frontal lobe in the left dominant hemisphere. Magnan (1880) noted aphasia in a patient with destruction of the posterior F_1 and F_2 and two-thirds of the motor strip in the left hemisphere near a large parasagittal meningioma; the third frontal gyrus was preserved. Jackson (1882) published a case in which a tumor was found on the mesial surface of the left frontal lobe, which was characterized by paresis of the right leg and a transient episode of "speech loss" lasting three to four minutes. In a case described by Erickson and Woolsey (1951), a

meningioma on the mesial surface of the left frontal lobe produced Jacksonian seizures consisting of intermittent vocalization.

Liepmann and Maas (1907), Critchley (1930), Poppen (1939), and Nielsen (1946) described similar speech disorders in patients with cerebral vascular disease and destruction by an infarction or hemorrhage of the posterior-superior part of the left frontal lobe in the territory of the left anterior cerebral artery. In a case presented by Nielsen, a 46-year-old woman suddenly developed akinetic mutism and complete apathy. She lay on her bed without any movement but was conscious. The patient occasionally said, usually after energetic stimulation, one word: "water." Death due to bronchopneumonia occurred on the thirty-fourth day after the stroke onset. The autopsy showed a cerebral infarction in the left cingulate gyrus and the adjacent part of the corpus callosum.

These and similar cases remained unnoticed in the literature for decades until new data were published about the development of a transient speech disorder during electrostimulation of the posterior part of the mesial frontal lobe. Brickner (1940) was the first to describe speech arrest with stereotyped perseveration of "err, err, . . ." during electrostimulation of the area on the mesial surface of the left hemisphere, anterior to the motor leg area.

This reaction to electrostimulation of the various parts of the hemisphere was systematically studied by Penfield and his colleagues beginning in the early 1950s. They showed that there is a supplementary motor area in the upper part of the mesial surface of the hemisphere anterior to the motor leg area and to Vogt's area 6 α, β. Electrostimulation of this area produces unusual movements of the legs, a notable reaction of the autonomic nervous system, and abnormal phonation. The patient keeps on pronouncing an initial vowel or repeating the word he had started to say at the moment of stimulation. This cortical representation of phonation is bilateral; unilateral removal of one of the supplementary motor areas does not disturb phonation. Penfield and Roberts (1959) described an aphasia disorder during electrostimulation of the supplementary motor area in the left dominant hemisphere. A similar type of aphasic response was obtained by the electrostimulation of the classic aphasic areas, posterior F_3 and posterior T_1 in the left hemisphere.

These well-known experiments served to increase interest in the clinical study of speech disorder in patients with a lesion of the supplementary motor area. Petit-Dutaillis *et al.* (1954) and Botez (1962) described patients with a lesion of the superior-posterior part of the frontal lobe in the left, dominant hemisphere who had a speech disorder manifested by decreased speech activity and difficulty in initiating speech. Their comprehension as well as reading and writing abilities were preserved. Guidetti (1957), Rubens (1975), Alexander and Schmitt (1980), and Masdeau *et al.* (1978), on the other hand, noted in their patients with a lesion of the upper-posterior part of the frontal lobe in the left hemisphere the presence of some aphasic signs, including a mild or moderate degree of anomia, agraphia, and alexia as well as marked impairment of speech initiation. Most of the authors classified these speech disorders as instances of transcortical motor aphasia, or dynamic aphasia according to our scheme.

Localization of the lesion in the supplementary motor area has been anatomically and histopathologically proven in Case MC, published by Tonkonogy and Ageeva (1961), described in chapter 3 and in the case of Masdeau *et al.* (1978). In both cases, the lesion involved the mesial surface of the posterior F_1 in the left hemisphere. Therefore the lesion destroyed the supplementary motor area in the left hemisphere. The lesion also spread, however, to the adjacent part of the cingulate gyrus and the caudate nucleus in both cases.

In our two cases with dynamic aphasia, Case 7, MC, and Case 8, MA, the localization of the lesion in the supplementary motor area and adjacent part of the posterior F_1 in the left hemisphere has been anatomically and histopathologically proven. Similar cases have been described by Rubens (1975) and by Alexander and Schmitt (1980). Infarction in the territory of the left anterior cerebral artery was confirmed by an isotope brain scan in Rubens's case and with a CT scan in the case of Alexander and Schmitt. In both our anatomically studied cases, the lesion involved the mesial surface of the posterior F_1 in the left hemisphere. In Case 7, MC, however, the main site of cerbral infarction was the cingulate gyrus with spreading to the adjacent part of the posterior F_1. On the other hand, a large cerebral infarction destroyed the posterior part of the first frontal gyrus and the paracentral lobule of the left hemisphere in Case 8, MA, but spared the cingulate gyrus. General akinesia was a notable feature of Case 7, MC, with a lesion of the cingulate gyrus, but was absent from Case 8, MA, with a spared cingulate gyrus. Dynamic aphasia, a primary disorder of speech initiation, probably develops because of a lesion of the posterior part of the first frontal gyrus in the left hemisphere corresponding to the supplementary motor area. A lesion of the anterior part of the cingulate gyrus is probably responsible for the development of general akinesia with a secondary disorder of speech initiation.

Extension of the lesion toward the cingulate gyrus and the caudate nucleus usually increases the general akinesia and speech disturbance, whereas involvement of the posterior part of the convexital surface of the F_1 in the left hemisphere and especially expansion of the lesion to the posterior F_2 gives rise to the more noticeable aphasic components in this primarily akinetic speech disorder.

Signs of decreased speech activity are often noted in patients with Broca's and global aphasia, especially in the acute stage of stroke. Nonetheless, in our anatomically studied cases of global or severe Broca's aphasia a cerebral infarction extended to the caudal part of the second and first frontal gyri, including the mesial surface of the left frontal lobe in one (Case 17, VN) of 11 cases with global aphasia. The mesial surface of the left frontal lobe and cingulate gyri was also involved in two out of four anatomical cases of Broca's aphasia (Case 2, FN, and Case 5, CA). However, extension of the cerebral edema and similar pathological processes from the infarcted Broca's area, the insula, and the Rolandic operculum to the region of the supplementary motor area cannot be excluded, especially in the acute stage of stroke.

The posterior part of the second frontal gyrus (area 6) was described as an isolated center of writing by Exner (1881). Wernicke (1903) and Déjerine (1914) denied, however, that any isolated lesion of posterior F_2 in the left hemisphere resulted in agraphia. Henschen (1920–22) selected from the literature five cases of isolated agraphia with a lesion of the left posterior F_2 anterior to the arm representation in the motor strip in patients with motor agraphia and with a lesion of the angular gyrus in patients with sensory agraphia. The precise role played by the lesion in the posterior F_2 in the development of isolated agraphia remains unclear, since in most of the published cases of such agraphia the lesion extended to Broca's area and other adjacent regions of the frontal lobe, and Broca's aphasia was present in those cases with occasional secondary worsening of the agraphia. In our own Case 8, MA, the isolated lesion of the posterior F_2 with partial involvement of the posterior F_3 (Broca's area) in the left hemisphere did not produce agraphia.

In most of the cases with involvement of the left posterior F_2 and sparing of Broca's area, some degree of aphasia is present. This type of aphasia has been considered a dynamic or "transcortical motor aphasia" (Kleist 1934; Luria 1947, 1966; Penfield and Roberts 1959). Electrical stimulation of the left posterior F_2 has also produced an aphasic type of response, according to Penfield and Roberts (1959). They considered it an indirect involvement of the adjacent posterior F_3 due to the spreading of electrical excitation from the stimulated area of the posterior F_2, although this question requires further study.

Infarction in the Posterior Language Zone and Aphasia

This zone in the dominant left hemisphere includes the middle and

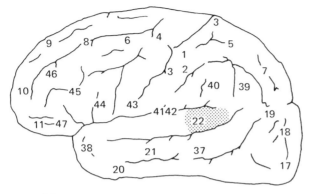

Figure 7.3
Transient Wernicke's aphasia. Small cerebral infarction in the posterior part of the first temporal gyrus of the left hemisphere.

posterior part of the first, second, and third temporal gyri, Heschl's gyri, and the inferior parietal lobule, with the supramarginal and angular gyri. The nuclear region of the posterior language zone is situated in the posterior part of T_1 of Wernicke's area and in the adjacent areas of the middle T_1, Heschl's gyri, the posterior T_2, and the angular gyri. A lesion of this region is responsible for the development of the language disorder in most of the patients with posterior aphasia.

Posterior Part of the First Temporal Gyrus (Area 22)
Wernicke (1874) was the first to describe sensory aphasia in cases with a lesion of the posterior T_1 in the left hemisphere. That is why this area is often called Wernicke's area. Three of Wernicke's ten cases were anatomically studied; the autopsy showed a diffuse generalized cortical atrophy in two cases as well as a lesion of the adjacent area of T_2 in one case. In these three cases, just as in Broca's cases, the lesion was not confined to the posterior T_1. No author, however, has seriously challenged the role of the lesion in the posterior T_1 in the development of Wernicke's aphasia, as has been done with Broca's area and Broca's aphasia. Nonetheless, in our own experience, a small lesion restricted to the posterior T_1 produced only a transient Wernicke's aphasia (Case 9, KZ, chapter 4) (Fig. 7.3). On the other hand, a cerebral infarction of the posterior T_1 extended to the other temporal and parietal region of the left hemisphere (Fig. 7.4) in all our three cases with persistent severe or moderate Wernicke's aphasia (Case 10, DD; Case 11, NE; Case 12, GV). Hopf (1957) presented a detailed serial anatomical and histopathological study of 17 cases of various types of posterior aphasia. In four cases of Wernicke's aphasia the lesion extended from the posterior

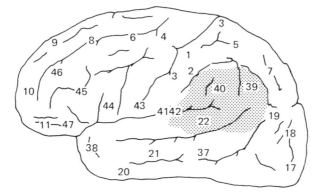

Figure 7.4
Severe Wernicke's aphasia. Localization of the large infarcts in the posterior language zone of the left hemisphere.

T_1 in the left hemisphere to the caudal part of T_2 and to Heschl's transversal gyri.

A crucial role in the development of Wernicke's aphasia has to be attributed to the posterior T_1 in the left hemisphere, since Wernicke's aphasia has not been described in cases without a lesion of that area. The role of the lesion in the adjacent part of the posterior language zone in Wernicke's aphasia must be studied further, especially because Wernicke's aphasia includes a large spectrum of language disorders, such as anomia, logorrhea, "word salad," verbal paraphasia, prevalence of small functional words, disturbance of the auditory component in phonological analysis, alienation of word meaning, etc. It is difficult to explain all these symptoms only as manifestations of the disorder related to a lesion of the one cytoarchitectonically homogenized part of Brodmann's area 22 in the left hemisphere.

Middle Part of the First Temporal Gyrus (Area 22)
A unilateral lesion of this area in the left hemisphere has been considered responsible for the development of conduction or repetition aphasia. As in Wernicke's or Broca's aphasia, no persistent aphasia has been described in cases with an isolated lesion of the middle T_1 in the left hemisphere, and the lesion often extends to Heschl's gyri or further to the adjacent area of the inferior parietal lobule. Hopf (1957) described an incomplete lesion of the caudal half of the T_1 and Heschl's gyri in his four anatomically studied cases of what he called "conduction" aphasia. Hopf considered this aphasia a stage of recovery from Wernicke's aphasia. One of our two anatomically studied cases of repetition

aphasia resulted from a cerebral infarction in the middle part of the T_1 with extension to Heschl's gyri in the left hemisphere, so that the lesion site was congruent with the lesion in Hopf's cases. In our second case of repetition aphasia, a small encapsulated hemorrhage was noted in the white matter of the middle T_1 in the left hemisphere. Edema and compression of the adjacent areas played a more prominent role in this case. A bilateral lesion of the middle T_1 has been described in cases with phonemic-sensory aphasia or "word deafness" (Henschen 1920–22, Kleist 1934, Brain 1965). This lesion was partly extended to the adjacent Heschl's gyri in most of the cases. In our own case of phonemic-sensory aphasia (Case 14, RL) autopsy showed a bilateral infarction in the middle T_1 with involvement of the anterior part of Heschl's gyri in the left hemisphere and complete destruction of Heschl's gyri in the right hemisphere.

Heschl's Transverse Gyri (Area 41 and Area 42)
These gyri are primarily projection areas of the auditory pathway to the temporal cortex. They occupy the inner surface of the temporal lobes deep in the Sylvian fissure. A bilateral lesion of Heschl's gyri does not produce any noticeable changes in the elementary auditory function, and an audiogram of patients with such a lesion does not markedly differ from that of a matched control group (Lemoyne and Mahoudeau 1959, Tonkonogy 1973). Recognition of individual phonemes and of syllables, however, may be markedly disturbed, and the syndrome of "word deafness" or phonemic-sensory aphasia has been described in cases with a bilateral lesion of the middle T_1 and the adjacent part of Heschl's gyri. An isolated unilateral lesion of Heschl's gyri in the left hemisphere does not usually produce a persistent, severe syndrome of phonemic-sensory aphasia, but in cases with severe Wernicke's aphasia, extension of the lesion in the left hemisphere from the posterior to the middle T_1 and Heschl's gyri often produces a striking disorder of recognition and repetition of single phonemes and syllables, just as in cases with phonemic-sensory aphasia or "word deafness." In our Case 10, DD, single-phoneme recognition and repetition was disturbed, but Heschl's gyri were preserved. Probably the disorder of single-phoneme recognition in that case developed because of the extension of the posterior T_1 lesion to the middle T_1. A lesion of Heschl's gyri may be partly responsible for the development of nonverbal auditory agnosia, sensory aprosody, and gesture agnosia, especially in cases with bilateral damage of these gyri. At the same time, no sign of aphasia is present in many patients with nonverbal auditory agnosia; the cause of this discrepancy remains unclear.

Caudal Half of the Second and Third Temporal Gyri (Area 21 and Area 37)

Anomic-sensory aphasia develops in patients with a lesion of these areas in the left, dominant hemisphere. Localization of the lesion in this region in cases with a similar aphasia syndrome has been shown by Hopf (1957), Luria (1947, 1966), and Kertesz *et al.* (1982). In cases with a lesion adjacent to the posterior T_1, anomic-sensory aphasia resembles Wernicke's aphasia by reason of the prominent disorder of expressive speech with marked verbal paraphasia and predominance of small functional words. Comprehension is also severely impaired. At the same time, phonological analysis, differentiation, recognition, and repetition of phonemes and words remains mildly disturbed in anomic-sensory aphasia, so that the term "transcortical sensory aphasia" has been used to describe such cases by many authors (Geschwind *et al.* 1968, Benson and Geschwind 1976, Goodglass and Kaplan 1983, Whitaker 1976, Albert *et al.* 1981). A similar clinical picture was present in our Case 15, RR, with an infarction in the white matter of the posterior T_1 and posterior T_2 as well as in the white and partly in the gray matter of the angular gyrus in the left hemisphere. Nonetheless, if a lesion of the caudal half of T_2 and T_3 exists at the same distance from the posterior T_1, the components of Wernicke's aphasia are less prominent, and anomia with alienation of word meaning represents the major clinical manifestation of aphasia. Our Case 16, GN, with a lesion of the middle-posterior part of the hippocampal and parahippocampal gyri adjacent to the caudal half of the third temporal gyri in the left hemisphere is an example of this type.

Supramarginal Gyrus (Area 40)

No major types of aphasia have been attributed to lesions of this area. Extension of the lesion in the middle part of the first temporal gyrus to the supramarginal gyrus of the dominant, left hemisphere was noted, however, in many cases of conduction or repetition aphasia (Green and Howes 1977). On the other hand, Luria (1947, 1966) stressed the involvement of the lower sensory strip and the adjacent part of the supramarginal gyri in the development of what he called afferent motor aphasia, resembling aphemia or articulation aphasia. Head (1926) postulated the more independent role of the supramarginal gyrus and suggested that its lesion in the left hemisphere produced semantic aphasia in his patients with sequelae of a head injury during World War I. Therefore quite different types of anterior and posterior aphasia have been described in some connection with a lesion of area 40 in the left hemisphere. A lesion of this area was also revealed in all but one of our anatomical cases of global aphasia. Possibly apraxia of articulation in articulation aphasia and literal paraphasis in repetition aphasia somehow relate to a lesion of the supramarginal gyrus, since this region is well known for its role in the development of ideomotor apraxia, and some authors believe that a lesion of this area and the lower sensory strip in the left hemisphere produces afferent motor apraxia and the corresponding syndrome of afferent motor aphasia (Luria 1947, 1966). However, no reliable cases of aphasia with an isolated lesion of the supramarginal gyrus have been published, and the role of the lesion in this area in the development of aphasia still has to be clarified.

Angular Gyrus (Area 39)

A lesion of this area does not produce any major aphasia syndrome. Anomia and anomic-spatial or semantic aphasia are probably related to this lesion site, however. Language disorders in patients with a lesion of the angular gyrus in the left hemisphere are characterized by a severe disorder of naming as well as alienation of word meaning for body parts and space-time relationship, called semantic aphasia by Head (1926) and Luria (1940, 1947, 1966), or anomic-spatial aphasia according to our classification. A lesion of the supramarginal gyrus also has to be suggested in such cases, and the relative role of damage of area 39 and area 40 is still unclear, especially because most of the authors do not even recognize the existence of a specific disorder of the space-time relationship in the language.

A lesion of the posterior T_1 often extends to the adjacent part of the angular gyrus in cases of Wernicke's aphasia. This extension may be easily missed, since the borderline between posterior T_1 and the angular gyrus is not clearly marked on the surface of the hemisphere. Such destruction of the angular gyrus is probably a factor in causing severe alexia and agraphia in some patients with Wernicke's aphasia because damage of area 39 is a main cause of the syndrome called "alexia with agraphia."

Cerebral Dominance and Localization Diagnosis in Aphasia

Cerebral Dominance for Language and Movement in Right-Handers

Various aphasia syndromes result from a left-hemisphere lesion in almost all right-handed persons. Benson and Geschwind (1976) noted that more than 99% of right-handed patients developed aphasia after a left-hemisphere lesion. Ettlinger *et al.* (1955) reviewed 15 published cases of aphasia in right-handed persons with a lesion of the right hemisphere. A personal and family history of left-handedness was found in 13 out of 15 cases, and the authors came to the conclusion that some degree of ambidexterity had to be suggested in those 13 cases. Cerebral dominance for language and handedness is believed to coincide in almost all right-handed persons (Boller 1973, Boller et al. 1977).

Dissociation of cerebral dominance for language and movement in left-handers occurs in approximately half of aphasia cases. In their famous paper, Goodglass and Quadfasel (1954) reviewed 110 cases from the literature and 13 original cases of left-handed persons with unilateral hemisphere lesion and aphasia. They found that a lesion of the left hemisphere resulted in aphasia in 53% of the cases. Aphasia was produced by a right-hemisphere lesion in 47% of the left-handed patients. Albert et al. (1981) stated that their review of several series showed that 20–30% of left-handed persons with aphasia had a right-hemisphere lesion. A left-hemisphere lesion results in aphasia in more than 50% of left-handed persons with aphasia (Goodglass and Quadfasel 1954, Luria 1966, Hécaen and Albert 1978, Albert and Obler 1978).

Many of these authors suggested that language has a bilateral representation in left-handed persons and that this (language ambidexterity) led to the development of a milder and less persistent aphasia in left-handed patients because of the compensatory role of the spared language zone in the opposite hemisphere. On the other hand, aphasia due to a unilateral lesion of the right hemisphere is rarely noted in right-handed patients.

Anatomical Asymmetries and Cerebral Dominance
Functional dominance of the hemispheres for language and movement may be related to underlying anatomical asymmetries of each hemisphere; the search for such asymmetries was begun early in the study of cerebral dominance. Progress in this study has been made only within the last 10 to 15 years, however. Certain asymmetries in the planum temporale mentioned by Pfeiffer (1936) were carefully studied by Geschwind and Levitsky (1968). The planum temporale, the cortical area bound anteriorly by Heschl's gyri and posteriorly by the caudal end of the Sylvian fissure, was found by Geschwind and Levitsky (1968) to be larger on the left side in 65 out of 100 adult brains, equal in 24 brains, and larger on the right in 11 brains. The left planum was five or more times larger than the right planum in some cases. The planum asymmetry seems to be inborn, since this asymmetry is present in the fetus and in the newborn (Wada 1969, Chi et al. 1977). The role of this asymmetry may be better appreciated in view of the fact that the planum temporale represents the area of the auditory association cortex (Galaburda and Sanides 1980, Galaburda and Pandya 1982). Galaburda et al. (1978) speculated that the planum asymmetries may

reflect cytoarchitectonic asymmetries in the auditory association cortex. The authors used the cytoarchitectonic method for mapping and measuring that area (Tpt) in the right and left hemispheres in four brains from the Yakovlev collection. This area occupies the posterolateral portion of the planum and extends to the posterior half of the first temporal gyrus corresponding to Brodmann's area 22 and Economo's and Koskinas' area TA. In some specimens the Tpt area also spreads to the posterior end of the Sylvian fissure and onto the parietal lobe. Galaburda *et al.* found the larger volume of the Tpt area in the left hemisphere in all four cases. They showed that the size of the asymmetries matched that of planum asymmetries. The size of the planum temporale thus may reflect the difference of asymmetries in the volume of the corresponding cytoarchitectonic areas in the association auditory cortex representing the anatomical substrate of language function. Unfortunately, lesions of the planum temporale did not draw the attention of aphasia researchers in the past, and anatomical and histopathological descriptions of this area are absent from most published aphasia cases. In cases of Wernicke's aphasia the lesion of Wernicke's area in the posterior part of the first temporal gyrus often spreads to the adjacent planum temporale. Since Geschwind and Levitsky (1968) and others have shown distinct hemisphere asymmetry in this area, it is evident that this area deserves further intensive study.

On the other hand, when studying amusia and sensory aprosody one has to take into account that the right superior planum temporale often contains a second transverse gyrus, whereas a single transverse gyrus is usually observed in the left hemisphere (Galaburda *et al.* 1978). Architectonic asymmetry has also been noted in the anterior language zone. Galaburda (1980) studied the pigmentoarchitectonic area in the pars opercularis of the third frontal gyrus (Brodmann's area 44) in 10 adult and juvenile brains. This area is characterized by the peculiar clumping of lipofuscin in the cytoplasm of the large pyramidal cells. The author noted that the pigmentoarchitectonic area, lying over most of area 44, was larger on the left in nine out of ten brains, including six specimens with the pigmentoarchitectonic area larger by more than 30% on the left. The existence of hemisphere asymmetries has been shown by angiographic and CT scan studies, with special emphasis on the relationship between distribution of asymmetry and hand preference. Using angiographic criteria to compare the length of the left and right Sylvian fissures, LeMay and Culebras (1972) and Hochberg and LeMay (1975) observed that the left Sylvian fissure is longer in 67% and shorter in 8% of right-handed persons. Sylvian fissures were symmetrical in 71.5% of left-handed persons. Furthermore, Ratcliff *et al.* (1980) showed more prominent Sylvian asymmetry in 39 out of 50 patients with dominant left hemisphere demonstrated by the Wada test.

LeMay and Kido (1978) measured Polaroid images of CT studies of 80 right-handed and 85 left-handed persons. The plane of scanning was about 20° above the orbitomeatal line. The authors found that the left occipital pole is wider in 71% of right-handed persons and protrudes more posteriorly than the right pole in 75% of right-handed patients. The right frontal region is wider than the left in 58% of right-handed persons and equal in another 30%. In left-handed persons almost equal distribution was found between the patients with wider right occipital regions (32%), left occipital regions (34%), and equal width of the occipital region (34%). Nonetheless, the correlation between CT scan asymmetry and handedness was not observed by Chui and Damasio (1980). This discrepancy in the results of the two similar studies may be partly explained by the difference in the scanning angle of the two studies, above 20° in LeMay and Kido's study and 15° in that of Chui and Damasio. On the other hand, Koff et al. (1984) noted a greater width of the left occipital regions in most patients whether they were right-handed or left-handed.

8

Aphasia Syndromes and Vascular Pathology

The type and extent of the brain pathology play a substantial role in the development and clinical course of the aphasia syndromes. The amount of edema surrounding the lesion, the rate of development of brain pathology, the degree of generalization of the pathological process, and other factors may be related to the particular manifestation and persistence of the aphasia syndrome. For example, severe edema around the lesion in the dominant, left hemisphere may precipitate the development of aphasia in persons with hemorrhage deep in the subcortical structures some distance from the cortical areas of the language zone. Aphasia tends to be more severe and persistent in persons with a diffuse cerebral atrophy in addition to an infarction within the cerebral language zone. The rate of development of the pathological processes may also influence the evolution of aphasia syndromes. In patients with tumors the brain lesion grows more slowly than does brain-tissue softening in cerebral infarction or destruction and compression of that tissue in cerebral hemorrhage, and function of the destroyed language area seems to be more easily compensated for in patients with cerebral tumor compared with those with acute vascular pathology. That is why the same size and site of a tumor may result in a milder aphasia syndrome in one case than in another.

Vascular Supply of the Language Zone

The vascular supply of the anterior and posterior language zone is provided by the left middle cerebral artery. The left anterior cerebral artery is only partly responsible for the blood supply of the anterior part of the language zone, nourishing the posterior part of the first frontal gyrus on the convexital and mesial surface of the hemisphere.

The posterior cerebral artery supplies the inferior temporal gyrus, a part of the posterior language zone.

The middle cerebral artery is the direct continuation of the internal carotid artery. Subcortical branches of the middle cerebral artery (Fig.

8.1) include the lenticulostriate arteries. These arteries supply the putamen, the lateral part of the globus pallidus, the anterior limb of the internal capsule, and the caudate nucleus, except for its head and tail. The corpus striatum and the internal capsule are partly supplied by the medial striate artery of Heubner, arising from the anterior cerebral artery. Heubner's artery nourishes the rostroventral part of the head of the caudate nucleus and adjacent portions of the putamen and internal capsule.

In the anterior language zone, cortical branches of the left middle cerebral artery (Fig. 8.1) supply the third and the second frontal gyri, and the lower two-thirds of the motor and sensory strips (Fig. 8.2). The orbitofrontal artery nourishes the pars triangularis and the anterior half of the pars opercularis of the inferior frontal gyrus as well as the anterior part of the middle frontal gyrus. The precentral or pre-Rolandic artery supplies the posterior portion of the pars opercularis of the third frontal gyrus and the anterior half of the lower two-thirds of the precentral gyrus. The central or Rolandic artery nourishes the lower two-thirds of the motor and sensory strips in areas adjacent to the Rolandic sulcus. The anterior parietal or post central artery supplies the lower two-thirds of the posterior half of the sensory strip and the anterior portion of the supramarginal gyrus.

The temporal and posterior parietal branches of the left middle cerebral artery nourish the posterior language zone. The anterior temporal artery supplies the anterior third of the first and second temporal gyri and the temporal pole. The posterior temporal artery provides the blood supply to the middle and posterior portions of the superior and middle temporal gyri. The posterior or inferior parietal artery nourishes the supramarginal gyrus and the lower part of the upper parietal lobule, extending caudally to supply the anterior part of the superior occipital gyrus. The artery supplies the angular gyrus and in some patients also the anterior part of the lateral occipital gyrus.

Branches of the anterior cerebral artery nourish the posterior part of the first frontal gyrus and are partly responsible for the blood supply of the anterior language zone. Thus the blood supply of the cortical language area may be provided by two branches of the middle cerebral artery, and each of these branches also nourishes a part of another language area, i.e., the pars opercularis of the third frontal gyrus receives its supply from the orbitofrontal and precentral arteries, and the lower part of the motor strip is supplied by the precentral and central arteries. On the other hand, the posterior temporal artery supplies at least three of the posterior language areas, including the posterior part of the first temporal gyrus, the middle part of the same gyrus, and the posterior part of the second temporal gyrus. Probably because of these peculiarities

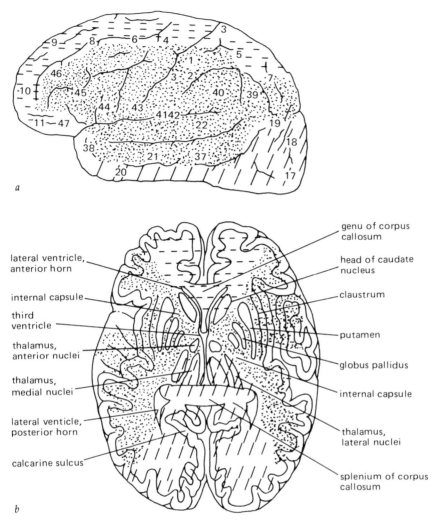

Figure 8.1
The vascular supply of the cerebral hemispheres: middle cerebral artery (dots), anterior
cerebral artery (dashes), posterior cerebral artery (slashes).

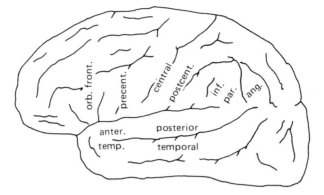

Figure 8.2
The blood supply of the cortical language zone in the left hemisphere by branches of
the middle cerebral artery.

of cerebral blood supply, a cerebral infarction seldom occurs in one
language area alone, and most aphasia syndromes develop in patients
with an overlapped infarction of two or three language areas.

Types of Vascular Pathology and Aphasia Syndromes

These extensive cerebral infarcts frequently occur in cases of occlusion
and stenosis of the left internal carotid artery or the left middle cerebral
artery. Thrombosis of the carotid arteries of the neck may be asymptomatic in 10–15% of cases. In many patients, however, a large cerebral
cortical and subcortical infarction develops after extracranial and especially intracranial thrombosis of the internal carotid artery. This infarction usually involves the territory of the middle cerebral artery. The
region nourished by the anterior cerebral artery is less often involved,
since it may have a collateral blood supply from the carotid artery of
the opposite side through the anterior communicating artery. Stenosis
of the internal carotid artery often leads to a less extensive cerebral
infarction, resulting from the emboli produced by the ulcerated atherosclerotic plaques in the wall of the stenotic carotid artery. Those
emboli also cause repeated transient ischemic attacks. In some cases
stenosis of the carotid arteries may be completely asymptomatic for
many years.

Thrombosis and stenosis of the middle cerebral artery lead to the
development of cerebral infarcts varying in their site and size. Such
infarcts may involve an entire region supplied by the middle cerebral
artery or be confined to one or two branches of this artery. Thrombosis

of individual arteries branching from the middle or anterior cerebral arteries produces a small cerebral infarction in approximately 20–25% of patients. Aphasia is often transient in such cases and may pass unnoticed if the patient is evaluated only two or three months after the stroke onset.

Cerebral hemorrhage resulting in aphasia usually occurs in the subcortical structures and deep white matter of the left hemisphere. A hemorrhagic stroke seldom occurs in the cortex and rarely produces aphasia. In patients with subcortical hemorrhage aphasia mainly results from the extension of the edema to the cortical language areas. The role of the subcortical speech disorder cannot be excluded as an additional component in the clinical picture of cortical aphasia.

Global Aphasia
In cases of cerebral infarction, a thrombotic occlusion of the left internal carotid artery often leads to the development of global aphasia because of great destruction of the cortical and subcortical structures in the left hemisphere, mainly in the territory of the left middle cerebral artery (Fig. 8.3). This cerebral infarction extends to the territory of the left anterior cerebral artery in some cases. Thrombosis with complete occlusion of the left internal carotid artery was noted in seven out of our ten cases of global aphasia studied anatomically. Marked narrowing of the lumen by the thrombus in the left internal carotid artery was seen in one of these ten cases. The carotid arteries were extended, enlarged, and twisted in Case 10, DD, with development of Wernicke's aphasia followed by global aphasia. The pathology of the left carotid artery was slight in one of the ten cases of global aphasia. Angiographic examination by Stolyarova (1973) showed a high percentage of occlusion of the left internal carotid artery (7 out of 22 cases of global aphasia) and the stem of the left middle cerebral artery (13 of the 22 cases). Stenosis of the left internal carotid artery was revealed only in only 2 of these 22 patients. More frequent thrombotic occlusion of the left internal carotid artery compared with the occlusion of the left middle cerebral artery in our anatomically studied cases may be related to the high level of mortality caused by the acute thrombotic occlusion to the carotid arteries in our cases. Angiography, however, seems to indicate more realistically the distribution of vessel pathology in patients with global aphasia. Both autopsy and angiography revealed complete occlusion of the main arteries supplying the left hemisphere in most of the patients with global aphasia. Such occlusions seem to be distributed between the left internal carotid and middle cerebral arteries, with most patients having occlusion of the stem of the middle cerebral artery.

Global aphasia may also result from cerebral hemorrhage in the

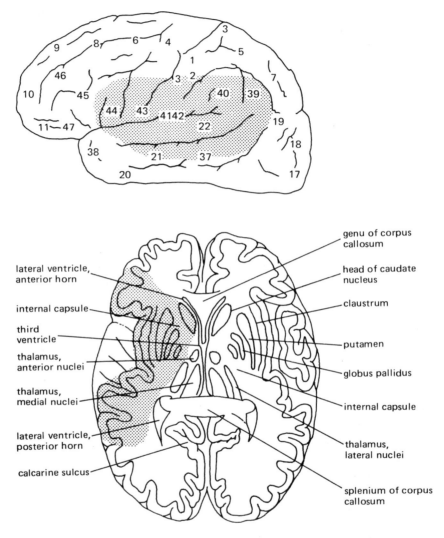

Figure 8.3
Global aphasia. Localization of the large cortical-subcortical infarcts in the left hemisphere.

subcortical structures of the left hemisphere (see chapter 6). In patients with hypertension the source of such hemorrhage is often the putaminal artery, which Charcot called the "hemorrhagic artery," a branch of the middle cerebral artery; this hemorrhage destroys the putamen, the globus pallidus, the external and the extreme capsules, the claustrum, and the adjacent white matter of the left hemisphere in the frontal, partietal, or temporal lobe. Cortical areas are not directly involved by this subcortical hemorrhage. Aphasia development in those cases is mainly related to the edema spreading from the subcortical focus of the hemorrhage to the cortical language zone. The role of direct damage to the subcortical structures cannot be excluded, since this destruction may be responsible for the development of such components of notable aphasia syndromes as aphonia, severe dysarthria, and dysprosody. In patients under 40 years of age a cerebral hemorrhage producing global aphasia usually results from an arteriovenous malformation of a ruptured aneurysm in the white matter of the left hemisphere. Another source of cerebral hemorrhage may be the thalamic arteries from the vertebrobasilar vascular system.

In three of our cases of global aphasia due to cerebral hemorrhage, a lateral striatal hemorrhage was revealed in two cases and a mixed striatal–thalamic hemorrhage in one case, that of a left-handed patient whose hemorrhage was in the right hemisphere (Case 31, KC).

Stolyarova (1973) showed in 16 anatomically studied cases with "hemorrhagic" global aphasia that a cerebral hemorrhage destroyed the subcortical structures in 15 cases, the deep white matter of the frontal lobe in 7 cases, of the parietal lobe in 7 cases, and of the temporal lobe in 8 cases. Global aphasia develops less often and language disorders are usually transient in cases with deeper localization of hemorrhage (the thalamus and the internal capsule). A relatively persistent global aphasia develops in cases with large striatal or striatal–thalamic hemorrhages. If the patient survives the acute stage, he or she may have good or even complete speech recovery two to three months later. In cases of global aphasia with deeper restricted hemorrhages, striking speech recovery may be noted in the first day or two after the stroke onset. Surgical removal of the hematoma often increases the survival rate. Global aphasia, however, tends to persist for a long time after surgery. An almost complete recovery was observed by Stolyarova in 16 out of 23 such cases without surgery and in 4 out of 11 cases with surgical removal of the hemorrhage of the left hemisphere.

Anterior Aphasia and Mixed Nonglobal Aphasia
A complete occlusion of the left internal carotid artery occurs less frequently in patients with Broca's aphasia than in those with global

aphasia. Broca's aphasia may also be observed in approximately as many patients with thrombosis of the stem of the left middle cerebral artery and stenosis of the left internal carotid artery. Stolyarova (1973) presented the following distribution of 15 cases of Broca's aphasia as observed with angiography: Six cases had occlusion, and five cases had stenosis of the left internal carotid artery; four cases had occlusion of the left middle cerebral artery. The autopsy in our own seven anatomically studied cases of Broca's aphasia showed a complete thrombotic occlusion of the left internal carotid artery in two cases, stenosis of this artery in three cases, thrombotic occlusion of the left middle cerebral artery in one case, and severe atherosclerotic stenosis of this artery in one case.

The same distribution of vascular pathology (thrombotic occlusion of the left internal carotid or middle cerebral arteries and stenosis of the left internal carotid artery) occurs in patients with dynamic aphasia, especially in the chronic stage of stroke, since such patients may appear to have global or severe Broca's aphasia in the first one or two months after stroke onset. Angiographic data showed that nine cases of dynamic aphasia included three cases with occlusion and three cases with stenosis of the left internal carotid artery, and three cases with occlusion of the left middle cerebral artery (Stolyarova 1973).

Mixed nonglobal aphasia is relatively seldom related to cerebral infarction and may be observed in all aforementioned types of vascular pathology, probably more frequently in patients with stenosis of the left internal carotid artery.

On the other hand, cerebral hemorrhage in the left hemisphere produces mixed nonglobal aphasia more often than Broca's or any other anterior aphasia. Stolyarova described deep limited striatal or striatal-thalamic hemorrhages in all six anatomically studied cases of mixed nonglobal aphasia and in three cases of Broca's aphasia.

Posterior Aphasia

In patients with anomic-sensory or repetition aphasia, thrombotic occlusion of the left internal carotid artery does not occur, at least according to our anatomical and Stolyarova's angiographic data. A stenosis of the internal carotid artery seems to occur more often in patients with Wernicke's aphasia. Such stenosis was revealed in three out of four of our anatomically studied cases and in five out of seven cases with Wernicke's aphasia studied by angiography. An occlusion of the left middle cerebral artery was found on an angiogram in two out of seven cases of Wernicke's aphasia. Stenosis of the left internal carotid artery may also be noted in patients with anomic-sensory aphasia. In one of our anatomically studied cases (Case 16, GN), anomic-sensory aphasia developed after thrombotic occlusion of the left posterior cerebral artery with cerebral infarction in the base of the left occipital and temporal lobes.

The fact that there is no occlusion of the left internal carotid artery in patients with posterior aphasia may be explained by the compensatory role of the cerebral circulation from the posterior vertebrobasilar arterial system through the left posterior cerebral artery. Patients with posterior aphasia, however, often have a stenosis of the left internal carotid artery. Another explanation is related to the development of the large cortico–subcortical cerebral infarcts in cases with left carotid occlusion, so that mixed and anterior aphasia is covering, effacing a clinical manifestation of the single posterior aphasia.

Posterior aphasia in patients with cerebral hemorrhage is rare. No case of posterior aphasia was described by Stolyarova out of 25 anatomically studied cases of aphasia due to cerebral hemorrhage. One of our four cases of repetition aphasia resulted from a small hemorrhage in the middle part of the left superior temporal gyrus (see Case 13, LE, in chapter 4). This patient died after a second large hemorrhage in the subcortical structures and the white matter of the left hemisphere. Those small hemorrhages had probably been missed in the pre-CT scan era, since the death rate in such cases is relatively low compared with that in patients with large subcortical hemorrhages. Even with the advantages of the CT scan, it is unlikely that the number of described cases of posterior aphasia with cerebral hemorrhage will sharply increase, because anatomical data have clearly shown over many years of stroke study that hemorrhages in the cortical gray and white matter developed in only a few cases of CVA, and that the vast majority of the cerebral hemorrhages occurred in the subcortical structures and adjacent white matter of the hemispheres.

There is no occlusion or stenosis of the left internal carotid artery or left middle cerebral artery in approximately one-fifth to one-fourth of the cases of global, anterior, or posterior aphasia. Embolic occlusion of the cortical and subcortical branches of the left middle cerebral artery is present in such cases. The cardiac source of emboli may be responsible for such stroke development in patients with atrial fibrillation. Ulcerated atherosclerotic plaques in the wall of the carotid arteries have also been considered by some authors as a possible source of repeated cerebral embolization.

References

Adams, R. D., and M. Victor, 1981. *Principles of Neurology*. New York: McGraw-Hill Book Company, 2nd edition.

Ajuriaguerra, J. de, and H. Hécaen, 1949. *Le Cortex Cérébral*. Paris: Masson.

Alajouanine, T., and F. Lhermitte, 1964. Les Composantes Phonémiques et Sémantiques de la Jargonaphasie. *Intern. J. Neurol.* 4:277–286.

Alajouanine, T., T. A. Ombredane, and M. Durand, 1939. *Le Syndrôme de Désintegration Phonétique dans l'aphasie*. Paris: Masson.

Alajouanine, T., P. Pichot, and M. Durand, 1949. Dissociation des altérations phonétiques avec conservation relative de la langue ancienne dans un cas d'anarthrie pure chez un sujet français bilingue. *Éncephale* 28:245–246.

Alajouanine, T., O. Sabouraud, and B. de Ribaucourt, 1952. Le Jargon des Apasiques. *J. Psychol.* 45:158–180, 293–329.

Albert, M. L., and D. Bear, 1974. Time to understand. A case study of word deafness with reference to the role of time in auditory comprehension. *Brain* 97:383–394.

Albert, M. L., H. Goodglass, N. A. Helm, A. B. Rubens, and M. P. Alexander, 1981. *Clinical Aspects of Dysphasia*. Wien-New York: Springer-Verlag.

Albert, M. L., and L. K. Obler, 1978. *The Bilingual Brain: Neurolinguistic and Neuropsychological Aspects of Bilingualism*. New York: Academic Press.

Alexander, M. P., and S. R. LoVerme, 1980. Aphasia after left hemisphere intracerebral hemorrhage. *Neurology* 30:1193–1202.

Alexander, M. P., and M. A. Schmitt, 1980. The aphasia syndrome of stroke in the left anterior cerebral artery territory. *Arch. Neurol.* 37:97–100.

Auerbach, S. H., T. Allard, M. Naeser, M. P. Alexander, and M. L. Albert, 1982. Pure word deafness: Analysis of a case with bilateral lesions and a defect at the prephonemic level. *Brain* 105:271–300.

Balonov, L. Y., and V. L. Deglin, 1976. *Hearing and Speech of the Dominant and Non-Dominant Hemispheres* (in Russian). Leningrad: Nauka.

Baru, A. V., G. V. Gershuni, and J. M. Tonkonogy, 1964. Detection of tone signals of various duration in the diagnosis of temporal lobe lesions (in Russian). *Korsakoff's J. Neurol. Psychiat.* 4:481–486.

Baru, A., and T. Karaseva, 1972. *The Brain and Hearing: Hearing Disturbances Associated with Local Brain Lesions*. New York: Plenum Press.

Bastian, H. C., 1897. Some problems in connection with aphasia and other speech defects. *Lancet* 1:933–942, 1005–1017, 1132–1137, 1187–1194.

Bazhin, E. F., Y. A. Meerson, and J. M. Tonkonogy, 1973. On the peculiarities of probabilistic prognosis in some mental and nervous diseases (in Russian). *Korsakoff's J. Neurol. Psychiat.* 5:701–705.

Benson, D. F., 1979. *Aphasia, Alexia and Agraphia*. New York: Churchill Livingstone.

Benson, D. F., and N. Geschwind, 1976. The aphasias and related disturbances. In *Clinical Neurology*. A. B. Baker, L. H. Baker, eds., vol. 1, Hagerstown: Harper and Row, pp. 1–28.

Benson, D. F., W. A. Sheramata, R. Bouchard, J. M. Segarra, D. Price, and N. Geschwind, 1973. Conduction apahasia: A clinicopathological study. *Arch. Neurol.* 28:339–346.

Blumstein, J. E., 1973. *A Phonological Investigation of Aphasic Speech*. The Hague: Mouton.

Blumstein, J. E., E. Baker, and H. Goodglass, 1977. Phonological factors in auditory comprehension. *Neuropsychologia* 15:19–30.

Blumstein, J. E., and W. Cooper, 1974. Hemispheric processing of intonational contours. *Cortex* 10:146–158.

Boller, F., 1973. Destruction of Wernicke's area without language disturbance. A fresh look at crossed aphasia. *Neuropsychologia* 11:243–246.

Boller, F., M. Cole, P. B. Vrtunski, M. Patterson, and Y. Kim, 1979. Paralinguistic aspects of auditory comprehension in aphasia. *Brain Lang.* 7:164–174.

Boller, F., Y. Kim, and J. L. Mack, 1977. Auditory comprehension in aphasia. *Studies in Neurolinguistics*. H. Whitaker and H. A. Whitaker, eds., vol. 3. New York: Academic Press, pp. 1–63.

Botez, M. I., 1962. *Afazia si Sindroamele Corelate in Procesele Expansive Intracraniene* (in Rumanian). Bucarest: Ed. Acad. Rep. Popul. Romine.

Bradley, D. C., M. F. Garett, and E. B. Zurif, 1980. Syntactic deficit in Broca's aphasia. In *Biological Studies of Mental Processes*, D. Caplan, ed. Cambridge, MA: MIT Press, pp. 269–286.

Brain, W. R., 1965. *Speech Disorders*. London: Butterworths, 2nd edition.

Brickner, R. M., 1940. A human cortical area producing repetitive phenomena when stimulated. *J. Neurophysiol.* 3:128–130.

Broca, P., 1861a. Perte de la parole, ramollissement chronique et destruction partielle du lobe antérieur gauche du cerveau. *Bull. Soc. Anthr. Paris* 2:235–237.

Broca, P., 1861b. Remarques sur le siége de la faculté du langage articulé suivies d'une observation d'aphémie. *Bull. Soc. Anthr. Paris* 6:330–357.

Brown, J. W., 1972. *Aphasia, Apraxia and Agnosia*. Springfield, Ill.: Charles C. Thomas.

Brown, J. W., 1979. Language representation in brain. In *Neurobiology of Social Communication in Primates*, H. D. Stecklis and M. J. Raleigh, eds. New York: Academic Press, pp. 133–195.

Cairns, H., R. Oldfield, J. Pennybacker, and D. Whitteridge, 1941. Akinetic mutism with an epidermoid cyst of the third ventricle. *Brain* 64:273–277.

Caplan, D., 1981. On the cerebral localization of linguistic functions: Logical and empirical issues surrounding deficit analysis and functional localization. *Brain and Language* 14:120–137.

Caplan, L. R., 1980. Top of the basilar syndrome. *Neurology* 30:72–79.

Castaigne, P., A. Buge, J. Cambier, R. Escourolle, P. Brunet, and J. D. Degos, 1966. Démence thalamique d'origine vasculaire par ramolissement bilateral, limité au territoire du pédicule rétromamillaire. *Rev. Neurol.* 114:89–107.

Castaigne, P., F. Lhermitte, A. Buge, R. Escourolle, J. J. Hauw, and O. Lyon-Caen, 1981. Paramedian thalamus and midbrain infarcts: Clinical and neuropathological study. *Ann. Neurol.* 10:127–148.

Castaigne, P., F. Lhermitte, J. L. Signoret, and R. Albanet, 1980. Description et étude scannographique du cerveau de Leborgne. La découverte de Broca. *Rev. Neurol.* 136:563–583.

Chedru, F., V. Bastard, and R. Efron, 1978. Auditory micropattern discrimination in brain-damaged subjects. *Neuropsychol.* 16:141–149.

Chi, J. G., E. C. Dooling, and F. H. Gilles, 1977. Gyral development of the human brain. *Ann. Neurol.* 1:86–93.

Chui, H. C., and A. R. Damasio, 1980. Human cerebral asymmetries evaluated by computed tomography. *J. Neurol. Neurosurg. Psychiat.* 43:873–878.

Chusid, J. G., G. G. Gutierrez-Mahoney, and M. P. Margules-Lavergne, 1955. Speech disturbances in association with parasagittal frontal lesions. *J. Neurosurg.* 11:193–204.

Ciemins, V. A., 1970. Localized thalamic hemorrhage: A cause of aphasia. *Neurology* 20:776–779.

Comte, A., 1900. Des paralyses pseudo-bulbaires. Dissertation, 8, No. 436. Paris: Steinheil.

Critchley, M., 1930. The anterior cerebral artery and its syndromes. *Brain* 53:120–165.

Critchley, M., 1952. Articulatory defects in aphasia. *Laryngol. Otol.* 66:1–17.

Critchley, M., 1953. *The Parietal Lobes*. London: Arnold.

Daly, D., and J. Love, 1958. Akinetic mutism. *Neurology* 8:238–242.

Damasio, A. R., H. Damasio, M. Rizzo, N. Varney, and F. Gersh, 1982. Aphasia with non-hemorrhagic lesions in the basal ganglia and internal capsule. *Arch. Neurol.* 39:15–20.

Déjerine, J., 1908. Discussion sur l'aphasie. *Rev. Neurol.* 16:611, 974.

Déjerine, J., 1914. *Sémiologie des Affections du Système Nerveux*. Paris: Masson.

DeRenzi, E., A. Piecuro, and L. Vignolo, 1966. Oral apraxia and aphasia. *Cortex* 2:50–73.

DeWitt, L., A. Grek, J. P. Kistler, D. N. Levine, K. Davis, T. J. Brady, and F. Buonanno, 1984. Nuclear magnetic resonance imaging and neurobehavioral syndromes: Five illustrative cases. *Neurology* 34:88–188.

Dubois J., H. Hécaen, R. Angelergues, A. Maufras du Chatelier, and P. Marcie, 1964. Etude neurolinguistigue de l'aphasia de conduction. *Neuropsychologia* 2:9–44.

Erickson, T. C., and C. N. Woolsey, 1951. Observations on the supplementary motor area of man. *Trans. Amer. Neurol. Assoc.* 76:50–56.

Ettlinger, G., C. V. Jackson, and O. L. Zangwill, 1955. Dysphasia following right temporal lobectomi in a right-handed man. *J. Neurol. Neurosurg. Psychiat.* 18:214–217.

Exner, J., 1881. *Untersuchungen über die Lokalisation der Funktionen in der Grosshirnrinde des Menschen*. Wien: W. Braumüller.

Feigenberg, I. M., 1963. Probability prognosis in cerebral activity (in Russian). *Voprosy Psychologii* 2:59–67.

Fisher, C. M., 1965. Pure sensory stroke involving face, arm, and leg. *Neurology* 15:76–80.

Fisher, C. M., 1978. Thalamic pure sensory stroke: A pathologic study. *Neurology* 28:1141–1144.

Fisher, C. M., 1979. Capsular infarcts: The underlying vascular lesions. *Neurology* 36:65–73.

Foix, C., and M. Levy, 1927. Les ramolissements sylviens: syndrômes des lésions en foyer du territoire de l'artère sylvienne et de ses branches. *Rev. Neurol.* 2:1–51.

Frantsuz, A. G., J. M. Tonkonogy, and I. Y. Levin, 1964. Computer application in the differential diagnosis of aphasia (in Russian). *Korsakoff's J. Neurol. Psychiat.* 2:1759–1765.

Freud, S., 1891. *Für Auffassung der Aphasien*. Wien: Deuticke.

Freund, C., 1889. Über optische Aphasie und Seelenblindheit. *Arch. Psychiat. Nervenkr.* 20:276–297, 371–416.

Galaburda, A. M., 1980. La région de Broca: Observations anatomiques faites un siècle après la mort de son découvreur. *Rev. Neurol. Paris* 136:609–616.

Galaburda, A. M., M. LeMay, T. L. Kemper, and N. Geschwind, 1978. Right–left asymmetries in brain. *Science* 199:852–856.

Galaburda, A. M., and D. N. Pandya, 1982. Role of architectonics and connections in the study of primate brain evolution. In *Primate Brain Evolution: Methods and Concepts*, E. Armstrong and D. Falk, eds. New York: Plenum, pp. 203–216.

Galaburda, A. M., and F. Sanides, 1980. Cytoarchitectonic organization of the human auditory cortex. *J. Comp. Neurol.* 190:597–610.

Galaburda, A. M., F. Sanides, and N. Geschwind, 1978. Human brain: Cytoarchitectonic left–right asymmetries in the temporal speech region. *Arch. Neurol.* 35:812–817.

Gardner, H., M. L. Albert, and S. Weintraub, 1975. Comprehending a word: The influence of speed and redundancy on auditory comprehension in aphasia. *Cortex* 11:155–162.

Gershuni, G. V., A. V. Baru, T. A. Karaseva, and J. M. Tonkonogy, 1971. The role of the temporal lobe in perception of short auditory signals. In *Sensory Processes at the Neuronal and Behavioral Level*, G. V. Gershuni, ed. New York: Academic Press, pp. 287–300.

Gerstmann, J., 1924. Fingeragnosie: Eine umschriebene Störung der Orientierung am eigenen Körper. *Wien. Klin. Wschr.*, pp. 1010–1012.

Gerstmann, J., 1927. Fingeragnosie und isolierte Agraphie: Ein neues Syndrome. *Ztschr. Neurol. Psychiat.* 108:152–177.

Geschwind, N., 1965. Disconnexion syndromes in animals and man. *Brain* 88:237–294, 585–644.

Geschwind, N., and W. Levitsky, 1968. Human brain: Left–right asymmetries in temporal speech region. *Science* 161:186–187.

Geschwind, N., F. Quadfasel, and J. Segarra, 1968. Isolation of the speech area. *Neuropsychologia* 6:327–340.

Gleser, V. D., K. N. Dudkin, A. M. Kuperman, I. Leushina, A. A. Nevskaya, N. F. Podvigin, and N. V. Prasdnikova, 1975. *Visual Recognition and Its Pathophysiological Mechanisms*. Leningrad: Nauka.

Goldstein, K., 1927. Die Lokalisation in der Grosshirnrinde. *Handb. Norm. Pathol. Physiol.*, A. Bethe, ed. Berlin: Springer, vol. 10, pp. 600–842.

Goldstein, K., 1934. *Der Aufbau des Organismus*. The Hague: Mouton.

Goldstein, K., 1948. *Language and Language Disturbances*. New York: Grune and Stratton.

Goodglass, H., and E. Baker, 1976. Semantic field, naming and auditory comprehension in aphasia. *Brain and Language* 3:359–374.

Goodglass, H., and E. Kaplan, 1983. *The Assessment of Aphasia and Related Disorders*. Philadelphia: Lea and Febiger, 2nd edition.

Goodglass, H., and F. Quadfasel, 1954. Language laterality in left-handed aphasics. *Brain* 77:521–548.

Graff-Redford, N. R., P. E. Eslinger, A. R. Damasio, and T. Yamada, 1984. Nonhemorrhagic infarction of the thalamus: behavioral, anatomic, and physiologic correlates. *Neurology* 34:14–23.

Green, E., and D. H. Howes, 1977. The nature of conduction aphasia: A study of anatomic and clinical features and of underlying mechanisms. In *Studies in Neurolinguistics*, H. Whitaker and H. A. Whitaker, eds. New York: Academic Press, vol. 3, pp. 123–156.

Guberman, A., and D. Stuss, 1983. The syndrome of bilateral paramedian thalamic infarction. *Neurology* 33:540–546.

Guidetti, B., 1957. Désordres de la parole associés à des lésions de la surface interhémispherique frontale postérieure. *Rev. Neurol.* 97:121–131.

Head, H., 1926. *Aphasia and Kindred Disorders of Speech*. London: Cambridge University Press.

Hécaen, H., 1972. *Introduction à la Neuropsychologie*. Paris: Larousse.

Hécaen, H., and M. L. Albert, 1978. *Human Neuropsychology*. New York: Wiley.

Hécaen, H., and J. Consoli, 1973. Analyse des troubles du langage au cours des lésions de l'aire de Broca. *Neuropsychologia* 2:377–388.

Heilman, K. M., R. Sholes, and R. T. Watson, 1975. Auditory affective agnosia. Disturbed comprehension of affective speech. *J. Neurol. Neurosurg. Psychiat.* 38:69–72.

Henschen, S. E., 1920–1922. *Klinische und anatomishe Beiträge zur Pathologie des Gehirns*. Stockhom: Almquist and Wiksell.

Hier, D. B., K. R. Davis, E. P. Richardson, and J. P. Mohr, 1977. Hypertensive putaminal hemorrhage. *Ann. Neurol.* 1:152–159.

Hochberg, F. H., and M. LeMay, 1975. Arteriographic correlates of handedness. *Neurology* 25:218–222.

Hopf, A. Z., 1957. Architektonische Untersuchungen um sensorischen Aphasien. *J. Hirnforsch.* 3:276–530.

Jackson, J. H., 1878–1879. On affections of speech from disease of the brain. *Brain* 1:304–330, 2:203–222, 323–356.

Jackson, J. H., 1882. Localized convulsions from tumor of the brain. *Brain* 5:364–374.

Jackson, J. H., 1884. On the evolution and dissolution of the nervous system. *Lancet* 1:555–558, 652–679, 739–744.

Jakobson, R., 1964. Towards a linguistic typology of aphasic impairments. *Disorder of Language.* Ciba Foundation Symposium. London: Ciba Foundation, pp. 21–41.

Jakobson, R., and M. Halle, 1956. *Fundamentals of Language.* The Hague: Mouton.

Jerger, J., 1964. Auditory tests for disorder of the central auditory mechanisms. In *Neurological Aspects of Auditory and Vestibular Disorders.* W. J. Fields and B. R. Alfordi, eds. Springfield, Ill.: Charles C. Thomas, pp. 77–86.

Kandel, E. R., 1982. Brain and Behavior. In *Principles of Neural Science.* E. R. Kandel and J. H. Schwartz, eds. New York: Elsevier-North Holland, pp. 3–13.

Kertesz, A., 1979. *Aphasia and Associated Disorders: Taxonomy, Localization and Recovery.* New York: Grune and Stratton.

Kertesz, A., W. Harlock, and R. Coates, 1979. Computer tomographic localization, lesion size and prognosis in aphasia and nonverbal impairment. *Brain Lang.* 8:34–50.

Kertesz, A., R. Sheppard, and R. MacKenzie, 1982. Localization in transcortical sensory aphasia. *Arch. Neurol.* 39(8):475–478.

Kinsbourne, M., 1972. Behavioral analysis of repetition deficit in conduction aphasia. *Neurology* 22:1126–1132.

Kleist, K., 1934. *Gehirnpathologie.* Leipzig: Barth.

Koff, E., M. A. Naeser, J. M. Pieniadz, A. L. Foundas, and H. Levine, 1984. CT scan hemispheric asymmetries in right and left-handed males and females. (to be published)

Kussmaul, A., 1877. Disturbances of speech. *Cyclop. Pract. Med.* 14:581–875.

Lashley, K. J., 1929. *Brain Mechanisms and Intelligence.* Chicago: University of Chicago Press.

Lashley, K. J., 1933. Integrative functions of the cerebral cortex. *Physiol. Rev.* 13:1–42.

LeCours, A. R., and F. Lhermitte, 1976. The "pure form" of the phonetic disintegration syndrome (pure anarthria); anatomical-clinical report of a historical case. *Brain Lang.* 3:88–113.

LeMay, M., and E. Culebras, 1972. Human brain. Morphological differences in the hemisphere demonstrable by carotid arteriography. *N. Engl. J. Med.* 287:168–170.

LeMay, M., and D. K. Kido, 1978. Asymmetries of cerebral hemispheres on computed tomograms. *J. Comp. Ass. Tomogr.* 2:471–476.

Lemoyne, J., and D. Mahoudeau, 1959. A propos d'un cas d'agnosie auditive pure avec surdité corticale associée à une dysphonie fonctionelle. Observation anatomo-clinique. *Ann. Oto-Laryngol.* 4:293–310.

Levine, D. N., and J. P. Mohr, 1979. Language after bilateral cerebral infarctions: Role of the minor hemisphere in speech. *Neurology* 29:927–938.

Lichtheim, L., 1884. Über Aphasie. *Dtsch. Archiv. klin. Med.* 36:204–208.

Lichtheim, L., 1885. On aphasia. *Brain* 7:433–484.

Liepmann, H., and O. Maas, 1907. Fall von einseitiger Agraphie und Apraxie bei rechtsseitiger Lähmung. *J. Psychiat. Neurol.* 10:214–227.

Liepmann, H., and M. Pappenheim, 1914. Über einen Fall von Sogennanter Leitungsaphasie mit anatomischen Befund. *Zeitschr. ges. Neurol. Psychiat.* 27:1–41.

Luria, A. R., 1940. The study of aphasia in the light of cerebral pathology (in Russian), vol. 1, Temoral (acoustic) aphasia. Sc. D. Dissertation, Kiev Medical Institute, vol. 2, Parietal (semantic) Aphasia, unpublished.

Luria, A. R., 1947. *Traumatic Aphasia* (in Russian). Moscow: USSR Academy of Medical Sciences Press.

Luria, A. R., 1966. *Higher Cortical Functions in Man*. New York: Basic Books.

Magnan, D. R., 1880. On simple aphasia, and aphasia with incoherence. *Brain* 2:112–123.

Marie, P., 1906a. Revision de la question de l'aphasie: L'aphasie de 1861 à 1866; essai de critique historique sur la genèse de la doctrine de Broca. *Sem. Méd.* 26:565–571.

Marie, P., 1906b. Revision de la question de l'aphasie: La Troisième convolution frontale gauche ne joue aucun rôle spécial dans la fonction du langage. *Sem. Méd.* 26:241–247.

Marie, P., 1906c. Revision de la question de l'aphasie: Que faut-il penser des aphasies sous-corticales (aphasies pures)? *Sem. Méd.* 26:493–500.

Masdeau, J. C., W. C. Schoene, and H. Funkenstein, 1978. Aphasia following infarction of the left supplementary motor area: A clinico-pathologic study. *Neurology* 28:1220–1223.

Mettler, F. A., 1949. *Selective Partial Ablation of the Frontal Cortex: A Correlative Study of the Effects on Human Psychotic Subjects*. New York: Paul B. Hoeber.

Mills, R. P., and P. D. Swanson, 1978. Vertical oculomotor apraxia and memory loss. *Ann. Neurol.* 4:149–153.

Mohr, J. P., 1973. Rapid amelioration of motor aphasia. *Arch. Neurol.* 28:77–82.

Mohr, J. P., 1976. Broca's area and Broca's aphasia. In *Studies in Neurolinguistics*, H. Whitaker and H. A. Whitaker, eds. New York: Academic Press, vol. 1, pp. 201–236.

Mohr, J. P., 1980. Personal communication.

Mohr, J. P., 1983. Thalamic lesions and syndromes. In *Localization in Neuropsychology*. A. Kertesz, ed. New York: Academic Press, pp. 269–293.

Mohr, J. P., H. Funkenstein, S. Finkelstein, M. Pessin, G. W. Duncan, and K. Davis, 1975. Broca's area infarction versus Broca's aphasia. *Neurology* 25:349–349.

Mohr, J. P., C. S. Kase, R. J. Meckler, and C. M. Fisher, 1977. Sensorimotor stroke. *Arch. Neurol.* 34:739–741.

Mohr, J. P., M. J. Pessin, J. Finkelstein, H. H. Funkenstein, G. W. Duncan, and K. R. Davis, 1978. Broca's aphasia: Pathologic and clinical. *Neurology* 4:311–324.

Mohr, J. P., W. L. Watters, and G. W. Duncan, 1975. Thalamic hemorrhage and aphasia. *Brain Lang.* 2:3–17.

Monakow, C., 1914. *Die Lokalisation um Grosshirn und der Abbau der Function durch corticale Herde*. Wiesbaden: Bergmann.

Monrad-Krohn, G. H., 1947. Dysprosody or altered "melody of language." *Brain* 70:405–415.

Moutier, F., 1908. *L'Aphasie de Broca*. Paris: Steinheil.

Naeser, M. A., M. P. Alexander, N. Helm-Estabrook, H. L. Levine, S. A. Laughlin, and N. Geschwind, 1982. Aphasia with predominantly subcortical lesion sites. *Arch. Neurol.* 39:2–14.

Naesar, M. A., and R. W. Hayward, 1978. Lesion localization in aphasia with cranial computed tomography and Boston Diagnostic Aphasia Examination. *Neurology* 28:545–551.

Newcombe, F., R. C. Oldfield, and R. Windfield, 1971. The recognition and naming of object—drawing by men with focal brain wounds. *J. Neurol. Neurosurg. Psychiat.* 34:329–340.

Nielsen, J. M., 1946. *Agnosia, Apraxia, Aphasia: Their Value in Cerebral Localization*. New York: Hoeber.

Niessl von Mayendorf, 1911. *Die Aphasischen Symptome und ihre Kortikale Lokalisation*. Leipzig: Barth.

Niessl von Mayendorf, 1926. Über die sogenannte Brocasche Windung und ihre angebliche Bedeutung für den motorischen Sprachact. *Mschr. Psychiat. Neurol.* 61:129–146.

Niessl von Mayendorf, 1930. *Vom Lokalisation Problem der Articulierten Sprache.* Leipzig: Barth.

Ojemann, G. A., and H. Whitaker, 1978. Language localization and variability. *Brain and Language* 6:239–260.

Pavlov, I. P., 1949. *Pavlov's Wednesdays.* vols. 1–3. Moscow: USSR Academy of Sciences Press.

Penfield, W., and T. Rasmussen, 1950. *The Cerebral Cortex of Man.* New York: Macmillan.

Penfield, W., and T. Rasmussen, 1958. *The Excitable Cortex in Conscious Man.* Springfield, Ill.: Charles C. Thomas.

Penfield, W., and L. Roberts, 1959. *Speech and Brain Mechanisms.* Princeton: Princeton University Press.

Penfield, W., and K. Welch, 1951. The supplementary motor area of the cerebral cortex: A clinical and experimental study. *AMA Arch. Neurol. Psychiat.* 66:289–317.

Petit-Dutaillis, D., G. Guiot, R. Meising, and C. Bourdillon, 1954. A propos d'une aphémie par attente de la zone motrice supplémentaire de Penfield, au cours de l'évolution d'un anévrisme artério-veineux. *Rev. Neurol.* 2:95–106.

Pfeiffer, R. A., 1936. Pathologie der Hörstrahlung und der corticalen Hörsphäre. In *Handbuch der Neurologie,* O. Bumke and O. Forster, eds. Berlin: Springer, pp. 523–626.

Pick, A., 1931. Aphasie. In *Handbuch der normalen und pathologischen Physiologie,* A. Bethe, ed. Berlin: Springer, vol. 15, pp. 1416–1524.

Pitres, A., 1898. *L'aphasie amnésique et ses variétés cliniques.* Paris: Alcan.

Pool, J. L., R. G. Heath, F. A. Mettler, and H. H. Gass, 1949. Neurology. In *Selective Partial Ablation of the Frontal Cortex,* F. A. Mettler, ed. New York: A. B. Hoeber, pp. 403–452.

Poppen, V. L., 1939. Ligation of the anterior cerebral artery. *Arch. Neurol. Psychiat.* 41:495–503.

Pribram, K. H., 1971. *Languages of the Brain: Experimental Paradoxes and Principles in Neuropsychology.* Englewood Cliffs, N.J.: Prentice-Hall.

Ratcliff, G., C. Dila, L. Taylor, and B. Milner, 1980. The morphological asymmetry of the hemispheres and cerebral dominance for speech: A possible relationship. *Brain Lang.* 11:87–98.

Reynolds, A. F., P. T. Turner, A. B. Harris, A. Ojemann, and G. A. Davis, 1979. Left thalamic hemorrhage with dysphasia: A report on five cases. *Brain Lang.* 7:62–73.

Ross, E. D., 1981. The aprosodias: Functional-anatomic organization of the affective components of language in the right hemisphere. *Arch. Neurol.* 38:561–569.

Ross, E. D., and M.-M. Mesulam, 1979. Dominant language functions of the right hemisphere: Prosody and emotional gesturing. *Arch. Neurol.* 36:144–148.

Rubens, A. B., 1975. Aphasia with infarction in the territory of the anterior cerebral artery. *Cortex* 11:239–250.

Sameral, A., T. L. Wright, S. Sergay, and H. R. Tyler, 1976. Thalamic hemorrhage with speech disorder. *Trans. Amer. Neurol. Assoc.* 101: 283–285.

Schiff, H. B., M. P. Alexander, M. A. Naeser, and A. M. Galaburda, 1983. Aphemia: Clinico-pathological correlations and brain mechanisms. *Arch. Neurol.* 6:27–41.

Schuell, H. M., J. J. Jenkins, and E. Jiméniz-Pabón, 1964. *Aphasia in Adults: Diagnosis, Prognosis and Treatment.* New York: Hoeber.

Schuster, P., 1936–1937. Beiträge zur Pathologie des Thalamus opticus. *Arch. Psychiat. Nervenkr.* 105:358–432, 106:13–53, 107:201–233.

Schuster, P., and H. Taterka, 1926. Beiträge zur Anatomie und Klinik der reinen Worttaubheit. *Ztschr. ges. Neur. Psychiat.* 105:494–538.

Stengel, E., 1936. Zur Lehre von den transkorticalen Aphasien. *Ztschr. ges. Neurol. Psychiat.* 154:778–782.

Stengel, E., 1947. A clinical and psychological study of echo-reactions. *J. Ment. Sci.* 93:598–612.

Signoret, J. L., P. Castaigne, F. Lhermitte, R. Abelanet, and P. Lavorel, 1984. Rediscovery of Leborgne's brain: Anatomical description with CT scan. *Brain Lang.* 22:303–319.

Stolyarova, L. G., 1964. Some peculiaties of the aphasic disorders in thrombosis and stenosis of the internal carotid and middle cerebral arteries (in Russian). *Korsakoff's J. Neurol. Psychiat.* 2:225–231.

Stolyarova, L. G., 1973. *Aphasia in Cerebral Stroke* (in Russian). Moscow: Medicina.

Tallal, P., and F. Newcombe, 1978. Impairment of auditory perception and language comprehension in dysphasia. *Brain Lang.* 5:13–24.

Tonkonogy, J. M., 1964. Aphasia in cerebral vascular disease (in Russian). D. Sc. Dissertation, The Bekhterev Psychoneurological Research Institute, Leningrad.

Tonkonogy, J. M., 1968. *Stroke and Aphasia* (in Russian). Leningrad: Medicina.

Tonkonogy, J. M., 1973. *Introduction to Clinical Neuropsychology* (in Russian). Leningrad: Medicina.

Tonkonogy, J. M., and A. N. Ageeva, 1961. On kinetic disorders of speech in a case with infarction in the territory of the left anterior cerebral artery (in Russian). In *Problems of Localization and Localization Diagnosis in Psychiatry and Neurology.* G. B. Abramovich and G. J. Levin, eds. Leningrad: The Bekhterev Institute Press.

Tonkonogy, J. M., and H. Goodglass, 1981. Language function. Foot of the third frontal gyrus and Rolandic operculum. *Neurology* 38:486–490.

Tonkonogy, J. M., and S. I. Kaidanova, 1963. Detection of tone signals in noise by patients with local brain lesions (in Russian). *Korsakoff's J. Neurol. Psychiat.* 11:1614–1619.

Tonkonogy, J. M., and I. I. Tsukkerman, 1966. An information-theoretical approach to the study of perceptual disturbances. *Soviet Psychol. Psychiat.* 3:26–32.

Trousseau, A., 1864. De l'aphasie, maladie décrite récemment sous le nom impropre d'aphémie. *Gaz. Hop. Paris.* 37:13, 25, 37, 49.

Tzortis, C., and M. L. Albert, 1974. Impairment of memory for sequences in aphasia. *Neuropsychologia* 12:355–366.

Victoria, M., 1937. Un cas de lésion de la troisième frontale gauche sans aphasie. *Encéphale* 32:85–92.

Wada, J. A., 1969. Interhemispheric straining and shift of cerebral speech function. *Exc. Medica Intern. Congress Series* 193:296–297.

Walshe, T. M., K. R. Davis, and C. M. Fisher, 1977. Thalamic hemorrhage: A computer tomographic-clinical correlation. *Neurology* 27:217–222.

Warrington, E. K., V. Logue, and R. T. C. Pratt, 1971. The anatomical localization of selective impairment of auditory verbal short-term memory. *Neuropsychologia* 9:377–387.

Warrington, E. K., and T. Shallice, 1969. The selective impairment of auditory verbal short-term memory. *Brain* 92:885–896.

Weisenburg, T. S., and K. E. McBride, 1935. *Aphasia: A Clinical and Psychological Study.* New York: The Commonwealth Fund.

Wernicke, C., 1874. *Der Aphasische Symptomencomplex.* Breslau: Cohn and Weigert.

Wernicke, C., 1903. Ein Fall von isolierter Agraphie. *Mtschr. Psychiat. Neurol.* 13:241–265.

Wernicke, C., and C. Friedlander, 1893. A case of deafness as a result of bilateral lesions of the temporal lobe. In *Wernicke's Works on Aphasia,* G. H. Eggert, ed. New York: Mouton, pp. 164–172.

Whitaker, H., 1976. A case of the isolation of the language function. In *Studies in Neurolinguistics,* H. Whitaker and H. A. Whitaker, eds. New York: Academic Press, vol. 2, pp. 1–59.

Whitty, C. W. M., 1964. Cortical dysarthria and dysprosody of speech. *J. Neurol. Neurosurg. Psychiat.* 27:507–510.

Zurif, E. B., 1980. Language mechanisms: A neuropsychological perspective. *Scient. Amer.* 3:305–311.

Zurif, E. B., and A. Caramazza, 1976. Psycholinguistic structures in aphasia: Studies in syntax and semantics. In *Studies of Neurolinguistics*, H. Whitaker and H. A. Whitaker, eds. New York: Academic Press, vol. 1, pp. 261–292.

Index

(Italicized page numbers refer to figures.)

⊒⊔ Bradford Books

Natalie Abrams and Michael D. Buckner, editors. MEDICAL ETHICS.
Peter Achinstein and Owen Hannaway, editors. OBSERVATION, EXPERIMENT, AND HYPOTHESIS IN MODERN PHYSICAL SCIENCE.
Jon Barwise and John Perry. SITUATIONS AND ATTITUDES.
Ned J. Block, editor. IMAGERY.
Steven Boër and William G. Lycan. KNOWING WHO.
Myles Brand. INTENDING AND ACTING.
Robert N. Brandon and Richard M. Burian, editors. GENES, ORGANISMS, POPULATIONS.
Paul M. Churchland. MATTER AND CONSCIOUSNESS.
Robert Cummins. THE NATURE OF PSYCHOLOGICAL EXPLANATION.
Daniel C. Dennett. BRAINSTORMS.
Daniel C. Dennett. ELBOW ROOM.
Fred I. Dretske. KNOWLEDGE AND THE FLOW OF INFORMATION.
Hubert L. Dreyfus, editor, in collaboration with Harrison Hall. HUSSERL, INTENTIONALITY, AND COGNITIVE SCIENCE.
K. Anders Ericsson and Herbert A. Simon. PROTOCOL ANALYSIS.
Owen J. Flanagan, Jr. THE SCIENCE OF THE MIND.
Jerry A. Fodor. REPRESENTATIONS.
Jerry A. Fodor. THE MODULARITY OF MIND.
Morris Halle and George N. Clements. PROBLEM BOOK IN PHONOLOGY.
John Haugeland, editor. MIND DESIGN.
Norbert Hornstein. LOGIC AS GRAMMAR.
William G. Lycan. LOGICAL FORM IN NATURAL LANGUAGE.
Earl R. Mac Cormac. A COGNITIVE THEORY OF METAPHOR.
John Macnamara. NAMES FOR THINGS.
Charles E. Marks. COMMISSUROTOMY, CONSCIOUSNESS, AND UNITY OF MIND.
Izchak Miller. HUSSERL, PERCEPTION, AND TEMPORAL AWARENESS.
Zenon W. Pylyshyn. COMPUTATION AND COGNITION.
W. V. Quine. THE TIME OF MY LIFE.
Irvin Rock. THE LOGIC OF PERCEPTION.
George D. Romanos. QUINE AND ANALYTIC PHILOSOPHY.
George Santayana. PERSONS AND PLACES.
Roger N. Shepard and Lynn A. Cooper. MENTAL IMAGES AND THEIR TRANSFORMATIONS.
Elliott Sober, editor. CONCEPTUAL ISSUES IN EVOLUTIONARY BIOLOGY.
Elliott Sober, THE NATURE OF SELECTION.
Robert C. Stalnaker. INQUIRY.
Stephen P. Stich. FROM FOLK PSYCHOLOGY TO COGNITIVE SCIENCE.
Joseph M. Tonkonogy. VASCULAR APHASIA.
Hao Wang. BEYOND ANALYTIC PHILOSOPHY.